# Shakespearean Biofiction on the Contemporary Stage and Screen

# SHAKESPEARE AND ADAPTATION

*Shakespeare and Adaptation* provides in-depth discussions of a dynamic field and showcases the ways in which, with each act of adaptation, a new Shakespeare is generated. The series addresses the phenomenon of Shakespeare and adaptation in all its guises and explores how Shakespeare continues as a reference-point in a generically diverse body of representations and forms, including fiction, film, drama, theatre, performance and mass media. Including sole authored books as well as edited collections, the series embraces a mix of methodologies and espouses a global perspective that brings into conversation adaptations from different nations, languages and cultures.

### Series Editor:
Mark Thornton Burnett (Queen's University Belfast, UK)

### Advisory Board:
Professor Ariane M. Balizet (Texas Christian University, USA)
Professor Sarah Hatchuel (Université Paul-Valéry Montpellier, 3, France)
Professor Peter Kirwan (Mary Baldwin University, USA)
Professor Douglas Lanier (University of New Hampshire, USA)
Professor Adele Lee (Emerson College, USA)
Dr Stephen O'Neill (Maynooth University, Ireland)
Professor Shormishtha Panja (University of Delhi, India)
Professor Lisa Starks (University of South Florida)
Professor Nathalie Vienne-Guerrin (Université Paul-Valéry Montpellier 3, France)
Professor Sandra Young (University of Cape Town, South Africa)

### Published Titles:
*Lockdown Shakespeare: New Evolutions in Performance and Adaptation*
Edited by Gemma Allred, Benjamin Broadribb and Erin Sullivan

*Women and Indian Shakespeares*
Edited by Thea Buckley, Mark Thornton Burnett, Sangeeta Datta and Rosa García-Periago

*Adapting Macbeth: A Cultural History*
William C. Carroll

*Liberating Shakespeare: Adaptation and Empowerment for Young Adult Audiences*
Edited by Jennifer Flaherty and Deborah Uman

Romeo and Juliet, *Adaptation and the Arts: 'Cut Him Out in Little Stars'*
Edited by Julia Reinhard Lupton and Ariane Helou

*Shakespeare's Histories on Screen: Adaptation, Race and Intersectionality*
Jennie M. Votava

**Forthcoming Titles:**

*Shakespeare and Comics: Negotiating Cultural Value*
Edited by Jim Casey and Brandon Christopher

*Shakespeare, Ecology and Adaptation: A Practical Guide*
Alys Daroy and Paul Prescott

*Shakespeare and Ballet: Gender, Sexuality, Race and Politics on Stage*
David Fuller

*Classicizing Shakespeare: Jean-François Ducis, Adaptation and Eighteenth-Century European Theatre*
Michèle Willems

# Shakespearean Biofiction on the Contemporary Stage and Screen

*Edited by*
*Edel Semple and Ronan Hatfull*

THE ARDEN SHAKESPEARE
LONDON • NEW YORK • OXFORD • NEW DELHI • SYDNEY

THE ARDEN SHAKESPEARE
Bloomsbury Publishing Plc, 50 Bedford Square, London, WC1B 3DP, UK
Bloomsbury Publishing Inc, 1385 Broadway, New York, NY 10018, USA
Bloomsbury Publishing Ireland, 29 Earlsfort Terrace, Dublin 2, D02 AY28, Ireland

BLOOMSBURY, THE ARDEN SHAKESPEARE and the Arden Shakespeare logo are trademarks of Bloomsbury Publishing Plc

First published in Great Britain 2024
This paperback edition published 2025

Copyright © Edel Semple, Ronan Hatfull and contributors, 2024

Edel Semple and Ronan Hatfull have asserted their right under the Copyright, Designs and Patents Act, 1988, to be identified as editors of this work.

For legal purposes the Acknowledgements on p. xii constitute an extension of this copyright page.

Cover image: Kenneth Branagh in the © Sony Pictures Classics new movie: All Is True (2018). LANDMARK MEDIA / Alamy

All rights reserved. No part of this publication may be: i) reproduced or transmitted in any form, electronic or mechanical, including photocopying, recording or by means of any information storage or retrieval system without prior permission in writing from the publishers; or ii) used or reproduced in any way for the training, development or operation of artificial intelligence (AI) technologies, including generative AI technologies. The rights holders expressly reserve this publication from the text and data mining exception as per Article 4(3) of the Digital Single Market Directive (EU) 2019/790.

Bloomsbury Publishing Inc does not have any control over, or responsibility for, any third-party websites referred to or in this book. All internet addresses given in this book were correct at the time of going to press. The author and publisher regret any inconvenience caused if addresses have changed or sites have ceased to exist, but can accept no responsibility for any such changes.

A catalogue record for this book is available from the British Library.

A catalog record for this book is available from the Library of Congress.

ISBN: HB: 978-1-3503-5920-8
PB: 978-1-3503-5924-6
ePDF: 978-1-3503-5922-2
eBook: 978-1-3503-5920-8

Series: Shakespeare and Adaptation

Typeset by Deanta Global Publishing Services, Chennai, India

For product safety related questions contact productsafety@bloomsbury.com.

To find out more about our authors and books visit www.bloomsbury.com and sign up for our newsletters.

# CONTENTS

*Note on contributors* ix
*Acknowledgements* xii
*Note on the text* xiv

Introduction: Shakespeare and his social circle on the stage and screen, 1998–2023 *Edel Semple* 1

**PART ONE Author** 17

1. Shakespeare regrets: Redefining the heritage biopic in *All Is True* *Clara Calvo* 19

2. 'I'll drown my book': Imagining Shakespeare's *Long Lost First Play* *Austin Tichenor* 28

3. 'Scarce . . . a blot in his papers': Shakespearean inspiration on screen *Judith Buchanan* 38

4. Interview on co-writing and performing in *Bill* (dir. Bracewell, 2015) *Laurence Rickard in conversation with Ronan Hatfull and Edel Semple* 48

5. 'The thing is, you're a douche': Fourth wave feminist representations of Shakespeare in *Emilia* and *& Juliet* *Gemma Kate Allred* 58

**PART TWO Family** 67

6. Shakespeare's dead, long live his widow! One-woman plays about Anne Hathaway *Edel Semple* 69

7. Interview on playing Sue Shakespeare in *Upstart Crow* (BBC, 2016–21) *Helen Monks in conversation with Ronan Hatfull and Edel Semple* 78

8  Father Shakespeare: Grieving for Hamnet on stage and screen  *Katherine Scheil*  86

9  Shakespeare and son in *All Is True* and O'Farrell's *Hamnet*  *Paul Franssen*  95

10  Interview on writing the play *Shakespeare's Sister* (2015)  *Emma Whipday in conversation with Ronan Hatfull and Edel Semple*  104

## PART THREE  Theatre  115

11  'Not the fashion': Imagining the formative presence of early modern women in Shakespeare's circle  *Naomi J. Miller*  117

12  'That's power': Representations of performance in Shakespearean biofiction  *Stephen Purcell*  126

13  Reverse engineering Shakespeare with biofiction: TNT's *Will* as repertory studies criticism  *Aaron Proudfoot*  136

14  Enter Burbage: The origin story of an acting superhero in Craig Pearce's *Will*  *Michael D. Friedman*  145

15  '#Sharlowe': Connecting Shakespeare and Marlowe in *Only Lovers Left Alive*, *Upstart Crow* and *Will*  *Ronan Hatfull*  155

## PART FOUR  Afterlives  165

16  More 'Shakespeare' than Shakespeare: The notion of 'Uber-Shakespeare' in *The Lego Movie*  *Benjamin Broadribb*  167

Afterword: Global Shakespearean biofictions  *Ramona Wray*  177

*Index*  187

# CONTRIBUTORS

**Gemma Kate Allred** is Doctoral Researcher Université de Neuchâtel, Switzerland. She is the co-editor of *Lockdown Shakespeare: New Evolutions in Performance and Adaptation* (2022). Her examination of celebrity and Shakespeare, '"Who's There?" Britain's Twenty-First-Century Obsession with Celebrity *Hamlet* (2008–2018)', was published in *Shakespeare Survey* (2020).

**Benjamin Broadribb** completed his PhD at The Shakespeare Institute, University of Birmingham, UK. His research focuses on twenty-first-century screen adaptations and appropriations of Shakespeare, and how these create cultural artefacts. With Gemma Kate Allred and Erin Sullivan, he co-edited *Lockdown Shakespeare: New Evolutions in Performance and Adaptation* (2022).

**Judith Buchanan** is Master of St Peter's College Oxford and Professor of Literature and Film in the English Faculty of the University of Oxford, UK. She is the author of *Shakespeare on Film* (2005) and *Shakespeare on Silent Film* (2009) and the editor of *The Writer on Film: Screening Literary Authorship* (2013).

**Clara Calvo** is Professor of English Studies at the University of Murcia, Spain. Her research interests include Shakespeare and the First World War, adaptation and cultural memory. She has edited *The Spanish Tragedy* for Arden with Jesús Tronch (2011) and *Celebrating Shakespeare: Commemoration and Cultural Memory* with Coppélia Kahn (2015).

**Paul Franssen** is a retired lecturer at Utrecht University, the Netherlands, specializing in Shakespeare. The author of *Shakespeare's Literary Lives: The Author as Character in Fiction and Film* (2016), he has also co-edited books on *Shakespeare & His Biographical Afterlives* (2020), *Shakespeare and War* (2008), *Shakespeare and European Politics* (2008) and *The Author as Character* (1999).

**Michael D. Friedman**, Professor of English at the University of Scranton, United States, is the author of *"The World Must Be Peopled": Shakespeare's Comedies of Forgiveness* (2002) and the volume devoted to *Titus Andronicus* in the Manchester University Press Shakespeare and Performance Series (2013), as well as numerous scholarly articles.

**Ronan Hatfull** is Senior Associate Tutor in Theatre and Performance Studies at the University of Warwick, UK, and Lecturer in Shakespeare on the Elizabethan Stage: Text and Performance at NYU London. He has published on Shakespeare's cultural afterlife and is currently preparing books on the Reduced Shakespeare Company and hip-hop Shakespeares. Ronan is the co-founder of the theatre company Partners Rapt.

**Naomi J. Miller** is Professor of English and the Study of Women and Gender at Smith College, United States. She has published ten books about Renaissance women and the early modern world. Her debut novel, *Imperfect Alchemist* (2020), launches Shakespeare's Sisters, a series of novels about Renaissance women authors.

**Aaron Proudfoot** is a PhD candidate at the University of Connecticut, United States. His research focuses on Shakespearean biofiction, adaptation studies, early modern history plays, and the ways Shakespeare continues to be adapted both directly and indirectly in the developing, streaming-based digital media ecosystem.

**Stephen Purcell** is Associate Professor in English and Comparative Literary Studies at the University of Warwick, UK. His major publications include *Popular Shakespeare: Simulation and Subversion on the Modern Stage* (2009), *Shakespeare and Audience in Practice* (2013), and *Shakespeare in the Theatre: Mark Rylance at the Globe* (2017). He is a founding member of the theatre company The Pantaloons.

**Katherine Scheil** is Professor of English at the University of Minnesota, United States. She is the author of *Imagining Shakespeare's Wife: The Afterlife of Anne Hathaway* (2018), *She Hath Been Reading: Women and Shakespeare Clubs in America* (2012) and *The Taste of the Town: Shakespearian Comedy and the Early Eighteenth-Century Theater* (2003).

**Edel Semple** is Lecturer in Shakespeare Studies at University College Cork, Ireland. She is co-editor of *Staged Normality in Shakespeare's England* (2019), *Staged Transgression in Shakespeare's England* (2013) and a special issue of *Early Modern Literary Studies* (2017). Her research focuses on gender in early modern drama and in Shakespeare on screen.

**Austin Tichenor** is an actor, playwright and co-artistic director of the Reduced Shakespeare Company who writes about Shakespeare in popular culture for the Folger Shakespeare Library. Co-author of the illustrated children's book *Pop-Up Shakespeare*, Austin hosts the world's longest-running theatre podcast, the Reduced Shakespeare Company Podcast.

**Ramona Wray** is Professor of Shakespeare and Early Modern Literature at Queen's University Belfast, UK. She is the author of *Women Writers of the Seventeenth Century* (2004), co-author of *Great Shakespeareans: Welles, Kurosawa, Kozintsev, Zeffirelli* (2013) and co-editor of *Screening Shakespeare in the Twenty-First Century* (2006) and *Shakespeare, Film, Fin de Siècle* (2000).

# ACKNOWLEDGEMENTS

In the film *Shakespeare in Love*, the theatrical impresario Henslowe and his financial backer Fennyman have the following exchange:

> HENSLOWE   Mr. Fennyman, allow me to explain about the theatre business. The natural condition is one of insurmountable obstacles on the road to imminent disaster.
> FENNYMAN   So what do we do?
> HENSLOWE   Nothing. Strangely enough, it all turns out well.
> FENNYMAN   How?
> HENSLOWE   I don't know. It's a mystery.

The natural condition of editing and publishing is as adverse as the early modern theatre business, though it is no mystery to how it all turns out well – getting a volume into print takes the hard work, generosity and cooperation of many people.

The inception of this book benefitted from the encouragement of Pete Kirwan, who offered sage advice in early 2020 on the seminar we proposed for the Shakespeare Association of America conference. That SAA seminar, 'Shakespearean Biofiction on the Stage and Screen', took place online in April 2021 with contributors and auditors from across the globe engaging in a lively discussion – a conversation so good that we just had to keep it going.

Thus, from this SAA seminar was born the Shakespeare Biofiction Bookclub, an international group of Shakespeare enthusiasts we hosted online to discuss a range of media from novels like Maggie O'Farrell's *Hamnet* and David Blixt's *Her Majesty's Will: A Tale of Kit and Will*, to TV series like *Upstart Crow*, to films like *Gnomeo and Juliet*. As the Covid-19 pandemic presented us with many tragedies and challenges, the bonhomie, collaborative spirit, and stimulating analysis of the contributors to the 2021 SAA and to the Bookclub was a sustaining positive force in our lives. Thank you to every person who attended those gatherings.

A profound thanks to our contributors, who enthusiastically took on the challenge of writing chapters of approx. 4,000 words, enabling the inclusion of multiple voices, texts and viewpoints within these pages. A special note of appreciation to the contributors who were part of the SAA seminar and the Bookclub; thanks for sticking with us across changes in time, geography and media.

We would like to extend our hearty thanks to Mark Thornton-Burnett, the Series Editor of Shakespeare and Adaptation, for his support and guidance as this volume developed.

We are also grateful to The Arden Shakespeare team at Bloomsbury, especially Ella Wilson and Mark Dudgeon for their considered advice and understanding.

Finally, we owe an immeasurable debt of gratitude to our families, friends and colleagues for their encouragement and sympathetic ears. Edel especially wishes to thank Bríd Murphy, Anna Pilz, Miranda Corcoran, Dee Ryan and Austin Tichenor. Ronan especially wishes to thank Natalie Diddams, Douglas Lanier, Paul Prescott, Stephen Purcell and, once again, Austin Tichenor.

# NOTE ON THE TEXT

All quotations from Shakespeare's plays refer to *Arden Shakespeare Third Series Complete Works* (2020), A. Thompson, D. S. Kastan, H. R. Woudhuysen and R. Proudfoot (eds), London: The Arden Shakespeare.

# Introduction

# Shakespeare and his social circle on the stage and screen, 1998–2023

## *Edel Semple*

Four hundred years after his death and the publication of the First Folio which disseminated his likeness, William Shakespeare has never been more visible.[1] In the twenty-first century Shakespeare, and indeed those connected to him like his wife, children, and friends, are commonplace characters on stage and screen. These fictional Shakespeares are often conscious of their influence, legacy and celebrity. For instance, the Reduced Shakespeare Company's comedy *William Shakespeare's Long Lost First Play (abridged)* captures the magic of writing by positioning Shakespeare as the most potent of theatrical magicians. He proudly informs the theatre audience and onstage auditors that his 'greatest gift' is to confer immortality on his characters; their 'tales will be told again and again', meaning that they will even outlive their creator (2018: 110). Such literary puissance is attractive to contemporary artists who often co-opt Shakespeare's name to further their own agendas or to render themselves, by association, 'Shakespearean' – a word which has become an 'all-purpose adjective, meaning great, tragic, or resonant' and which may or may not have 'any real relevance to Shakespeare' (Garber 2008: xiv). Reflecting on fiction and history in the plot of the Bard biopic *All Is True* (2018), the film's director Kenneth Branagh remarks:

> Hamnet died when he was 11 years old. In a way [Shakespeare] opens that wound again. There were sexual scandals involving his daughters, legal difficulties, money difficulties, and he had to come to terms also with the effect of his father's disgrace. Family issues come home to roost

in this story. All the gloves are off. It's the kind of thing Shakespeare would write about, for sure. Maybe we get to have a go at the story he didn't have time to write. ('*All Is True* / Exclusive Featurette', 2018)

Branagh's comment suggests that the biopic is both Shakespearean in content and a work of imagination. The film is legitimized by being about Shakespeare, by being Shakespearean in its approach to biography, by Shakespeare's cultural cachet – his brand association with authority, quality, high culture (Lanier 2007) – as well as by virtue of its status as historically informed fiction. Moreover, because Branagh, a renowned Shakespearean actor and filmmaker, produces and directs *All Is True* and plays its hero and casts Shakespearean acting royalty (Judi Dench and Ian McKellen), the project has the implicit approval of the Bard himself. (In promotional 'behind the scenes' footage, we even see Branagh in Shakespeare costume directing the action.) The suggestion is that the story of *All Is True* – the story of Shakespeare's final years – is Shakespearean and Shakespeare *would* have chronicled his life but, in the absence of his autobiography, 'we get to have a go'.

Although Shakespeare has appeared as a fictionalized character in Britain since the seventeenth century, and in European literature since the late eighteenth century, in recent years more and more artists are 'having a go' at telling his life story.[2] Fictional Shakespeares are part of a larger literary trend – a rise in the popularity of biofiction, a term which 'refers to fictionalizations of actual figures whether on the page or in performance' (Fitzmaurice, Miller, and Steen 2022: 13).[3] The veritable boom in Anglo-American Shakespearean biofiction was inaugurated by the release of *Shakespeare in Love* (dir. Madden) in 1998. As Courtney Lehmann and Lisa Starks recognized soon after the release of Madden's box-office hit, it 'usher[ed] in a new age of Bardolatry in Hollywood [. . .] recreat[ing] Shakespeare as both cultural icon and cult figure' (2002: 11). For the narrativization of the lives of historical figures especially, Madden's Oscar-winning film was definitive. After it, audiences viewed icons 'skeptically, askance, playfully' (Hackett 2009: 4), and it 'shifted the literary biopic into the contemporary age in terms of how it interacts with cultural and screen preoccupations of the last few decades, and positions the ongoing cultural fascination with the identity and figure of the author for the modern age' (Shachar 2019: 32). The film has been echoed, evoked and parodied in subsequent representations of the playwright's life, while its financial and critical success proved that remaking Shakespearean's biography could be commercially viable. Even the film's screenplay 'boasted impressive sales figures', in part thanks to its 'dramatist co-author Tom Stoppard' (Erne 2013: 66). In short, then, the success, awards-haul, media reception, international dissemination, and enduring mainstream popularity of *Shakespeare in Love* mean that it is *the* instigating primogenitor for a generation of Shakespearean biofictions.

In the wake of *Shakespeare in Love*, a concentrated and diverse range of plays, musicals, films and television imagining Shakespeare's life, many of which are in dialogue with one another, emerged from North America and the British Isles. This is unsurprising given that the British Isles and North America are particularly invested in Shakespeare as a monumental figure long embedded in their national histories, arts and culture, media, educational systems and economies. As Helen Hackett observes, England's Shakespeare mythology 'was adopted and adapted by Americans', and the cultural dominance of the United States has ensured the survival and spread of these myths (2009: 4). This is evident at several points in *Shakespeare in Love* but especially in its final shots which portray the hero as a shared Anglo-American property. '[I]nspired by his vision of the new world' (Cartmell 2016: 72), an invigorated Will picks up his quill to write *Twelfth Night*, while a dissolve reveals his muse Viola walking on a beach that 'looks surprisingly like Southern California and, by extension, Hollywood' (Lehmann and Starks 2002: 11).

Subsequent biofictions have followed this pattern of presenting Shakespeare as more or less Anglicized and/or Americanized according to their needs. For instance, Will appears as an Anglo rock god in the Broadway musical *Something Rotten!* (2015). Its hero, Nick Bottom, an Americanized average guy seeking fame and fortune, begrudgingly admires the genius's works. The issues of creative originality, the anxiety of influence, and competing national claims to Shakespeare arise when Nick uses a soothsayer to steal Shakespeare's next big hit – which the prophecy garbles as *Omelette* – and in turn Will steals this work, which inspires his masterpiece, *Hamlet*. The finale reveals that banished from England, Nick is the New World's latest citizen. His genius is no longer confined or misunderstood, Nick is 'living the dream' in 'America where everything is new', including Nick's great invention: the musical. While the Old World has prestige associations with genius, history and high culture, it also represents elitism, traditionalism and antiquated attitudes which the hero must escape to succeed. *Something Rotten!*'s Shakespeare is thus a foil to the lovable Nick, who embodies pop culture, the future (where the audience lives), and the American values of innovation, opportunity and democracy. On screen, the sitcom *Upstart Crow* (BBC, 2016–20) and biopic *All Is True*, both written by Ben Elton, 'reif[y] a particular Englishness as essential to William Shakespeare' (Blackwell 2021: 145). As Branagh has pursued 'a "quintessentially English" identity' throughout his career (Lehmann 2002: 173), his involvement in Elton's projects only furthers Shakespeare's Englishness.[4] In contrast to Madden's Shakespeare, Branagh's Shakespeare is embedded in rural verdure so that as Calvo argues in her chapter in this volume, Stratford appears as a national idyll. Likewise, Douglas Lanier proposes that *Upstart Crow* engages in an 'insistent Englishing of Shakespeare' as a reassertion of 'a specifically British context for reading Shakespeare's works' and as a resistance to the process of globalization (2021). Shakespeare's universality, canonicity and status as a national and international icon will be recurrent concerns throughout this volume.

While *Shakespeare in Love* is its starting point, contemporary Shakespearean biofiction has since been animated by a series of influential occasions including Shakespeare topping a 1999 poll to be titled the Man of the Millenium; the 2012 Cultural Olympiad; Shakespeare 450 and Marlowe 450 in 2014; the high-profile and worldwide commemorations in 2016 for the quatercentenary of Shakespeare's death; and in 2023, the quatercentenary of Anne Hathaway's death and the publication of the First Folio, whose portrait helped make the author a globally recognizable icon. Linked to these anniversaries, and a further influence on Bard biofictions, were a 'high number of academic and semi-fictional biographies [ . . . which] re-opened ancient controversies on Shakespeare's life and on the authorship of the plays, but also called into question the very nature of biography as a genre' (Petrina 2020: 116). From the abundance of Shakespearean biofictions produced between the twenty-five-year period 1998–2023, this volume includes discussions of most of the following: the plays *William Shakespeare's Haunted House* (Faux Real Theater Company, 1998–2019), *Shakespeare's Will* (Thiessen, 2005), *I am Shakespeare* (Rylance, 2007), *Shakespeare Unbound – a Gift to the Future* (Reese, 2008, 2023), *The Second Best Bed* (Rowlands, 2012), *Shakespeare in Love* (adaptation by Hall, 2014), *Shakespeare's Sister* (Whipday, 2015–16), *William Shakespeare's Long Lost First Play (abridged)*, *The Bed* (FitzGibbon, 2016), *Hamnet* (Dead Centre, 2017), *The Book of Will* (Gunderson, 2017), *Emilia* (Lloyd Malcolm, 2018), *The Upstart Crow* (Elton, 2020, 2022), *Born With Teeth* (Duffy Adams, 2022), and *Hamnet* (RSC, 2023); TV including the *Doctor Who* episode 'The Shakespeare Code' (BBC, 2007), the series *Will* (TNT, 2017), *Upstart Crow*; *Something Rotten!* and the West End musical *& Juliet* (2019); and the films *A Waste of Shame* (BBC, 2005), the conspiracy period drama *Anonymous* (dir. Emmerich, 2011), the family comedy *Bill* (dir. Bracewell, 2015), and *All Is True*.

Aside from these biofictions, Shakespeare and those in his social circle have frequently had cameo roles (some of which are explored in the chapters by Miller, Hatfull and Broadribb). To name just a few such appearances, Shakespeare can be found in an episode of MTV's claymation series *Celebrity Deathmatch* (1999), *Blackadder Back & Forth* (1999), *St Trinian's 2: The Legend of Fritton's Gold* (dirs. Thompson and Parker, 2009),[5] *Horrible Histories* (2009–13), *Gnomeo and Juliet* (dirs. Stevenson and Asbury, 2011), Key and Peele's sketch 'They Really Did That to Othello' (Comedy Central, 2013), *The Lego Movie* (dirs. Lord and Miller, 2014), series 29 episode 14 of *The Simpsons* (Fox, 2018), *Good Omens* (Amazon Prime, 2019), in adaptations such as *The Complete Deaths* (Spymonkey and Tim Crouch, 2016), *Much Ado About Nothing* (Rough Magic, Ireland, 2019) and *Romeo and Juliet* (Cyclone Rep, Ireland, 2019), while Shakespeare and Christopher Marlowe appear in *Staged 1592* (BBC, 2021) and *Sandman* (Netflix, 2022),

Marlowe cameos in *Only Lovers Left Alive* (dir. Jarmusch, 2013) and Marlowe and Mary Sidney appear in *A Discovery of Witches* (Sky, 2021). As should by now be evident, Shakespearean biofiction on the stage and screen is a thriving and diverse literary form. Generically complex, Shakespearean biofiction freely and knowingly draws on a whole host of media, forms and genres to breathe new life into a long-dead genius. For instance, *Bill* mixes biopic conventions with 'edutainment and slapstick' (Földváry 2020: 271), in *Upstart Crow* the format of the sitcom is used self-reflexively and with irony (Blackwell 2021: 138), and chapters in this volume by Calvo, Buchanan, Scheil, Franssen, Miller, Proudfoot and Friedman identify further connections between Shakespearean biofiction and other media and genres.

As public interest in Shakespeare was sparked by Madden's film and fuelled by the landmark anniversaries in the 2010s, so too has scholarly interest turned to the afterlives of the playwright and his social circle. Amongst a range of disciplinary approaches and theoretical lenses, studies of pop culture, the early modern era, gender, adaptation, film theory, the literary biopic, celebrity, cultural history, and performance are common frameworks for examining Shakespearean afterlives in the collections *The Writer on Film: Screening Literary Authorship* (2013), *Shakespeare and his Biographical Afterlives* (2020) and *Authorizing Early Modern European Women: From Biography to Biofiction* (2022), and in monographs such as Lanier's *Shakespeare and Modern Popular Culture* (2002), Lehmann's *Shakespeare Remains: Theater to Film, Early Modern to Postmodern* (2002), Hackett's *Shakespeare and Elizabeth: The Meeting of Two Myths* (2009), Franssen's *Shakespeare's Literary Lives: The Author as Character in Fiction and Film* (2016), Scheil's *Imagining Shakespeare's Wife: The Afterlife of Anne Hathaway* (2018) and Castaldo's *Fictional Shakespeares and Portraits of Genius* (2022). The present volume builds on this wealth of scholarship, including the rich repository of studies on *Shakespeare in Love*, but distinctively focuses on the Anglo-American stage and screen and on a specific twenty-five-year period. This focus enables an assessment of Shakespearean biofiction as it develops across the related media of theatre, TV and film; its place within the contemporary pop culture canon; and its continuing appeal as a source for creative invention. Moreover, as film has frequently dominated critical discussions of Shakespeare's afterlives, this volume seeks to redress that balance by reflecting on how contemporary theatre-makers have responded to Shakespeare's biography and to biofictions in other media.

This volume aims to broaden the discussion of Shakespearean biofiction beyond the academy by bringing together an interdisciplinary group of voices, both critical and creative. The volume includes conversations with Laurence Rickard, co-writer of *Bill*, a British-made family film about young Shakespeare; with Helen Monks, a writer and actor who has played Shakespeare's eldest daughter, Sue, in the sitcom *Upstart Crow* since 2016 and who went on to perform the character in *The Upstart Crow* on the West

End stage; and with Emma Whipday, a scholar of Renaissance literature and author of the play *Shakespeare's Sister*. Beyond these conversations, the creative and critical intermingle further in the chapters by Austin Tichenor and Naomi J. Miller. Rather than being separated by discipline, the chapters written by artists and academics, and the conversations between creatives and critics, are spread across the volume. This structure reveals that actors, dramatists, novelists, and literary and performance scholars share interests and questions such as: Why are artists drawn to Shakespeare as a character? To what uses is he put in the twenty-first century? What kinds of stories are generated from imagining his life? How do theatre and screen media mediate his status as literary genius?

Uniquely, this volume discusses biofiction about Shakespeare and those in his social circle, in which there has been growing interest. (Edmondson and Wells's 2015 collection and Scheil's work have been influential on this front.) The importance and impact of broadening the biofictional focus beyond Shakespeare can be seen in two recent high-profile occurrences. The first is the addition of Anne Hathaway, Shakespeare's wife of thirty-four years, and his daughters Susanna Hall and Judith Quiney to the *Oxford Dictionary of National Biography*, a move which 'gives importance to the role of women in family life, and legitimizes their contributions to "the life of the nation"' (Scheil 2021). The second noteworthy occasion is the creation in 2022 of a memorial for Hamnet and Judith in Stratford's Holy Trinity church graveyard, which came about in response to Maggie O'Farrell's *Hamnet* (2020). The international media attention garnered by this memorial and the popularity of O'Farrell's award-winning biofictional novel has led to a stage adaptation of *Hamnet*, due to premiere in 2023 at the Royal Shakespeare Company in Stratford (announced just as this book was completed). In these events, Shakespeare is a useful selling point that grabs an audience, a market and media attention, but that attention is then directed to an adjacent subject. Broadening awareness to include those in Shakespeare's social circle, enables new stories to be told and heard. As Benjamin Broadribb observes elsewhere in this volume, even in Shakespeare's briefest appearances, like those in *The Lego Movie*, he is freighted with 'massive cultural and commercial capital' (175). Attending to biofictional depictions of early modern people, to those who do not have Shakespeare's capital or instant name recognition, offers counter narratives and alternative perspectives that are obscured when the individual genius is the sole focus. Foregrounding Shakespeare's social circle can even pave the way to recovery, awareness and greater understanding of the lives of the marginalized, neglected and forgotten of history.

*Shakespearean Biofiction on the Contemporary Stage and Screen* is structured in four parts. Part One examines depictions of Shakespeare as an author at different points in his life. Clara Calvo's chapter looks at *All Is True*, the most recent cinematic outing for Shakespeare the man and the only one that focuses solely on his latter years. Calvo argues that the film's generic hybridity, although a contributing factor in its lukewarm reception, is central to its interpretation. By drawing on the documentary form, the film can explore the meaning of truth, and blend fact and fiction to arrive at an emotional truth, if not a historical one. Through the conventions of heritage drama, Calvo suggests, *All Is True* foregrounds its hero's middle-class Englishness and the painful consequences of the choices he made as a younger man. Next, Shakespeare's youth is studied in Austin Tichenor's chapter and in our conversation, about *Bill*, with Laurence Rickard. Tichenor deliberates on his co-writing of the RSC's *Long Lost Shakes*, a comedy in which the novice writer Shakespeare grapples with his burgeoning genius, and indeed his own creations. Although the play stages a teen Shakespeare, and dozens of his characters and plotlines, biofiction, Tichenor suggests, often reveals as much about its creator as it does about its subject. Judith Buchanan's chapter considers the authorial iconography in the First Folio before tracing how Shakespeare's writing process appears in three films: *Shakespeare Writing Julius Caesar* (1907), *Prospero's Books* (1991), and *Shakespeare in Love*. Buchanan proposes that Shakespeare's inspiration, genius and legacy may be celebrated or unsettled in these films, but in the end, their audiences are reassured of Shakespeare's monumental literary greatness. Part One closes with Gemma Allred's chapter on theatrical depictions of Shakespeare as a selfish artist. Analysing *Emilia* and *& Juliet*, Allred outlines how Will's sexism and male privilege are exposed by his treatment of his wife Anne, lover Aemilia Lanyer and his female characters.

Progressing from Shakespeare as an individual, Part Two: Family and Part Three: Theatre broaden the focus to explore his social circle in biofiction, including his real and imagined family, friends, lovers, inspirations, colleagues and audiences. Edel Semple begins Part Two by examining how three plays, by a Canadian, British and Irish dramatist, kill off Shakespeare so that his wife, Anne Hathaway, can tell her story. By staging Anne as a newly minted widow, Semple proposes, the plays meditate on women and grief, sexuality and family, and the legacy of literary genius. Three chapters then turn to Shakespeare's children, beginning with Susanna – discussed in the editors' conversation with Helen Monks – and then moving to Hamnet, a child who has been the subject of several biofictions in the last decade (Semple 2023b). Focusing on Shakespeare's relationship with Hamnet, Katherine Scheil discusses how the *pater* of English literature is imagined as a flawed and loving father in *Upstart Crow*, *All Is True*, the play *Hamnet* and the novel *Hamnet*. In his consideration of depictions of father and son, Paul Franssen finds that biofictions on the page and screen pillory the author, but he is ultimately redeemed. Amidst the absolutory process, traditional and radical views of gender roles and art are reconciled. Part Two closes with a conversation with Emma Whipday who reflects on her dramatic imagining of a sister for Shakespeare whose writerly ambitions see her enter the theatre industry and unite with a community of women, but end in tragedy.

Picking up this thread, Part Three: Theatre considers characters and groups who were, or potentially could have been, part of Shakespeare's theatrical sphere. The contributors here discuss texts that share a need to 'redistribute "greatness" among the community' (Blackwell 2021: 134), crediting those who helped create Shakespeare's works, whether this community comprises early modern women (Miller), Shakespeare's theatre company (Purcell, Proudfoot), or those who existed within his performative eco-system (Friedman, Hatfull). Naomi J. Miller's chapter analyses how women writers in Shakespeare's circle are frequently cast as types – lover, muse, shrew – 'often with little regard for the women's own voices and roles in the historical record' (118). Through her biofictional novels, Miller seeks to redress these issues and raise awareness of authors like Mary Sidney Herbert and Aemilia Lanyer. Stephen Purcell's chapter shows that the politics of a particular Shakespearean biofiction can often be revealed in its treatment and depiction of early modern performance. Whether on television or the big screen, Shakespearean drama is typically presented as being a unifying force for both elite and popular audiences. However, Purcell proposes, diversity and inclusivity have often been lacking in depictions of Shakespeare's players and his audiences. Next, Aaron Proudfoot considers how the series *Will* works as a piece of early modern repertory studies criticism which uses 'reverse appropriation' to illuminate the professional and material contexts of the early modern playhouse. The series, Proudfoot contends, decentres its eponymous hero to recognize the importance of the material contexts, professional challenges and social networks to the production of Shakespeare's art. Michael D. Friedman continues the discussion of *Will* but turns to the actor Richard Burbage for his chapter. Using conceptions of the superhero, supervillain and the origin story, *Will*, Friedman argues, engages its audience and articulates Burbage's transformation from average actor to great tragedian. Part Three concludes with Hatfull's discussion of the playwright Christopher Marlowe, who is often depicted as Shakespeare's opposite. Hatfull proposes that Marlowe, despite being acknowledged as infamous and a genius, is sustained in the consciousness of today's screen audiences only by the spectral and persistent presence of Shakespeare.

The volume closes with Part Four: Afterlives which explores Shakespeare's cultural afterlife in figurative form and the futures of Shakespearean biofiction. Recalling issues raised in Part One of the volume, Benjamin Broadribb's chapter opens by considering Shakespeare's portrait and the identifying marks of the Shakespeare brand in cartoon, webcomic and animated film. Examining Shakespearean creativity, individuality, and authenticity, Broadribb proposes that the Bard minifigure in *The Lego Movie* simultaneously pushes 'at the extremes of what is and is not Shakespeare' and blurs 'the boundaries between the two', becoming a prime example of what Broadribb terms 'uber-Shakespeare' (169). Ramona Wray's Afterword reflects on the chapters in this volume and considers the origins of biofiction and its future. Wray speculates on the cultural work of Shakespeare's afterlives when they are transferred to transnational, non-Anglophone domains. Turning to world cinema, Wray attends closely to

Shakespeare's appearances in the Belgian/Dutch short film *To be or not to be* (dir. Woditsch, 1999), the Spanish heritage film *Miguel and William* (dir. París, 2007), and *Angoor* (dir. Gulzar, 1982) and *Local Kung Fu 2* (dir. Basumatary, 2017), respectively Hindi and Assamese language adaptations of *The Comedy of Errors*.

In the rest of this Introduction, I identify preoccupations in theatrical and screen Shakespeares from the period 1998 to 2023 which recur throughout this volume. Shakespeare's genius and the gaps in his biography have prompted many writers to, as Branagh puts it, 'have a go at [telling his] story'. As remarked by the editors of *The Shakespeare Circle*, 'biography, in its quest to tell the truth, articulates at the same time its own sense of longing, which makes itself felt, in part, through speculation' (Edmondson and Wells 2015: 5). Shakespearean biofiction is animated by the longing to fill in biographical gaps and, in this, speculation is an absolute necessity. Contemporary producers of biofiction and audiences alike have a powerful 'cultural craving' (as Buchanan asserts (39)) to unearth Shakespeare's origins, his feelings and inspirations and the truth behind his genius. *All Is True* provides an example of just such an impulse when it has a fan visit Shakespeare to comically bombard him with questions. Shakespeare informs the enquiring fan that if he engages in honest self-reflection, it will mean that 'all is true' in his writing. Biofiction's relationship to truth, though, is always partial and compromised, and this is a boon to writers as they speculate on the lives of real historical people 'to offer new insight into many fields of intellectual inquiry' (Lackey 2022: 271). Reflecting on her 'Shakespeare's Sisters' novels, Miller urges us to appreciate 'the potential for biofiction itself to serve as a transformative process' which results 'in fictional narratives with the capacity to conjure gold from elemental materials [that is, from] historical and biographical facts' (2022: 139). Shakespeare's struggles and early efforts in writing, as well as his so-called 'lost years' (*c*.1585–92), have been rich ground from which 'to conjure gold'. So too has Shakespeare's canon been invaluable in patching the fissures in his biography and transforming it to offer fresh ideas and find neglected truths.

The mystique of Shakespeare's genius has been fertile ground for biofictions since the nineteenth century. Recent fictions capitalize on contemporary concerns and trends in pop culture by using the Shakespeare Authorship Question to imagine a conspiracy surrounding Shakespeare's identity. For instance, the Oxfordian and Prince Tudor II theories are *Anonymous*'s raison d'etre; in *Only Lovers Left Alive*, Marlowe conceals his identity as the true author of Shakespeare's works as part of a larger conspiracy (the concealment of the existence of vampires); and in *St Trinian's 2*, an ancient misogynist cabal suppresses the truth that Shakespeare was a woman, before a group of British schoolgirls heroically reveal this secret to the world. Not all biofictions take such a light-hearted approach to the enigma of Shakespeare's inspiration. As demonstrated by Annalisa Castaldo, fictions of Shakespeare's genius often imagine it is concomitant with alienation, suffering and even madness (2022). This is a variety of 'the stereotype of the Tormented Artist' whose creativity is so destructive he (and it is typically a 'he', especially in biopics) essentially says to himself 'my martyrdom shall be the badge of my creative legitimacy' and goes on to tragically 'die young, blam[ing] creativity for having killed [him]' (Gilbert 2015: 39). For some creators of biofiction though, it is not Shakespeare's brilliance or his inspiration that is a mystery, but his withdrawal from an active creative life. When the fan in *All Is True* asks 'Why did you stop writing?', Shakespeare replies only 'Cheerio!' Of this moment, Castaldo surmises that '[i]t is as if Elton and Branagh can conceive of the cause and shape of genius, but cannot fathom the desire to ever let that genius rest' (2022: 103). Elton and Branagh are not alone in being bewildered by Shakespeare's apparent retirement. In 'Ten Reasons Why William Shakespeare is a Fraud', a promotional video for *Anonymous*, Roland Emmerich imagines a timeless continuity between creative artists when he declares that because he could never abandon his art and retire to his hometown, the man who did do this – Shakespeare – could not be the true author of the great works (Semple 2023a). Thus, as paradoxical as it seems, both an anti-Stratfordian and a Bardolotrous biodrama bear out Tichenor's contention, in this volume, that biofiction is always autobiographical (36).

While many Shakespeares, like those in *A Waste of Shame*, *The Second Best Bed* and *Will*, follow the pattern of Shakespearean singledom laid down in *Shakespeare in Love*, this has increasingly given way to portraits of him as a family man. Rather than show Shakespeare as an unattached lover-about-town, recent biofictions embed him within a social network of real and fictional figures, including his immediate family, personal contacts and professional associates. In contrast to *Anonymous*'s Oxford, who has relatives but is cast in the mould of the isolated genius, Shakespeare has close ties to his family in *Bill* and the plays *The Bed*, *Hamnet* and *Shakespeare's Sister*. As TV serials are ideal formats to expand Shakespeare's universe to include a range of networks and social situations, it is no surprise that domestic relationships are central to Elton's *Upstart Crow*. They are also at the heart of his *All Is True*; in this biopic, a decidedly mundane Will dines, gardens, walks and attends church with his family. When Shakespeare is depicted as paternal, biofictions inevitably show him being shaken by Hamnet's untimely death. To return briefly to the memorial dedication to Hamnet and Judith: O'Farrell saw this undertaking as a bittersweet, communal responsibility: 'We are honouring a child who died aged 11, but we are also happy to be paying them both tribute. They won't be forgotten' (Thorpe 2022). While it commemorates Shakespeare's twins, the Stratford memorial, like recent biofictions including O'Farrell's novel, constructs Shakespeare as a family man and, in the absence of any personal evidence, reassures us of his humanity and familiarity. Like Elton's biofictions, it says: Shakespeare was subject to the vagaries of fate, he suffered loss, he grieved his son, he remembered his children through his work. By having Shakespeare interact with his immediate family, biofictions ensure that audiences can quickly gain his measure; he becomes recognizable, knowable and just like us.

As simultaneously 'our friend, a normal bloke' and a celebrity 'mystery' (Hadfield 2016: 61), Shakespeare is an ideal subject with which to voice disenchantment with the notion of the 'Great Man'. For instance, Whipday's heroine Judith knows her brother William is destined for fame and fortune and bleakly reminds him of the unequal opportunities that have shaped their fates: 'Perhaps it is easier for me to die as a writer. I have no chance of living as one' (Whipday 2016: 80). Biofictional portraits like this can creatively reverse historical exclusions, push for inclusivity, deconstruct and question Shakespeare's legacy and feed conversations about cultural authority and authorship into contemporary movements, such as #MeToo. Contemporary feminist biofictions offer a reminder that historically male genius has relied on others' (read women's) labour and sacrifices, a fact that has been all too often effaced by the brightness of the Bard's brilliance. Biofictions that centre on female characters and have a feminist bent also encourage us to 'kick Shakespeare's pedestal', as Allred argues, so that audiences can, as the protagonist of *Emilia* urges, 'take the fire as [their] own' (66). Such is Shakespeare's cultural dominance though that some stories move him offstage or commit Bardicide so that others may take centre stage, representing a postmodern death of the author (Lehmann 2002).

It seems fair to say, then, that the position on Shakespeare as a singular genius has shifted for twenty-first-century artists, who write in an increasingly globalized world where, thanks to digital connectivity, the potential for collaboration is supposedly instant, easy and convenient. Whether or not the internet has dis/improved artistic connection, recent Shakespearean biofiction is notably preoccupied with enlarging the playwright's social sphere and making genius accessible through the process of democratization. For instance, Mark Rylance offers genius up as common property to the audience of *I Am Shakespeare*, while in another key entirely *The Lego Movie* introduces Shakespeare to a family audience as part of a collective of real geniuses and fantasy figures: the Master Builders. The collaboration involved in artistic creation is also acknowledged in *Bill* and in *Long Lost Shakes*'s 'shared universe' of Shakespearean characters. So too does *Will*, which carves out an 'origin story' for Shakespeare and his leading man Burbage, base its narrative around the artistic input of a theatrical ensemble. Nevertheless, audiences can remain excluded as Shakespearean exceptionalism persists in popular culture. In the *Doctor Who* episode 'The Shakespeare Code', for instance, the Doctor describes his hero as 'the most human human', with 'Shakespeare's humanity [. . .] so great it effectively makes him different than other humans' (Castaldo 2022: 100). Somewhat aptly for science-fiction, this moment may preserve his position atop the theatrical throne by alienating Shakespeare from modern audiences. Elsewhere, the early modern playwrights Dekker, Webster, Jonson, Kyd, Marlowe and Middleton appear in the song 'Welcome to the Renaissance' in *Something Rotten!*, but these authors are merely name-checked; as the chorus says, Shakespeare remains 'our brightest star'.

It appears then that even when biofictions have an iconoclastic approach to Shakespeare, Bardolatry always seeps in; perhaps it is innate to the form. This tension is apparent in *Shakespeare in Love*: 'while it aims to divest the Bard of his intimidating iconic status and make him readily understandable to everyone, it simultaneously endorses his work as a bearer of universal values couched in the greatest poetry ever written' (Klett 2001: 27). Thus, the film succeeds in having it both ways: 'bringing Shakespeare down to earth and setting him up on a pedestal' (Klett 2001: 27). Even 'Bard-baiting' depictions which 'gleefully denigrate the man Shakespeare' as lacking in artistic integrity, morality, or any 'proto-modern prescience or contemporaneity' ultimately, like their progenitor, 'resolve themselves into a tempered admission of the work's continued brilliance' (O'Brien 2020: 151, 159, 169). Thus, a corollary of the biofictional focus on Shakespeare is that his contemporaries are often reduced to bit-players and 'fanboys' (Kirwan 2014: 16), their biographies deemed unromantic, their work presented as unassimilable to modern sensibilities (as is the case for Ben Jonson, who is often cast 'as Shakespeare's stooge' (O'Brien 2016: 188)). Though this can also work in reverse. For instance, in a *Horrible Histories* sketch which formed part of *Shakespeare Live! From the RSC* (2016), a young Shakespeare is eager to learn from his contemporaries, who mockingly shout 'fanboy alert!' in response.

Since the release of Madden's film, Shakespearean biofiction on the stage and screen has made some strides towards greater representation for people of colour and the LGBTQ+ community. Biofiction affords artists some opportunity to use Shakespeare's economic and cultural capital, writing back to counter power imbalances and address representation, or the lack thereof, in his work. Do creative artists behind such portrayals of Shakespeare's life succeed in increasing awareness of the diversity which existed in Elizabethan and Jacobean England? In 'The Shakespeare Code' the presence of Martha Jones, and her seeing two women of colour as a normal part of London's urban life in 1599, does suggest that '[i]deas about the black presence in Elizabethan London and a black Dark Lady [of Shakespeare's sonnets] are slowly beginning to trickle down into the general consciousness' (Franssen 2016: 156). Martha, and her opposition to Shakespeare's bigotry, provide a voice and model for 'groups previously marginalized by or excluded from constructions of the "typical" Shakespearean audience' (Purcell 2009: 165). Efforts at diversity, equity and inclusivity are especially notable in the production, marketing and performance of *Emilia*, a play written 'specifically for a cast of diverse women' in which '[w]omen of all ages, of all skin colours, of all body types play women [and men]' (Williams 2022: 32). These efforts are apparent too in *& Juliet* and in *The Bed*, when characters eschew heteronormativity, while Starks notes that *Will* is notable for 'presenting a range of sexualities in the theatre world' including 'a queer Marlowe' (2019: 224).

Some biofictions, however, are less than successful in addressing issues of 'sexual preference, social exclusion, exploitation, sexism and racism [. . .] by confronting their hero with them' (Franssen 2016: 160). These include *A Waste of Shame* in which Lucy Negro, a mixed-race sex worker linked with Islam, embodies Western fears post-9/11 (Franssen 2016: 154). In *Upstart Crow* female characters are largely 'confin[ed] to gender and/or race stereotypes' (Petrina 2020: 122). To give just one example, with tongue-in-cheek, Elton's published script explains that Miss Lucy, who is based on a historical figure, is portrayed as a tavernkeeper, rather than a brothelkeeper, offering 'surprising evidence that Elizabethan writers followed modern BBC guidelines and avoided depicting black characters as sex workers' (Elton 2018: x).

Elton is similarly flippant regarding race in *All Is True*. Shakespeare reports how he weaponized an African actor who played *Titus Andronicus*'s Aaron – played by Nonso Anozie in a fleeting flashback – to intimidate John Lane, who had accused Susanna of adultery. Shakespeare admits to Anne that in reality, the actor 'was a lovely fella, but John Lane doesn't know that', following this with the quip 'I've never let the truth get in the way of a good story'. *All Is True* does treat with seriousness the homoerotic relationship between Will and the Earl of Southampton, here the 'Fair Youth' of the sonnets. Shakespeare's love for his patron is left unsatisfied, but not unspoken. Having declared that Sonnet 29 is no 'flattery [but] truth', Shakespeare intimates his hope that his love is reciprocated. Southampton quickly shuts down this possibility and dismisses his social inferior's feelings; he can admire the poet, but not the man Shakespeare. In a compensatory gesture, he offers his own recitation of Sonnet 29, before departing. The sober and repeated leave-takings in this film add weight to Kinga Földváry's contention that *All Is True* is an 'odd biographic lament' that may signal a waning of, or even an end to, the cinematic love affair with Shakespeare's character (2020: 279, 280).

In *Shakespeare and I*, Theodora Papadopoulou and William McKenzie advocate for self-investment in art and a more personal form of criticism. Part of this endeavour involves self-writing, a unique form that unites the academic 'critical voice' with the personal and one's 'personality [ . . . in the hope] that such *personable* writing could potentially reach readers and writers outside as well as inside the university, enabling productive dialogue between them' (2012: 12–13). It is in such a spirit that we as editors of this volume encouraged our contributors to pursue their interests as scholars, producers, and fans of Shakespearean biofiction, writing equally for academic audiences, consumers of popular culture and – the inevitable overlapping point between both worlds – themselves. Since its conception, this book has enabled new connections within and beyond academia, as well as productive dialogue across all sorts of boundaries. As this book encounters an even wider audience, we hope that it continues to offer creative practitioners, scholars, educators, students and the general reader a springboard for their own teaching, research, artistic reinterpretation and enjoyment of Shakespearean afterlives.

## Notes

1. My thanks to Ronan Hatfull for his editorial efforts with this Introduction.
2. Shakespeare appeared as a ghost in the prologue of John Dryden's 1679 adaptation of *Troilus and Cressida*. For an overview of the history of Shakespearean biofiction in an international context, and its critical history, see Franssen (2016).
3. For more on the history and development of biofiction, see Lackey (2021).
4. Branagh made a guest appearance in *Upstart Crow*'s Christmas special in 2018.
5. Semple discusses Shakespeare in *St Trinian's 2: The Legend of Fritton's Gold* in a forthcoming publication. At the finale of this family adventure comedy, it is revealed that 'Shakespeare' was a nom de plume of a cross-dressing woman writer. The character is played by Rupert Everett, who also plays a headmistress and a ghost in the film.

## References

*All Is True* (2018), [Film] Dir. Kenneth Branagh, UK: Columbia.
'All Is True / Exclusive Featurette', *YouTube*, (2018). Available online: https://www.youtube.com/watch?v=WgptXvqr93w (accessed 1 December 2022).
Blackwell, A. (2021), 'Sympathise with the Losers: Performing Intellectual Loserdom in Shakespearean Biopic', in V. M. Fazel and L. Geddes (eds), *Variable Objects: Shakespeare and Speculative Appropriation*, 127–50, Edinburgh: Edinburgh University Press.
Cartmell, D. (2016), 'Marketing Shakespeare Films: From Tragedy to Biopic', in D. Shellard and S. Keenan (eds), *Shakespeare's Cultural Capital from the Sixteenth to the Twenty-first Century*, 57–76, London: Palgrave.
Castaldo, A. (2022), *Fictional Shakespeares and Portraits of Genius*, Amsterdam: ARC, Amsterdam University Press.
*Doctor Who* (2007), [TV series] 'The Shakespeare Code', BBC One, 7 April.
Edmondson, P. and S. Wells, eds (2015), *The Shakespeare Circle: An Alternative Biography*, Cambridge: Cambridge University Press.
Elton, B. (2018), *Upstart Crow: The Scripts*, London: Bantam Press.
Erne, L. (2013), *Shakespeare as Literary Dramatist*, Cambridge: Cambridge University Press.
Fitzmaurice, J., N. Miller, and S. Steen, eds (2022), *Authorizing Early Modern European Women: From Biography to Biofiction*, Amsterdam: Amsterdam University Press.
Földváry, K. (2020), 'Will, Bill and the Earl: Versions of the Author in Contemporary Biopics', in *Cowboy Hamlets and Zombie Romeos*, 247–84, Manchester: Manchester University Press.

Franssen, P. (2016), *Shakespeare's Literary Lives: The Author as Character in Fiction and Film*, Cambridge: Cambridge University Press.
Garber, M. (2008), *Shakespeare and Modern Culture*, New York: Pantheon Books.
Gilbert, E. (2015), *Big Magic: Creative Living Beyond Fear*, New York: Riverhead Books.
Hackett, H. (2009), *Shakespeare and Elizabeth: The Meeting of Two Myths*, Princeton, NJ: Princeton University Press.
Hadfield, A. (2016), 'William Shakespeare, My New Best Friend?', *Journal of Early Modern Studies*, 5: 53–68.
Kirwan, P. (2014), '"You Have No Voice!": Constructing Reputation Through Contemporaries in the Shakespeare Biopic', *Shakespeare Bulletin*, 32 (1): 11–26.
Klett, E. (2001), '*Shakespeare in Love* and the End(s) of History', in D. Cartmell, I. Q. Hunter, and I. Whelehan (eds), *Retrovisions: Reinventing the Past in Film and Fiction*, 25–40, London: Pluto.
Lackey, M. (2021), *Biofiction: An Introduction*, London: Routledge.
Lackey, M. (2022), 'Afterword', in J. Fitzmaurice, N. Miller, and S. Steen (eds), *Authorizing Early Modern European Women: From Biography to Biofiction*, 165–78, Amsterdam: Amsterdam University Press.
Lanier, D. (2007), 'Shakespeare™: Myth and Biographical Fiction', in R. Shaughnessy (ed), *The Cambridge Companion to Shakespeare and Popular Culture*, 93–113, Cambridge: Cambridge University Press.
Lanier, D. (2021), 'Schlubspeare: *Upstart Crow* and the Return of the British Bard', Unpublished paper from the 'Shakespearean Biofiction on the Stage and Screen' seminar at the Shakespeare Association of America conference.
Lehmann, C. (2002), *Shakespeare Remains: Theater to Film, Early Modern to Postmodern*, Ithaca, NY and London: Cornell University Press.
Lehmann, C. and L. S. Starks-Estes, eds (2002), *Spectacular Shakespeare: Critical Theory and Popular Cinema*, London: Associated University Presses.
Martin, R. and A. Tichenor (2018), *William Shakespeare's Long Lost First Play (abridged)*, New York: Broadway Play Publishing.
McKenzie, W. and T. Papadopoulou, eds (2012), *Shakespeare and I*, London: Continuum.
Miller, N. J. (2022), 'Imagining Shakespeare's Sisters: Fictionalizing Mary Sidney Herbert and Mary Sidney Wroth', in J. Fitzmaurice, N. Miller, and S. Steen (eds), *Authorizing Early Modern European Women: From Biography to Biofiction*, 129–40, Amsterdam: Amsterdam University Press.
O'Brien, R. (2016), '"Put not / Beyond the Sphere of Your Activity": The Fictional Afterlives of Ben Jonson', *Ben Jonson Journal*, 23 (2): 169–91.
O'Brien, R. (2020), 'The Bard-Baiting Model in *Upstart Crow* and *Something Rotten*', in P. Franssen and P. Edmondson (eds), *Shakespeare and his Biographical Afterlives*, 150–72, New York: Berghahn Books.
Petrina, A. (2020), '"Where Would you Fit the Coconuts?" The Reinstatement of Sexual Stereotypes in a Mock-Biopic', *Textus, English Studies in Italy*, 2: 11528.
Purcell, S. (2009), *Popular Shakespeare: Simulation and Subversion on the Modern Stage*, Basingstoke: Palgrave.
Semple, E. (2023a), '"A Darker Story": Two Shakespeares, Art, and History in Emmerich's *Anonymous*', *Borrowers and Lenders: The Journal of Shakespeare and Appropriation*, 15 (1).

Semple, E. (2023b), 'Hamnet Shakespeare: A Difficult Dead Celebrity Child', in B. Coleclough, R. Visser, and S. Michael-Fox (eds), *Difficult Death, Dying, and the Dead in Media and Culture*, Cham: Palgrave.

Scheil, K. (2021), '"Witty Above her Sex": Restoring Shakespeare's Women to the Record', *Women's History Network*, 26 November. Available online: https://womenshistorynetwork.org/witty-above-her-sex-restoring-shakespeares-women-to-the-record/ (accessed 1 December 2022).

Shachar, H. (2019), *Screening the Author: The Literary Biopic*, Cham, Switzerland: Springer.

*Shakespeare in Love* (1998), [Film] Dir. John Madden, USA: Miramax.

Starks, Lisa S. (2019), 'Queering Will and Kit: Slash and the Shakespeare Biopic', in K. Graha and A. Kolentsis (eds), *Shakespeare on Stage and Off*, 212–29, Montreal: McGill-Queen's University Press.

Thorpe, V. (2022), 'Shakespeare's Tragic Twins Memorialised in the Bard's Resting Place', *The Guardian*, 1 May. Available online: https://www.theguardian.com/culture/2022/may/01/shakespeares-tragic-twins-memorialised-in-the-bards-resting-place (accessed 1 December 2022).

Whipday, E. (2016), *Shakespeare's Sister*, London: Samuel French.

Williams, K. A. (2022), '"Burn the Whole f*cking House Down!": Black Feminist Lessons for Joyful Rage', in L. Kressly, A. Patient, K. A. Williams (eds), *Notelets of Filth: A Companion Reader to Morgan Lloyd Malcolm's Emilia*, 31–46, London and New York: Routledge.

# PART ONE

# Author

# 1

# Shakespeare regrets

# Redefining the heritage biopic in *All Is True*

## *Clara Calvo*

Kenneth Branagh and Ben Elton's biopic about Shakespeare's last years in Stratford, *All Is True*, premiered in 2018 to rather lukewarm reviews. Writing for *The Guardian*, Peter Bradshaw describes it as 'a sweet-natured, melancholy film' but also as sentimental, theatrical and 'unfashionable' (2018). In *The New York Times*, Jeannette Catsoulis deems it 'a slow and soothing tale of family secrets and festering resentments', which she finds 'A little soppy and a tad dull'. For Catsoulis, the film is more 'country soap than biopic' (2019). In Elton's script there are no doubt resonances of his Bard-sitcom *Upstart Crow* (2016–18). For viewers of both, it may feel as if *All Is True* offers in film the serious, melodramatic version of lively, hilarious family life that is so characteristic of *Upstart Crow*. Marital relationships in *All Is True* are the reversal of the relationship Shakespeare and Anne Hathaway have in *Upstart Crow* – whereas in the biopic the marital tension only gradually abates, every TV episode ends with husband and wife at day's end sharing a restful moment with a clay pipe. Despite the multiple echoes of *Upstart Crow* (Judith recalls both Susanna and Kate, Sir Thomas Lucy resembles Robert Greene), the generic roots of *All Is True* are to be found in neither soap nor sitcom. Detecting the family resemblance to other film genres and production trends enhances the audience's understanding and enjoyment of the film, whereas failure to do so partly accounts for the lukewarm film reviews.

In recent years, the biopic has increasingly been the subject of theoretical debate. Studies of the biopic have found it compelling to explore its relation to film genres, historical truth and national identity, together with its relation to the nature of the real and reality and to the practice of adaptation (Brown and Vidal 2013; Cartmell and Polasek 2020; Hollinger 2020; Minier and Pennacchia 2016; Pettey and Palmer 2018; Shachar 2019). Whether a genre or a production trend, given that they are more often the choice of producers than of 'auteur' filmmakers, biopics have been approached as a hybrid art form defined by a proliferation of subgenres, from the celebrity biopic to melodrama to the musical, and including forays into screen genres such as gangster, rom-com and the Western. Deborah Cartmell has succinctly summarized the challenge any theoretical approach to the biopic has to contend with: 'It is not always clear what qualifies as a biopic and whether or not it matters that there cannot be a precise definition' (2020: 93).

This chapter argues that the lack of critical recognition *All Is True* received is partly due to its complex generic nature, which combines the established literary or 'author' biopic with conventions, aesthetics, gender politics and patterns of framing and editing usually associated with the documentary or with heritage drama. An exploration of the features *All Is True* shares with these screen genres, such as re-enactment and the use of heritage or 'found' locations, suggests new angles from which to read and interpret Shakespeare's last-years biopic. It is precisely through its hybridity that the film achieves a more thorough exploration of the emotions that are usually found in other celebrity or author biopics and a purposeful blurring of the fact/fiction divide. The analysis will be informed by recent theories of the biopic as a hybrid, dynamic genre which aims to 'fill in the gaps' of traditional biographies and, while doing so, has to contend with the disparagement of historians and film critics and come to terms with its fluid relation to truth, history and national identity.

## The documentary tradition

Documentaries are not easy to define. For many, a documentary is a movie which is not a movie. Documentaries are then defined negatively, as something which is the opposite of a feature film: whereas the movie is fictional, the documentary involves a search for truth; whereas the first narrates, the second shows. This distinction can collapse quickly, but in the case of a biographical documentary or a documentary about a play, for instance, it is also counter-intuitive, as both require the narration of events. Other attempts to describe the difference between a documentary and a film draw on two other characteristics of documentaries, their educational and informative purpose and their insistence on veracity and credibility. Thus, a documentary, according to Patricia Aufderheide, is 'a movie that isn't fun, a serious movie, something that tries to teach you something' (2017:

1) which generally 'tells a story about real life with claims to truthfulness' (2017: 2). However, documentaries, like any other film or art object are constructs and as such they are 'constructed by artists and technicians who make myriad decisions about what story to tell to whom and for what purpose' (Aufderheide 2017: 2). Decisions may involve the use of poetic licence and the symbolic representation of reality, downplaying the genre's possible claims to 'real life' and 'truthfulness'. Documentaries, then, are best understood as 'a fair and honest representation of somebody's experience of reality' (Aufderheide 2017: 3) or in John Grierson's much-quoted definition as the 'creative treatment of actuality' (1933: 8; see also Kerrigan and McIntyre 2010). More important than defining the documentary, perhaps, is to acknowledge, as Trinh T. Mihn-ha proposes, that 'there is no such thing as documentary', but rather only 'the very visible existence of a documentary tradition' (1991: 29). This documentary tradition is just as hard to define, and it is difficult to go beyond suggesting that it is grounded in a series of standard documentary techniques which include: interviews with experts; anonymous voice-over narration; direct address; animated charts, maps and graphs; collages; didacticism; 'found' locations; re-enactment; and shots of symbolic objects. Many of these techniques are evident in *All Is True*.

*All Is True* shares with documentaries its seriousness and its complex claim to truthfulness. Throughout the film, truth is a porous signifier, qualified by poetic licence. In one scene Shakespeare claims 'Judith is 28 and a spinster. That is true' and in another he wittily says: 'I've never let the truth get in the way of a good story.' The film departs from Shakespeare's documented biography unashamedly and enters into the late nineteenth-century tradition of the *vie imaginaire*.[1] *All Is True*'s version of Shakespeare's last years in retirement in Stratford is highly fictionalized; for instance, Shakespeare didn't give up writing after *Henry VIII* (whose alternative title provides the film's), we can't be sure he retired to Stratford and left London for good, we know nothing about his feelings for his dead son. Truth, Shakespeare tells us, is an artistic concept. It is the process of creation (writing) that makes something true and real.

The film also makes use of some of the standard techniques of the 'documentary tradition' (Mihn-ha 1991: 29). A significant 'found location', for example, is the pond which plays a role in the childhood of Shakespeare and his children, shown in a long bird's eye view take, suggesting a connection between its myriad colours and artistic inspiration. Shots of symbolic objects include the swan gliding along the Avon, the poems attributed to Hamnet and the mercury that Susannah drops on the floor. The swan brings to mind Jonson's description of Shakespeare in his preliminary poem in the First Folio ('swan of Avon'), reminding us of his status as an English Bard; Hamnet's poems, which Shakespeare (Branagh) treasures, become a material symbol of his grief and regret; and the bag of mercury drops Susanna Hall (Lydia Wilson) picks up after it has revealed its contents on the shopfloor is a symbol of her extramarital sexual life.

In several scenes, prolonged silences help establish a similarity between some shots and the documentary's technique of re-enactment. A good deal of the family scenes inside New Place bring to mind re-enactment in Tudor documentaries: a family meal in front of a sparsely laid table, or a shot of Anne Hathaway (Judi Dench) with her daughter Judith (Kathryn Wilder) at 'work' by a lattice window, both echo the documentary's preference for foregrounding costume and period detail in static scenes in which movement or action is minimal. This is especially evident in the shot showing the guests at Judith's wedding, a scene with pictorial resonances which make it resemble a theatrical tableau. Another scene that resembles re-enactment comes towards the end of the film when Shakespeare is tenderly embraced by his wife and surrounded by his family.

## The heritage biopic

Heritage film is now a term used to refer to a wide set of period dramas which range from narratives about historical figures or events to literary adaptations. The genre initially gained visibility in the 1980s and 1990s with *Chariots of Fire* (Hugh Hudson, 1981) and *Gandhi* (David Attenborough, 1982), but it became a production trend with the Merchant-Ivory adaptations of literary works by E. M. Forster, Henry James, Kazuo Ishiguro and Jane Austen. In particular, the long list of film and TV adaptations of Austen's six major novels has been a substantial contribution to the heritage production trend. The trend's continuity is manifest in adaptations such as *Pride and Prejudice* (Joe Wright, 2005) and *Emma* (Autumn de Wilde, 2020) and in the 'Austen without Austen' phenomenon that has produced films such as *Bride and Prejudice* (Gurindher Chadha, 2004), and *Aisha* (Rashshree Ojha, 2010). Pertinent to this discussion, the genre stretches to two biopics, *Becoming Jane* (Julian Jarrold, 2007) and *Miss Austen Regrets* (Jeremy Lovering, BBC, 2008), which clearly show the influence of *Shakespeare in Love* (Cano and García-Periago 2008).

The steady success of the Austen on-screen industry has kept the heritage film trend alive and has cemented many of the genre's aesthetic features which are easily identifiable today: markers of quality (a canonical literary author, a British star cast), countryside locations, well looked-after gardens, authentic period detail, lavish costumes, spectacular sets and slow-paced narratives. These features recur in *All Is True*, which shares much with the two aforementioned Austen biopics, but particularly with *Miss Austen Regrets*. These three biopics share patterns of framing and editing, alternating landscape views with curated interiors, and the exploration of affect, particularly through the manifestations of resentment and regret.

*All Is True* signals the marital estrangement between Shakespeare and Anne when she directs her newly arrived husband to the guest room in a candle-lit scene shot from a low angle which is likely to make the viewer uneasy. When the couple sits in the garden of New Place, there is a mutual feeling of unrest. The topic of their dead son Hamnet is raised, leading to resentment on her part and regret on his. The scene is very similar to a shot in *Miss Austen Regrets* in which Rev. Brook Edward Bridges (Hugh Bonneville), who proposed to Jane Austen (Olivia Williams) and was rejected, tries to make her concede that she regrets her decision. In both films, regret comes out in restrained conversation, the scene framed by a garden or park, as if hidden and repressed sentiment can be released only in the presence of nature and open air. Both films frame the scene similarly: the seated couple, against a background of greenery, occupy the centre of the shot, which focuses on their individual facial expressions.

*All Is True* and *Miss Austen Regrets* share patterns of framing in using the 'significant walk', a moment in which two characters share emotions or thoughts while strolling in beautiful grounds. In *All Is True*, while walking in the shrubbery-lined avenues of New Place, Susanna comforts her father and discusses her mother's coldness and Judith's bitterness. In *Miss Austen's Regrets*, Cassandra and her sister take a walk in (presumably) the grounds at Chawton after Jane almost admits that she regretted not marrying Bridges. In both biopics, then, the 'significant walk' has the two human figures enveloped by green foliage, as if isolated from the rest of the world by protecting nature and, thus, enabling the expression of difficult or hidden sentiments. The aesthetic effect achieved is pleasing and the position of the figures in the frame invites the viewer to concentrate on the dialogue and the shared feelings between the biopic's protagonists.

## English verdure, English comfort

In her novel *Emma*, Jane Austen defined Englishness as 'English verdure, English culture, English comfort' (2012: 249).[2] For Austen, the green landscape of the English countryside not only provides a view that is 'sweet to the eye and to the mind', it is also the root of collective identity and national culture. In documentaries about English history and in adaptations of English literary classics, a green landscape purporting to be the English countryside often provides the opening gambit, simultaneously setting the scene and situating the film within its genre. The association of Englishness with wide-angle takes of green fields, enclosures and rolling slopes, dotted with sheep and men on horseback, continues to be a standard feature of heritage drama. This presentation of the English countryside and its idealized, pastoralized, rural life is a feature which adaptations of Austen's novels share with both historical documentaries from the Tudors to the Romantics and with heritage biopics.

In British period dramas, wide-angle long shots of rolling landscapes – which bring to mind William Blake's association of England with a green and pleasant land – are closely associated with the representation of national identity. In his study of heritage film, Andrew Higson (2003) questioned the 'Englishness' of costume drama and argued that literary adaptations and historically inflected cinema represented class, rather than national, identity, as they are typically concerned with the life of the gentry and aristocracy. Although heritage film may be read as a nostalgic, conservative genre which mostly represents the habitus of the privileged classes, the idea of a national idyll remains central to heritage films and TV series and permeates class division, as proven by the interest generated amongst audiences of *The Crown* (2016–) and *The Hollow Crown* (2012–16), for example. The continuing success of National Trust properties and the boom of heritage tourism testifies to the fact that large parks and blossoming gardens, together with the curated interiors of the country house, are integral to the representation of English culture.

Both *All Is True* and *Miss Austen Regrets* redefine heritage drama, appropriating English verdure for the professional middle classes who earn their living. At the beginning of *Miss Austen Regrets*, the heroine rejects the marriage proposal which would have made her a member of the gentry, for the sake of pursuing her writing career. Concern for how much money her novels make reveals that she sees her career in a different light from her brothers; writing, she believes, can support her and her family. At the end of *All Is True*, Shakespeare finally confronts the antagonistic Sir Thomas Lucy, exposing the useless life of the indolent aristocrat by contrasting it with the fruitful lifetime of a London actor, artist and theatre manager. In his visit to Stratford, Ben Jonson convincingly suggests that the Earl of Southampton is wrong when he refers to Shakespeare's life as 'the smallest life' or as Jonson says 'little'. Jonson bypasses aristocratic patronage and makes it clear that now the playwright's profession allows a direct relation between subject and king; art is championed as a worthy calling and as a profitable pursuit that can enable class mobility. These heritage biopics help redefine heritage drama, which is no longer, as Higson suggested, merely nostalgic and conservative in their representation of English verdure and national identity.[3]

In the heritage biopic, Englishness is established through frequent takes of green landscapes and historical period is signalled with views of rural activity. There are at least three consistent functions of 'English verdure': to establish the setting in England with wide-angle shots of rolling countryside; to offer an alternating contrast to dark or constrained interiors; and to provide relief for the biopic's protagonist, who finds in solitude and nature an environment that facilitates the release of emotion.

*All Is True* deploys all three of these functions of English verdure. The film opens with the burning of the Globe in 1613 and connects this event with the playwright's retirement to Stratford. Shakespeare is never portrayed leaving London. After showing him watching his theatre burn to the ground, the film presents him galloping through the countryside towards Stratford. This crucial change in his life is consistently linked to green landscapes. New Place is not the town house in the centre of Stratford it once was, but a gentleman's country seat, a true manor house with park and garden, surrounded by considerable grounds. Before he enters the house, Shakespeare is shown surveying the land, reconnecting to his rural origins.

In heritage drama, landscape is closely linked to the understanding of emotion, and particularly so in *Miss Austen Regrets* and *All Is True*. In both films, important moments and substantial conversations take place in gardens or in a natural setting. Shots of Shakespeare gardening are interspersed with his laconic exchanges with his wife, and Austen's conversations with her niece Fanny mostly take place outdoors; the pond in *All Is True* or the stream in *Miss Austen Regrets* provide the setting for crucial pieces of dialogue. Nature is where the pain of regretting comes to the surface: Austen regrets spinsterhood and the poverty it has brought her while she persuades herself that she did it to pursue writing; Shakespeare regrets not having been present when Hamnet died, and he clings to the belief that his son was a promising poet.

In *Miss Austen Regrets*, Austen goes for a soothing solitary walk after her mother has raised the emotional temperature in Chawton cottage, accusing her of selfishness and blaming her for their poverty and lack of economic independence, which could have been avoided if she had not rejected the advantageous marriage proposal. Shakespeare mourns in front of Hamnet's gravestone in the churchyard, contending with his pain and regret while surrounded by trees and grass. Both biopics find in nature the environment that allows affect, releasing emotions that have been long contained. In both biopics, the green world ultimately has a reparative effect. While working in the memorial garden he constructs for his son, Shakespeare grieves for Hamnet and finds solace in remembering him, just before he imagines he sees his son's ghost. Austen collapses with grief during her solitary walk in Chawton's grounds. English verdure provides a sanctuary for emotion to be released in, as Austen imagined for several of her fictional heroines, including Emma, who deals with emotional stress by retreating to the shrubbery in Hartfield.

## The usable past

*All Is True* shares with *Becoming Jane* and *Miss Austen's Regrets* the aesthetics of heritage film and the theme of regret in the protagonist's later life, but its relation to documented life and historical truth is far more elusive. 'Nothing' – Judith Shakespeare says – 'is ever true'. Elton's verbal games, his quipping and one-liners in *Upstart Crow* emerge here and there as the sign of the auteur. Taken from the alternative title of Shakespeare's *Henry VIII*, the film's title enables Elton to toy with the semantics of its three words. Historically true becomes artistically true. For Elton's Shakespeare, even if not true to history, all is true once it is true to art. Consciously altering historical evidence and creating fiction out of the gaps of documentary evidence, *All Is True* aims to persuade us that truth is not found in the past, but in the artistic present.

Literary biopics often strive to go beyond documented or scholarly biography and while *All Is True* is no exception, its playful postmodern blending of fact and fiction refuses Bardolatry and easy answers to the lacunae in Shakespeare's life story. Like a Shakespearean last play, *All Is True* revolves around reconciliation and second chances. The film begins with a Prospero-like Shakespeare who metaphorically drowns his books and gives up his magic so that he can return to his dukedom and duties as the head of the family. Shakespeare, like *The Winter's Tale*'s Leontes, loses his young son but recovers his Hermione, and the hieratic, laconic Anne Shakespeare softens as the film progresses – she even helps Shakespeare in the garden and learns to sign her name. Shakespeare cannot get his son back but instead retrieves his lost daughter. Judith becomes a sort of Perdita who marries her Florizel in a heritage-film-style wedding, even if the historical Shakespeare never trusted Tom Quiney, as the documented last-minute change of Shakespeare's will suggests. Like in Shakespeare's tragicomedies, someone is left out of the happy ending and Margaret Wheeler's story conveniently fits in. For all his sexual indiscretions, Quiney, like Isabella's brother in *Measure for Measure*, is forgiven – he is 'a good man', Judith says.

*All Is True* makes use of the conventions of documentary and heritage drama to explore the complex relationship biopics sustain with documented historical facts, national identity, artistic truth and the strategies of fictional narrative. Historical documentaries provide us with a version of the past, with a form of 'usable past', a narrative that helps us to understand ourselves (Aufderheide 2017: 91). Fictional biography gives audiences a sense of feeling and emotional depth, a layer that is often lacking in documentary lives. Together biography and fiction aim to satisfy contemporary needs. Wouldn't it have been nice if Southampton had visited Shakespeare in Stratford and, ignoring class barriers, had hinted at his affection; if Judith Shakespeare had written poems, a postmodern replacement of the imaginary sister Virginia Woolf gave Shakespeare in *A Room of One's Own*; if Shakespeare had won the game of one-upmanship against Sir Thomas Lucy of Charlecote Park? *All Is True* gives us a biopic for our times which is as much about Shakespeare as about ourselves and our 'likes'. Through its combination of history, art, truth and national identity, it gives us too an exploration of grief and regrets, showing the price paid by neglecting family obligations for the demands of a professional career. Unlike *Shakespeare in Love* and most instances of Shakespearean biofiction, *All Is True* imagines a mature Shakespeare forced to deal with the complex emotions and consequences of his life choices, a Shakespeare who shares our twenty-first-century concerns.

# Notes

1 Marcel Schwob's *Vie Imaginaries* (1896), a collection of short stories, helped establish the genre of fictional biography.

2 'It was a sweet view – sweet to the eye and to the mind. English verdure, English culture, English comfort, seen under a sun bright, without being oppressive' (*Emma*, III, 6, 249).

3 *All Is True*, nevertheless, is caught in a paradox: a film directed by Irish actor/director Kenneth Branagh, who has contributed more than any other English-speaking filmmaker to turn Shakespeare into a global author, construes him as an English gentleman, whose roots and only home rest in rural England.

# References

*All Is True* (2018), [Film] Dir. Kenneth Branagh, UK: Columbia.
Aufderheide, P. (2017), *Documentary Film: A Very Short Introduction*, Oxford: Oxford University Press.
Austen, J. (2012), *Emma*, edited by George Justice, New York and London: Norton.
Bradshaw, P. (2018), '*All Is True* Review: Kenneth Branagh and Ben Elton's Bard Poignant Biopic', *The Guardian*, 21 December. Available online: https://www.theguardian.com/film/2018/dec/21/all-is-true-review-ben-elton-kenneth-branagh-shakespeare (accessed 1 February 2023).
Brown, T. and B. Vidal (2013), *The Biopic in Contemporary Film Culture*, London: Routledge.
Cano López, M. and R. M. García-Periago (2008), 'Becoming Shakespeare and Jane Austen in Love: An Intertextual Dialogue Between Two Biopics', *Persuasions-On-Line*, 29 (1). Available online: https://www.jasna.org/persuasions/on-line/vol29no1/cano-garcia.html? (accessed 5 September 2022).
Cartmell, D. (2020), 'The Hollywood Biopic of the Twentieth Century: A History', D. Cartmell and A. D. Polasek (eds), *A Companion to the Biopic*, 89–102, London: John Wiley.
Cartmell, D. and A. D. Polasek (2020), *A Companion to the Biopic*, London: John Wiley.
Catsoulis, J. (2019), '*All Is True* Review: Regret is the Thing as Shakespeare Comes Home', *The New York Times*, 9 May.
Grierson, J. (1933), 'The Documentary Producer', *Cinema Quarterly*, 2 (1): 7–9.
Higson, A. (2003), *English Heritage, English Cinema: Costume Drama since 1980*, Oxford: Oxford University Press.
Hollinger, K. (2020), *Biopics of Women*, London: Routledge.
Kerrigan, S. and P. McIntyre (2010), 'The "Creative Treatment of Actuality": Rationalizing and Reconceptualizing the Notion of Creativity for Documentary Practice', *Journal of Media Practice*, 11 (2): 111–30.
Mihn-ha, T. T. (1991), 'The Totalizing Quest of Meaning', in *When the Moon Waxes Red: Representation, Gender and Cultural Politics*, 29–50, London: Routledge.
Minier, M. and M. Pennacchia (2016), *Adaptation, Intermediality and the British Celebrity Biopic*, 2nd edn, London: Routledge.
Pettey, H. B. and R. B. Palmer (2018), *Rule, Britannia!: The Biopic and British National Identity*, Albany: State University of New York Press.
Shachar, H. (2019), *Screening the Author: The Literary Biopic*, London: Palgrave.

# 2

# 'I'll drown my book'

# Imagining Shakespeare's *Long Lost First Play*

## *Austin Tichenor*

## Act 1: I'll call for pen and ink and write my mind

The things we don't know about William Shakespeare's life and methods would fill several internets, so authors eagerly step in to fill those historical gaps with creative hypotheses. Whether writing traditional biography, fan fiction or biofiction, the impulse is always what novelist Michael Chabon calls 'the classic fanfiction gesture: to find a hole in the quilt of canon, and patch it' (Chabon 2019). We're all trying to fill in the blanks of the story.

I, too, have taken up the biofictional needle and thread, most notably when I developed, co-wrote and performed the stage comedy *William Shakespeare's Long Lost First Play (abridged)*, which places forty-six of Shakespeare's characters into a storyline that borrows plot elements from *The Comedy of Errors*, *Much Ado About Nothing*, *Romeo & Juliet*, *Macbeth* and *The Tempest*, and also brings in the character of Shakespeare himself 'as a living/Post-modern and meta-theatrical/*Coup d'theatre deus ex machina*' (Martin and Tichenor 2018: 100).

*Long Lost Shakes* – as we refer to it – was the tenth stage production of the Reduced Shakespeare Company (RSC) and the ninth play written by me and my RSC partner Reed Martin. Since the mid-1990s, we have been artistic directors of the three-person comedy theatre troupe that takes large serious topics and reduces them into short comic entertainments in multiple media (plays, short films, radio series, books and podcasts). The company's entire identity is a Matryoshka doll of Shakespeare fan fiction: influences nested inside inspiration from not only Shakespeare's life and work but from how they're interpreted and performed by others. These include:

- the company name, a play on *Royal* Shakespeare Company (and the reason we're frequently referred to as 'the *other* RSC' to highlight the distinction) (Hatfull 2018);
- the company's very first performance, in 1981, of a twenty-minute reduction of *Hamlet* (inspired by Tom Stoppard's play *Dogg's Hamlet*) at the Renaissance Pleasure Faire in Novato, California;
- the company's signature work, *The Complete Works of William Shakespeare (abridged)* (written by founding members Adam Long, Daniel Singer and Jess Winfield), which premiered at the Edinburgh Festival Fringe in 1987;
- a three-hour BBC World Service radio series in which we comically dramatize various aspects of Shakespeare's life, including his 'little-known trip to America' (Long, Martin, and Tichenor 1994: episode 6);
- several books that parody Shakespeare academics and speculate comically about gaps in Shakespeare's biography; and
- an ongoing weekly podcast, begun in 2006, that in recent years has increasingly featured Shakespearean content.

Imagining narrative choices the young Shakespeare *didn't* make gave us insight into the ones he did, but our fan fiction project became biofiction when we decided to make Shakespeare an actual character who appears onstage, the first time we'd done that in any of our stage shows. Authors appearing in their own work is a hallmark of the RSC's performance style where, from the company's very first performance in 1981, RSC actors present themselves onstage using their own names, playing exaggerated versions of themselves. Founding member Long guesses the reason this practice started is 'because [in the early days] we were hanging out with mainly street performers and stand-up comics rather than theatre folk. So there was never any conceit about playing a character. First and foremost we were ourselves, and the picking up of wigs, costumes and accents was secondary' (Long 2021).

Authors appearing in their own plays creates an extratextual conversation between the story and the storyteller, involving the audience in not only the tale being told but in the arguments and backstory that inform the narrative choices being made. Performers using their actual identity in a narrative context onstage, rather than their character's, blurs the lines between actor, role and audience, enhancing the immediacy and theatricality of the performance. When Reed and I joined the RSC in 1989 and 1992 (replacing Singer and Winfield respectively), we defined the RSC's onstage personas as comic archetypes dating back to *commedia dell'arte* and felt using our actual names to identify our 'characters' was reminiscent of twentieth-century comedy teams like the Three Stooges and the Marx Brothers, who, even when playing characters with different names, are always recognizably Moe, Larry, Curly, Groucho, Chico and Harpo.

The inspiration to depict Shakespeare's first burst of artistic expression came in 2010 while Reed and I were performing with the RSC at the Kennedy Center in Washington DC. My wife, Dee Ryan, and I were given a private tour of DC's Folger Shakespeare Library vaults by then-Director Gail Kern Paster and Head of Reference Georgianna Ziegler. After viewing treasures historical and whimsical, including shelves of original quartos and folios, the following exchange occurred:

> DEE: If you were going to write a *Da Vinci Code* movie, what would your plot be?
>
> GEORGIANNA: My holy grail would be to find an actual manuscript of a Shakespeare play, in his hand. ('Episode 191' 2010)

The idea began to take shape even before we left the building. Since finding an actual Shakespeare manuscript in his own handwriting is unlikely (but not impossible, according to Paster), I realized we could write an RSC comedy in which 'we' (i.e. the by-now accustomed exaggerated versions of ourselves) find a lost play of Shakespeare's, in his own handwriting, and present it to the world. Since such a thing doesn't actually exist, this would require us also, crucially, to write the play we found.

When I proposed this to Reed, he immediately 'yes, anded' me, suggesting the lost play should be way too long and thus require us to reduce it to two hours.[1] I built on that saying that the reason it's so long is because it's Shakespeare's *first* play, written when he was very young and, while unquestionably a genius, still a neophyte in terms of craft. To me, Shakespeare's youth and inexperience explained both the play's length and its disappearance; once he realized the impracticality and unwieldiness of what he'd created, he would destroy the manuscript.

Reed and I were excited by the possibilities of what even then we were calling *Long Lost Shakes*, and though concern was expressed that writing another reduction of Shakespeare's plays would invite unwelcome comparisons to the RSC's first (and by many metrics, most well-known and successful) production, I wasn't worried. Every RSC script we write is in some way compared to *Complete Works*, and in several ways beyond the focus of this chapter – but in a few to which I've already alluded – *Long Lost Shakes* would become the most significantly different RSC script we'd yet created.

## Act 2: Do you believe in magic?

At our first formal writing meeting in 2014, I pitched to Reed the basic idea that Shakespeare's *Long Lost First Play* could begin with Antipholus and Dromio of Syracuse (from *The Comedy of Errors*), in search of their missing twin brothers, getting separated by the witches from *Macbeth* and thrown together with characters from other plays in the canon. I was excited by the possibilities of seeing all of Shakespeare's characters as part of a shared universe, an idea Shakespeare himself explored with his many prequels and sequels and, especially, the way he spun off Sir John Falstaff (what we might now call a 'breakout character') from two history plays into a domestic comedy. Seeing Shakespeare's characters in unexpected situations offers comic opportunities to parody some of the tropes Shakespeare used repeatedly and, by exploring how his characters might behave in alternate surroundings, shed new light on how Shakespeare crafted their narratives. I also hoped to ground these divergent storylines with as much actual Shakespearean text as possible, including what we could call first-draft versions of his most famous lines. (Richard III's climactic battle cry, for example, would instead become this glorious new entrance line for Falstaff: 'A whore, a whore! My kingdom for a whore!') (Martin and Tichenor 2018: 26). *Long Lost Shakes*, I thought, would be a traditional fan fiction exercise, a 'greatest hits' comedy in which we assemble Shakespeare's most popular characters and famous lines into a new and funny narrative, interspersed with the kind of meta comic arguments and vaudeville bickering for which the RSC is known.

But Reed then posed three fundamentally important dramaturgical questions, the answers to which focused my thinking and gave the whole project much-needed clarity. 'What's up with the witches?' Reed asked. 'Is magic a theme?' And finally, 'What's the point?'

Considering Reed's questions, I began to see how the story could develop more organically, beginning playfully but growing increasingly out of control, with greater and more powerful magicians, witches, fairies and sorcerers driving the narrative and escalating the conflict. In my email response to Reed's questions, I suggested the Antipholus and Dromio story should be hijacked by mischievous Puck instead, and that Puck should be

> challenged by Ariel, who claims her magic is stronger and [who's] even got a stronger sorcerer as a Master. In their competition, they keep sending the story in whichever directions we want[,] until the Weird Sisters finally appear with their greater and darker magic. In an effort to put *them* down, Prospero appears and creates a mighty tempest that pulls all the characters (including Lear) into a mighty vortex that ends Act One. (Maybe Ariel calls upon Prospero and Puck calls upon Titania and it's the battle between Prospero and Titania that creates the swirling tempest.) (Tichenor 2014)

'Act Two then', I continued, 'is the resolution of all the plot lines, with the final and greatest magician of all – Shakespeare himself – stepping into his own story and resolving things.'

Though I didn't realize it until later, I was describing here the plot and resolution of 'The Sorcerer's Apprentice', the third segment in the Disney film *Fantasia*, and casting Shakespeare in the role of the sorcerer. Shakespeare's control over his characters and his influence on films from Walt Disney Studios – and more broadly, contemporary popular culture – would eventually become two of the script's central themes and running gags.

Magic, therefore, was not just the play's narrative engine but its primary theme and subject, capable of answering both plot and biographical questions. My email concluded: 'Anything we can't explain – such as how an uneducated glover's apprentice and politician's son can create the greatest dramatic poetry, etc – we dismiss as magic or genius. *The play then is about the magic of Shakespeare specifically, and maybe the magic of theatre generally.*' (Tichenor 2014. Emphasis added.)

We decided Shakespeare was seventeen when he wrote his first play: bursting with stories, characters and (in Adam Long's memorable phrase from *The Complete Works*) 'a lot of — as Shakespeare would say — chutzpah' (Long, Singer, and Winfield 1987: 55). It was a slightly arbitrary age to choose and doesn't withstand overmuch scrutiny, but we thought of our Will as youthfully brash and enthusiastic, unencumbered by a wife and children (both of which he'd have the following year) and, while having strong opinions about how dialogue should be delivered, inexperienced with the actual practicalities of putting on a play . . . all of which we tried to suggest in the very first speech of Shakespeare's very first play.

## Act 3: Admit me, Chorus

*Long Lost Shakes* begins this way:

> *A cloaked hooded figure enters and commands the audience's attention. His face is unseen. He gestures and the house lights go down, then gestures to make a single special rise on him. With a flourish he removes his hood. This is* CHORUS. (Martin and Tichenor 2018: 1)

We don't know much about Chorus, but we know he can control the lights and possesses a theatrical flair. Are these genuinely magical abilities, or is he like an orchestra conductor, directing all we're about to see? Unclear. He then utters his first line, which is intended to establish the tone for all of what follows: 'O, if a Muse of fire be the food of love, let's eat!' (Martin and Tichenor 2018: 1). First of all, it doesn't scan. It's a seven-foot heptameter line, not the traditional five-foot ten-syllables of iambic pentameter. The first eleven words are famously Shakespeare's – a mash-up of two of his most famous opening lines – followed by two words that don't appear anywhere in the canon in this precise combination. Similar to their use in *Henry V*, the first six words are an invocation, a cry for divine inspiration from the creative muses, and combined with the metaphor from *Twelfth Night*, they also suggest a confidence and youthful swagger. The final two words are a rallying cry – in both the use of the first-person plural and a continuation of the food metaphor – for all of us to join in a feast of creative consumption: filling our minds, our imaginations and this specific venue. The next line continues as it does in *Twelfth Night*, 'Give me excess of it', suggesting the impatience of youth, a greedy hunger and a teenage metabolism; further clues to Chorus's true identity.

## Act 4: Things have changed

Chorus isn't quite so cocky and excited when he returns at the top of Act Two of *Long Lost Shakes*. After some physical business where his attempts to magically control the lights don't go as planned, Chorus starts his speech with the same words Shakespeare will later give to the character of Prologue in *Henry VIII* – 'I come no more to make you laugh' (Prologue, 1) – and ends with a warning that the trouble facing the massive cast of characters will soon get worse. It doesn't feel purely expositional: you sense Chorus is concerned not only about what's happening but also what's *about* to happen.

The next time we see him, Chorus is transformed. When the 'merry war' and 'ancient grudge' between Puck and Ariel reaches its angry peak, their clash of spells and impassioned calls for magical assistance don't summon Prospero, Oberon or the Weird Sisters. Instead, the cloaked figure reappears and removes his hood, revealing William Shakespeare himself.

How do we know it's him? According to the stage directions, the actor playing him 'wears the familiar ruff, hairpiece, and facial hair we associate with the known portraits of the Man from Stratford', and these physical signifiers are important. They ensure the audience recognizes and is introduced, not to a brand-new character, but a familiar person, known to us through portraits and previous pop culture appearances from *The Twilight Zone* to *The Simpsons* (Shakespeare in Action, n.d.), whose well-known image is being tweaked while previously unknown character traits are being revealed.

Puck and Ariel also helpfully spell out in dialogue that they're stunned by the appearance of what, to them, is their deity:

PUCK: Oh my Bard!
ARIEL: It is He!
PUCK: That greatest Magician –
ARIEL: The only Begetter of us all –

> PUCK: The Man from Stratford himself –
> BOTH: William Shakespeare!!
> *(Dropping to their knees)*
> We're not worthy, we're not worthy! (Martin and Tichenor 2018: 99–100).

When Shakespeare removes his hood, the first thing he sees is the audience and, in a moment ~~ripped off~~ inspired by the episode where Doctor Who brings Vincent Van Gogh forward to the present to see his artistic legacy and impact (*Doctor Who*), Shakespeare is visibly moved by the sight of so many people watching him and his characters onstage 400 years after his death. The poignancy of this moment is emphasized when Ariel and Puck apologize for the chaos they've created, and their benevolent creator accepts full responsibility. 'The fault, dear fairies', Shakespeare says, 'is not in your powers / But in ourself'. Shakespeare has discovered in his own work the source of his artistic difficulty, his depiction of out-of-control magical power being his own unconscious metaphor for his unrefined and untamed creative brilliance. 'Your magic's as wild and uncontrolled / As my genius is', he realizes. 'Yes, I'm young and bold, / But my skill's still naive and slightly daft. / My imagination o'erwhelms my craft.' In his guise as Chorus, he's been there all along, monitoring the story and worrying out loud about how it's going. Now, he feels compelled to step in and fix things: 'I wrote myself into a corner, so / I wrote myself into the play to get / Myself out of it' (Martin and Tichenor 2018: 100–1). He's revealed himself *to* himself, a thing sometimes only possible for a playwright once his work is fully alive and on its feet.

The rest of his soliloquy is a series of escalating epiphanies in which we see Shakespeare, in real time, chart the limits and potential of his power, and realize how the enormity of what he's created shouldn't be crammed into a single unproduceable epic. Picking up his manuscript and quoting Lear, Shakespeare declares, 'Because such greatness lies in every scene, / Divide we our play in three times thirteen', outlining how he'll expand the characters and stories from this one play into thirty-nine plays. Several of his realizations stem from the dawning awareness of the political realities of his day, ranging from the danger of questioning the Tudor Myth to the risks of casting his sovereign's father, Henry VIII, in anything but a flattering light ('I can't portray him abusing his power, / Not if I don't want to die in the Tower'); but some are personal ('Lord Hamlet, I think, shall get his own play. / I could watch him weigh his options all day'), illustrating that authors in every era, Shakespeare included, create the art they want to see (Martin and Tichenor 2018: 101–2).

Finally, Shakespeare flips the conventional wisdom that Prospero represents him at the end of his career by using Prospero's words to represent him at the *beginning* of his career. Realizing he must reject this maiden dramatic effort, he holds up the manuscript and says,

> So this rough magic I here abjure. I'll
> Bury it certain fathoms in the earth,
> And deeper than did ever plummet sound
> I'll drown my book in a hole in the ground. (Martin and Tichenor 2018: 102)

Shakespeare's appearance near the play's end – rather than squandering its power earlier – fulfils the promise of the play's premise in grand and surprising fashion. He exits, usually to applause, and appears one final time during the curtain call, when he bows extravagantly, 'mic drops' his quill pen, and dances off.

## Act 5: Reflections

Part of fan fiction's appeal is that it can often serve characters better than their creators by expanding their narratives, improving their love lives, giving them leading roles instead of supporting ones, and (to return to Chabon's metaphor) picking up dangling threads and knitting something wonderfully new out of them.

But exploring Shakespeare's characters and narrative choices from a fan fictional perspective can also reveal biofictional elements about the man and his methods. In *Long Lost Shakes*, as much as we reference Shakespeare's genius, we're primarily celebrating the great dramatic poet's *craft*: the craft of a writer who improved over time, learned from his mistakes and saw his youthful impulses mature. He also became a practical businessman who wrote for a specific company of players and famously borrowed plots and characters from Holinshed, Plutarch and others, taking what he needed and changing whatever he wanted.

Since Shakespeare is *our* Holinshed and Plutarch, we emulate him by taking what's useful from his work and his life and leaving the rest. In *Long Lost Shakes*, we embraced both the charms of fan fiction and the power of biofiction, which offers ways of understanding Shakespeare's life as a writer (and actor and husband and father and lover) in ways that standard biography can't.

And maybe shouldn't.

Though biofiction may be relatively new as a field of study, when it comes to Shakespeare it's been practised by *scholars* almost as much as novelists, playwrights and screenwriters. As I joked in 2006, 'Not knowing much about Shakespeare's life hasn't stopped everyone from cashing in, filling in the blanks with scholarly supposition when they can, and simply making it up when they can't. It's a shocking record, and we're proud to be part of it.' (Martin and Tichenor 2006: 3). Katherine Scheil argues more seriously in this volume that "the imagined circumstances of" the death of Shakespeare's son in 1596 have given "biographers . . . a way to sketch out an emotional life for Shakespeare" (87, 88). She cites Stephen Greenblatt's *Will in the World* as the most widely read example of the 'highly speculative fantasy' of what Shakespeare 'must have' done or 'undoubtedly' did while attending Hamnet's funeral, despite there being zero evidence he did any such thing (88). Though Greenblatt's novelistic flourishes are undoubtedly (!) responsible for the deserved popularity of *Will in the World*, they're easier to forgive in clearly fictional works.

Further, if biofiction is a form of fan fiction, then I submit that all fan fiction is inherently *autobiofiction*, a mirror that reveals as much of its author's nature as its subject's. Since we know so little about Shakespeare, we create the Shakespeare we want to see, giving him some of our own attributes and inevitably depicting him – in the absence of evidence proving otherwise – as a reflection of ourselves.

Making Shakespeare a character in his own play dramatizes our understanding that authors are always present in their work, for the only thing sillier than asking an author whether what they've written is autobiographical is not understanding that *everything* an author writes is autobiographical. Jessica McCall and Kavita Mudan Finn argue that fan fiction – and by extension, biofiction – 'offers an alternative form of both close reading and contextual *criticism* when applied to pre-modern writers' (2019: 38). As we hopefully demonstrated in *Long Lost Shakes*, when it comes to understanding historical figures like William Shakespeare, it might be better if authors of biofiction rush in where mere biographers should rightly fear to tread.

## Note

1 'Yes, And' is a term of art in improvisation, where actors accept the initiation of their partners and then add to it in order to build the scene.

# References

Chabon, M. (2019), 'The Final Frontier', *The New Yorker*, 11 November. Available online: https://www.newyorker.com/magazine/2019/11/18/the-final-frontier (accessed 17 July 2022).

*Doctor Who* (2010), 'Vincent and the Doctor' [TV series] BBC One, 5 June.

'Episode 191: Folger Shakespeare Library' (2010), Of the *Reduced Shakespeare Company* Podcast, [Podcast] 2 August. Available online: https://www.reducedshakespeare.com/2010/08/episode-191-folger-shakespeare-library/ (accessed 17 July 2022).

Hatfull, R. (2018), '"The Other RSC": The History and Legacy of the Reduced Shakespeare Company', PhD thesis, University of Warwick, UK.

Long, A. (2021), Email to Austin Tichenor, 21 January.

Long, A., R. Martin, and A. Tichenor (1994), *The Reduced Shakespeare Radio Show*, London: BBC World Service / Laughing Stock.

Long, A., D. Singer, and J. Winfield (1987), *The Complete Works of William Shakespeare (abridged)*, Los Angeles: Reduced Shakespeare Company in-house PDF.

Martin, R. and A. Tichenor (2006), *Reduced Shakespeare: The Complete Guide for the Attention-Impaired (abridged)*, New York: Hyperion Press.

Martin, R. and A. Tichenor (2018), *William Shakespeare's Long Lost First Play (abridged)*, New York: Broadway Play Publishing.

McCall, J. and K. Mudan Finn (2019), 'Exit, Pursued by a Fan: Shakespeare, Fandom, and the Lure of the Alternate Universe', in R. Conkie and S. Maisano (eds), *Shakespeare and Creative Criticism*, 38–53, New York: Berghahn Books.

*Shakespeare In Action* (2014), 'Shakespeare and *The Simpsons*', 13 May, Available online: https://shakespeareinaction.wordpress.com/tag/pop-culture/ (accessed 17 July 2022).

Tichenor, A. (2014), Email to Reed Martin, 7 December.

# 3

# 'Scarce . . . a blot in his papers'

# Shakespearean inspiration on screen

## *Judith Buchanan*

Chafing against the convention that 'the explanation of a work' should always be 'sought in the man or woman who produced it', in his seminal 1967 essay 'The Death of the Author', Roland Barthes argued that the author's effective erasure from the present-tense operations of a work is part of what publication means and achieves. No longer was a text to be understood as simply a transmission vehicle for a settled and stable meaning determined by an author and awaiting decoding in those terms; now it had become 'a multi-dimensional space in which a variety of writings, none of them original, blend and clash' – a place, in fact, 'where all identity is lost, starting with the very identity of the body writing' (1967: 142–8). The necessary corollary to these processes of semantic multiplicity and authorial loss, argued Barthes, was the empowerment of those receiving and encountering the work ('the reader').

Although Barthes did not, of course, fundamentally change how a text works in the world, he did alter the terms in which its operations are described, by making conspicuous what was already the case. A process of professional severance, author from work and work from author, is the necessary psychological, emotional, symbolic and material corollary to publication. Upon publication it becomes a thing apart and beyond authorial governance. Consciously or otherwise, that is the transaction authors make, and have always made, with their work.

While the work's disengagement from its author is true in formal terms, experientially, however, it has rarely been so simple. In making sense of a work, readers, audiences and spectators crave, and seek, origins, and the most potently desired expression of artistic origin is always personal. In terms that speak back to Barthes, it is, explicitly, the 'identity of the body writing' that draws our interest.

The higher the profile of the work, the greater the desire to identify and personalize its authorial provenance as part of the process of recovering its origin story. Unsurprisingly, therefore, a cultural craving for Shakespeare has proved particularly strong.

Here I discuss three films in which an interest in 'the identity of the body writing' finds concentrated expression in the depiction of Shakespeare at work. The films selected are taken from either end of the twentieth century: *Shakespeare Writing Julius Caesar* (Georges Méliès, 1907), *Prospero's Books* (Peter Greenaway, 1991), *Shakespeare in Love* (John Madden, 1999). In relation to each, I consider its engagements with Shakespeare's writing processes, reputation and legacy.

However, screen configurations of Shakespeare (satirical and earnest) depend, both by emulation and resistance, upon the ways in which his writing processes were being powerfully conjured long before the advent of cinema. And so I start there.

\* \* \*

## Configuring the playwright: the 1623 Folio

In the *Doctor Who* episode 'The Shakespeare Code' (2007), a time-travelling visitor to the Globe in 1599 shouts 'Author' from her standing position amongst the groundlings and – without recorded precedent on the early modern stage – the call is taken up by the crowd, resulting in an onstage appearance by Shakespeare himself. As a dramatic moment, the will to see and commend the playwright in person was too delicious an anachronism, and too good an on-screen joke, not to be emulated subsequently. In the animated feature film, *Gnomeo and Juliet* (2011), the talking statue of William Shakespeare (voiced by Patrick Stewart) fondly remembers the end of early performances of *Romeo and Juliet* ending with a 'standing ovation' and cries of 'author, author'. And in *Anonymous* (2011), at the end of a performance of *Henry V* (on offer here as a work secretly written by the Earl of Oxford), the audience takes up the chant 'Playwright, playwright, playwright'. It is this popular clamour that persuades Will Shakespeare (Rafe Spall), the charlatan non-playwright of this film, to claim the work as his own, in a fraudulent masquerade of authorship.

Late sixteenth-century audiences in London playhouses did not call for on-stage appearances by the playwright at the end of a performance. As printed plays, diary entries (Manningham MS: 18) and the Stationers' Register from the 1590s and early 1600s testify, the name of a playwright from the public stage was not yet foregrounded in either the public imagination or the formal record: unlike for poems or sermons, for example, the most common identifying badge for plays, beyond title, was the name of the playhouse in which they played and/or of the playing company that mounted them.[1] In comparison, the name of the playwright featured minimally.

By 1623, however, this had changed decisively. For the publication of the Shakespeare ('First') Folio, the desire for a clear and personalized authorial connection to wrap into the experience of reading Shakespeare's plays was, by then, emphatically determining how the edition was presented and marketed. With a canny eye on the anticipated preferences of its market in this respect, for the prefatory pages for the 1623 Folio, a directly configured image of Shakespeare himself in the form of the famous Droeshout engraving was included as the frontispiece. No allegorical engravings saturated in erudite references here of the sort that had, for example, graced the frontispiece of Ben Jonson's 1616 *Workes*: just a directly appreciable portrait of a man which, despite the paradoxical urging of the poetic address on the facing page to look 'Not on his Picture, but his Booke', still constitutes a powerful draw.

However, the prefatory pages of the 1623 Folio do more than invite us to gaze upon a representation of the man who authored the works to follow: they also allude directly to the idea of 'the body writing' – that is, to Shakespeare as the point of writerly origin for those works. John Heminges and Henry Condell, Shakespeare's former friends, fellow actors and business partners, and the collators and editors of the volume, reported in their prefatory address that Shakespeare's 'mind and hand went together, and what he thought he uttered with that easiness, that we have scarce received from him a blot in his papers'. It is an evocative image. The claim of unblotted papers effectively launched the myth of Shakespeare's natural genius, in which an undisrupted process of inspiration found its way unimpeded and fluently onto the page. Such an inspired process obviated the need for further reflection or revision: hence the reported absence of 'blots'.

Heminges and Condell's tribute to Shakespeare's unchecked fluency of compositional process was undoubtedly heartfelt, but it also took some licence. It was simultaneously a touching tribute to the quality and capacity of the mind of their former friend *and* a piece of strategic hyperbole that helped market the book that they were explicitly keen to sell. It has not, however, been as figurative tribute that the description then gained traction in the centuries that followed. Rather, choosing to interpret the claim of unblotted work as a literal first-hand description of Shakespeare's foul papers has fuelled the claims for Shakespeare's rare natural genius that later generations have fervently wished to adduce. Shakespeare's alleged lack of self-correcting marks on his manuscripts has been taken as evidence of his inspired genius, helping to feed an emergent industry of bardolatry (Wells

2003: 329). The processes of literary idealization and mythicization were consolidated across the centuries, both in literary accounts and in artistic representations. So settled an establishment 'truth' did Shakespeare's image become – the poet of nature, the natural genius (Bate 1997: 157–216) – that with near inevitability, it also, in the process, became ripe for debunking. By the twentieth century, the idea of Shakespeare as an inspired genius through whom the muse flowed easily was too tempting a target for filmmakers to resist.

## Genius: debunked and restored

The much-recycled image of the inspired genius craved an intervention and, in response, films with an interest in Shakespeare's writing processes have systematically disrupted the supposed unbroken line of inspired transmission from muse to quill. In its place, cinema has taken self-conscious pleasure in choosing to imagine versions of a more earthed Shakespeare whose 'mind and hand' do not always '[go] together' with the immediate 'easiness' so winningly claimed by his earliest publicists. Would it not be more dramatically interesting, successive filmmakers have implicitly posited, for a Shakespeare character to experience recognizable writerly frustrations, to have to overcome impediments before earning his break-throughs and to be, as yet, pleasingly incognizant of the 'Shakespeare' he would in due course become?[2] If both tension and flawed humanity are necessary ingredients of drama, problematizing the 'easiness' of the writing process could, after all, serve the overall dramatic energies of a Shakespeare biopic rather well. Moreover, given the brand stability of Shakespeare's genius (Bate 1997: 3–33), dismantling that as a starting premise has something innately, impishly appealing about it.

Notwithstanding the satisfaction to be found in such iconoclastic impulses, the view of the inspired author has nevertheless retained its powerful appeal. In Shakespearean biopics, as a consequence, the will to unstitch a retrospectively perfected 'Shakespeare' and add, in effect, wrinkles of anxiety to the Droeshoutian forehead has often been matched by an equally strong subsequent desire to reconstruct the familiar monumentality and consoling perfection of the inherited Shakespearean image, complete with untroubled brow.

## *Shakespeare in Love* (Madden, 1998)

One of the most high-profile expressions of this process of debunking of Shakespeare's romantic genius followed by its comprehensive reinstatement is to be found in *Shakespeare in Love*. Here, audiences are given the flattering privilege of knowing more 'Shakespeare' than the character Will Shakespeare

(Joseph Fiennes) himself yet does. The young, aspiring London playwright is not yet fully cognizant of his destiny. He throws screwed-up pages of a possible playscript across the room in despair at his own fettered imagination, sucks his quill fruitlessly, consults an early modern shrink about his writer's block, tries out 'Romeo and Ethel the Pirate's Daughter' as the proposed title of his next work on an unconvinced Kit Marlowe (Rupert Everett) and spends more time experimenting with versions of his own signature than in writing the promised play. His struggles are banal, writerly and humanly recognizable. This is not the near-deified poet feted in the prefatory pages to the 1623 Folio but rather, circumstantially at least, one of us: a flawed and frustrated individual contending with financial anxieties, a less than simple love life and an apparent inability to live up to his own creative aspirations.

It is not, however, with frustrated quill-scratchings that the film ends. Once Will has been artistically 'released' by personally living a version of the love story that he needs to write, the poetic muse is comprehensively restored and the image of the inspired playwright with unfettered quill is explicitly resummoned with all the romanticized force that big-budget scoring and high production value cinematography can deliver. Will reports to his love interest and muse, Lady Viola (Gwyneth Paltrow), that for him, she will 'never age . . . nor fade nor die', and later to himself that she will be 'my heroine for all time'. At the close of the film, we see her – as imagined by Will – walking up a long beach on the eastern shore of the Americas, both into the action of his new play, *Twelfth Night* and, more suggestively yet, into new as yet unrealized Shakespearean futures. In his DVD commentary (1999), director John Madden reports that he had flirted with showing 'the ghostly outline of modern Manhattan' rising above the treeline on the horizon towards which Viola walks. This modern-day skyline does not appear in the released film, but the sustained shot of the lone figure, the open beach and the distant horizon is intuitively understood, as Madden explicitly hoped it would be, as showing Viola 'walking away into history', embodying the legacy, both enduring and international, of the writing we have witnessed.

## *Shakespeare Writing Julius Caesar* (Méliès, 1907)

The screen representation of a Shakespeare struggling to write the play that we know will in due course be successfully launched upon the world, and concluding with a recognition of its own lasting historical resonance, is, however, a cinematic trope that long predates *Shakespeare in Love*. The 1907 French film *Shakespeare Writing Julius Caesar* (*Shakespeare Écrivant La Mort de Jules César*) from zany, experimental filmmaker Georges Méliès depicts a directly comparable story arc, if in sparer form.

Sadly, the Méliès film, like so many from the era, is now believed lost. Nevertheless, a detailed catalogue entry furnishes us with a clear indication of its action (Ball 1968: 35–6). In addition, two stills from the film survive, archived in the Library of Congress (Washington DC) and the Museum of Modern Art, New York (MOMA) respectively (Buchanan 2013: 8). The detailed description of the film's action, in combination with the two surviving stills, provide a clear sense of the film's design, its engaging taste for spatial transformation and the mechanism by which its transitions (from playwright's humdrum working space to realized dramatic scene and back again) were innovatively negotiated.

The film consisted of four scenes. Understanding their sequencing reveals the structural similarity to *Shakespeare in Love* and so speaks in broad terms to the comparable temptations being experienced, and opportunities being seized, by makers of Shakespeare biopics at both ends of the century.

The film's opening scene is set in Shakespeare's study. A temporarily uninspired Shakespeare (played by Méliès himself) sits at his desk trying, but failing, to write the assassination scene for *Julius Caesar*. In blocked frustration, he leaves his desk and papers and paces the room trying to catch and conjure the dramatic scene currently eluding him. 'At his wits' end', as the catalogue entry expresses it, 'he sits down in an armchair, crosses his legs, and leaning on his hand prepares for a good, long think'.

For the second scene, as confirmed by the MOMA still, Shakespeare remains seated in his armchair in right of frame. However, with the stop-motion transformative magic characteristic of so many Méliès films, Shakespeare's study has now vanished entirely. Without having moved, Shakespeare now finds himself transplanted from a position gazing unproductively at the walls of his own study to a ring-side seat in the Capitol with the high-octane scene of Caesar's assassination being played out before him. His previously blocked imagination seems now to have conjured, fully formed and dramatically enacted, the scene that was previously eluding him. The visitation of the muse, delivered in an idiom attuned to the capacities of the silent era, is one fully worthy of the inspired genius of the 1623 Shakespeare Folio's prefatory pages.

Once the climactic action is completed, the Roman scene fades and Shakespeare, still in his scene-shifting armchair, is magically absorbed back into the more prosaic surrounds of his study, leaving him joyously inspired about the scene he can now commit to paper. As the catalogue entry reports: 'the poet . . . realizes that he at last has come upon the required idea and begins to stalk about excitedly, going it all over for himself'. Ignoring a servant who has entered with a tray of food, Shakespeare 'keeps on tearing and ranting about the room in his passion . . . wind[ing] up by raising a knife and plunging it furiously into the loaf of bread which was on the table'. Shakespeare's own actions, as described here – tearing about the room, ranting and stabbing – show him almost comically inhabiting the assassination scene he now needs to write.

Via a final Méliès transformation, the closing scene then delivers the triumphant coda: '[Shakespeare] . . . folds his arms and the scene dissolves into a bust of William Shakespeare, around which all the nations wave flags and garlands.' This final dissolve is a double celebration of Shakespeare's monumentality (the bust) and universality (the community of 'all nations waving flags'). It is the fluidity and reach of his own sympathies as a writer – demonstrably, in this short film, enabling him to escape the containment of his modest study – that ushers in and legitimizes the breadth of this subsequent lasting international recognition.

Though delivered on a much more economical scale, the structural rhyme with the much later *Shakespeare in Love* is striking. Both films open on a Shakespeare whose imagination is blocked. Both suggest that the playwright needs personally to live the action (falling in love/plunging the knife in) in order to write it. Both films explore a degree of interchange between the writer's life and the dramatized scene. In both films, the previously blocked Shakespeare yields excitedly to the influence of the muse whose inspiration, once found, lands with ease. And in the closing moments of both films, the inspired work is enthusiastically celebrated as having both international reach and endurance.

## *Prospero's Books* (Greenaway, 1991)

In *Prospero's Books*, the central character (John Gielgud) sits in his Renaissance scholar's writing cell quietly eliding the functions and associations of Prospero (controlling the drama), Shakespeare (scripting it) and St. Jerome (the scholar-hermit, directly conjured through artistic reference) (Buchanan 2005: 225–30). The film's foundational conceit is that we are watching the processes of the composition of *The Tempest* into which the playwright scripts himself as the play's central protagonist. The play being written will, by the close of the film, grace the opening pages of the 1623 Shakespeare Folio.

As the Shakespeare-evocative figure composes the play from the calm haven of his scholarly study, he tries out lines in his head and on paper. The words he writes conjure the action that is then played out in the world beyond his writing space; enacted before his, and our, eyes. All other characters in the play are, therefore, his imaginative constructs and the action and dialogue are seen to follow the whims and determinations of his dramatic imagination.

Méliès, Madden and Greenaway all experiment with the image of the solitary genius seeking inspiration by excluding the world. But their sense of how inspiration arrives differs significantly. Madden's Shakespeare cannot thrive away from the world: he needs to be fully immersed in order to write 'truth' in the terms of the film. For Méliès' Shakespeare, the books and papers on the desk prove to be fettering and must be abandoned in order to 'release' the muse. Like the romanticized portraiture of Byron (Kenyon-

Jones 2008: 100), this Shakespeare needs to free himself from literary clutter and bookish distraction for his natural genius to find unimpeded expression.

By contrast, Greenaway's Shakespeare is ostentatiously learned. His compositional processes explicitly involve attentive encounters with other beautiful volumes that help to structure the film and inform the dramatist's mind. Rather than abandoning his books in order to compose, this Shakespeare immerses himself in them the more to write, advertising at every turn his art's dependence on erudition.

Greenaway's dramatist also reflects consciously and in detail on the specific words he writes. The text we watch emerging in *Prospero's Books* has not yet reached the publishable stability of the First Folio *Tempest*. The ongoing minor adjustments to a word or a line between spoken forms and written forms help to suggest that what we are witnessing is neither the rehearsed delivery of a text already complete, nor the unimpeded channelling of a muse's visitation, but rather the gradual and worked-for emergence of a text from the (stylized) throes of a creative process. The opening word of the play, 'boatswain', for example, is written and uttered many times by the dramatist, sometimes appearing with no punctuation, once with a question mark and once with an exclamation mark, as if the dramatist were still trying to establish what sort of dramatic charge it could most effectively carry. And as variants are considered and discarded (Buchanan 2005: 223), the text is refined in stages towards the First Folio version of the play that we know.

The end of the film is marked by a flamboyant, almost celebratory display of pyrotechnic book destruction. But the canonized and now completed Folio is kept safe from the surrounding carnage, rescued for posterity. The process we have been made privy to across the course of the film, through the considered work of the dramatist's quill is, therefore, the passage of the provisional into the monumental.

\* \* \*

The literal Shakespeare monument – the bust 'around which all the nations wave flags and garlands' – into which the action of Méliès' 1907 film dissolves at its end stills the freneticism of the preceding scenes into a tableau iconizing the ongoing, international reputation of the dramatist. It is apt that more than a century of movies about Shakespeare should have been launched by a film that so clearly showcased a triangulated interest in his process (Shakespeare writing), his output (the play) and his authorial legacy (the bust).

As the films considered here attest, the strength of the temptation to impede the processes of inspiration and writing, and to unsettle the sense of Shakespeare as a playwright exclusively characterized by an 'easiness' to his writing may be strong; but if that is so, the pull towards confirming the consoling and near-beatifying vision contained in the prefatory pages of the 1623 Folio may be yet stronger – its cultural power having been acquired and consolidated across many generations. As for Rosalind on her giddy trip to the Forest of Arden, or for Bottom in his overnight adventure in a wood near Athens, a time-bounded version of Shakespeare who is other than his settled self can, in these films at least, be temporarily entertained. As words, lines or whole scenes seem to elude him, we enjoy the disruptive fun of seeing him temporarily un-Shakespeared. But like those other holiday moments, the rhythms of the drama and of conservative expectation conspire to dictate an eventual return to things *as they should be*. Neither Rosalind in *As You Like It*, nor Bottom in *A Midsummer Night's Dream*, for example, can stay in their more convention-defying roles beyond the end of the drama: the weight of expectation requires their reabsorption back into the world of weddable womanhood/honest tradesman respectively. And an equivalent narrative arc, from convention-defying disruption to reasserted (and celebrated) conformity to expectation, is, in differing ways, felt in these Shakespeare films also.

As the failure to write cedes to the fully realized conjuration of the *Julius Caesar* scene and a transtemporal waving of international flags in Méliès, the slow and considered weighing of textual variants to the emergence of the Folio that must be saved for posterity in Greenaway, and unfruitful time at the desk to the fluently inspired writing of *Romeo and Juliet* and then *Twelfth Night* in Madden, allowing the work to walk 'away into history', Shakespeare is in each case returned to being the consolingly inspired 'Shakespeare' we have received from history. And with Shakespearean mind and hand thus restored to each other, and legacy thereby assured, his papers can once again bear scarce a blot.

## Notes

1 Of the significant run of 1590s published quarto plays which identify the work by playing company not by playwright, see, for example: 'The Tragedie of King Richard the third . . . As it hath been lately acted by the Right Honourable the Lord Chamberlaine his Servants' (1597). Note also that entries for Shakespeare plays in the Stationers' Register do not include his name until 1607.

2 On the Shakespeare/'Shakespeare' distinction, see Eagleton 1988: 204.

## References

*Anonymous* (2011), [Film] Dir. Roland Emmerich, USA: Columbia Pictures.
Ball, R. H. (1968), *Shakespeare on Silent Film*, New York: Theater Arts Books.
Barthes, R. ([1967] 1978), 'The Death of the Author', in *Image-Music-Text*, S. Heath (trans.), 142–148, New York: Hill and Wang.
Bate, J. (1997), *The Genius of Shakespeare*, London: Picador.

Buchanan, J. (2005), *Shakespeare on Film*, Harlow: Longman-Pearson.
Buchanan, J., ed. (2013), *The Writer on Film: Screening Literary Authorship*, London: Palgrave-Macmillan.
*Doctor Who* (2007), [TV series] 'The Shakespeare Code', BBC One, 7 April.
Eagleton, T. (1988), 'Afterword', in G. Holderness (ed), *The Shakespeare Myth*, Manchester: Manchester University Press.
*Gnomeo and Juliet* (2011), [Film] Dir. Kelly Asbury, USA: Touchstone Pictures.
Kenyon-Jones, C. (2008), *Byron: The Image of a Poet*, Newark: University of Delaware Press.
Madden, J. (1999), 'Director's Commentary', in *Shakespeare in Love*, London: UCA. DVD.
Manningham, J. (1602–1603), *Diary*, Harley MS 5353, London: British Library.
*Prospero's Books* (1991), [Film] Dir. Peter Greenaway, UK, Netherlands, France: Allarts.
*Shakespeare in Love* (1998), [Film] Dir. John Madden, USA: Miramax.
*Shakespeare Writing Julius Caesar* (1907), [Film] Dir. Georges Méliès, France: Star-Film.
*Stationers' Register* (1557–1640), Available online: http://stationersregister.online.
Wells, S. (2003), *Shakespeare: For All Time*, Oxford: Oxford University Press.

# 4

# Interview on co-writing and performing in *Bill* (dir. Bracewell, 2015) *Laurence Rickard in conversation with Ronan Hatfull and Edel Semple*

**Laurence Rickard:** is a BAFTA-winning comedy writer and actor. He co-wrote *Bill* (2015) with Ben Willbond and was a principal writer and star of *Horrible Histories*, which won more than twenty major awards, including National Comedy Awards, BAFTAs and the Prix Jeunesse. Laurence is also a co-creator, writer, and star of the BBC sitcom *Ghosts*.

**Ronan Hatfull:** Why did you choose the medium of film, a feature film rather than a television series for this project?

**Laurence Rickard:** I think there's something about getting to tell such different stories when you're doing something feature-length. Even though we were being loose with the facts, Shakespeare has this handy [biographical] hole where, for a year on either side of 1593, you can put anything in there and it's hard to disprove. That was such rich territory, and it wouldn't be enough to do it in half hour. We didn't want to rewrite history. There's this tiny, compact hole in the history, and we can, therefore, have the licence to fill that with whatever nonsense we want. So, it was a story that was too long for a half hour, but facts would start to hem it in if it became a series; a feature film felt like the natural territory.

**RH:** When did you hit upon the framework of a Spanish plot to murder Queen Elizabeth I to inform Shakespeare's lost years?

**LR:** We [Ben Willbond and I] were keen to do something Tudor and Rich [Bracewell], our director, was a big Shakespeare fan. So, we started talking early on about Shakespeare and, very quickly, we hit on the idea of doing early Shakespeare. The first thing we thought was 'okay, we're going to write a film about Shakespeare, let's do our research'. [Then] we realized how tricky it was to write about his early life because we can't find a lot about it; then we thought 'hang on, that's perfect!' Once we settled on 1593, we started researching around the historical and political contexts of that period and found these endless Catholic plots and invasions against Elizabeth. We thought 'well, that's a really good caper to get a small player pulled into it'. At this point, Shakespeare is so fresh to London and not yet embroiled in the court, we thought that to take this giant geopolitical plot and pull some bloke called Bill from Stratford into it would make for a big, fun, ridiculous story.

**Edel Semple:** Did you read around the character of Walsingham [Elizabeth's spymaster] or were you using your imagination? He reminded me of the six-fingered man from *The Princess Bride*, and his voice was like that of a hero in a spy movie!

**LR:** The six-fingered man played into it and the voice, well, whenever we're writing these characters who think they're brilliant, both and Ben and I would naturally fall into what Pierce Brosnan's James Bond did when he was trying to be overly dramatic; he would get very breathy. So, it's a really, really bad Pierce Brosnan impression! Walsingham's got the ridiculousness of the six-fingered man, he's got the slight arrogance of Brosnan's Bond, and then we dressed him, insofar as we could, like Batman! He's in this padded leather doublet, and he can't have Batman's mask, but he's got a little black hat. He really does think he's a superhero, to the point where he says that he's back from the dead.

**RH:** You've touched there on two of the genres, the spy and superhero movie, that I wanted to ask about in relation to *Bill*. Why did you open the film with what is essentially a 'cold open', and was the casting of Damian Lewis as adventurer-spy Sir Richard Hawkins anything to do with his notable role as a double agent in *Homeland*? Did you aim to evoke spy thrillers during this opening scene?

**LR:** With the opening scene, Hawkins stealing the gold was originally a battle between two Spanish galleons, with a boarding party, and he had all these quips about Spanish food. When we started looking at the budget, we realized that we'd have to do that in a slightly different way! But we liked the idea of a proper Bond-like spy hitting against an idiot, who likes to think he's a spy but has got lots and lots of goons around him. [The character of King Phillip II of Spain] outnumbers but doesn't outthink him. We loved that idea, and, for ages, we really wanted someone big in the role of Hawkins because your assumption is that this is someone who's going to play a significant role throughout, and then we use them for three minutes! And then, three-quarters of the way through the film, when everyone's forgotten about him, we remind the audience, and so we wanted someone big enough where that joke would land. We'd approached Damian, and then we had subsequently managed to get Helen McCrory to play Elizabeth, and Damian and the kids came up to York, when we were filming in Selby Abbey, and just saw how much fun we were having. And Helen went 'oh, you should do it', and so he agreed on the day. We wanted someone who could lend the gravitas of a proper spy film to something so ridiculous.

**RH:** Even though it's called *Bill*, is the film also Philip's story?

**LR:** Yes, absolutely. I think he's the peg that brings together the disparate blocks; it's very much about Phillip and his drive to take over and dethrone the Queen. The agent who brings about the most change in the story is Croydon, in the fact that it's him who brings together Phillip and Bill and by extension Marlowe. Without him, none of these things come together. The big political rivals are Walsingham and Philip playing against each other in this game of cat-and-mouse. Bill is this hapless pawn for the most part until it gets quite late into the film, and he frees Marlowe and unmasks Philip, but it's quite late into the film that it becomes Bill's story.

**RH:** You were working during the superhero movie boom – or what I'd describe as the mid-saturation point with superhero movies – when *Bill* came out. We were one year away from *Captain America: Civil War* and *Batman v Superman* (2016). Were there any tangible superhero influences behind the film and the inspiration to create a Shakespearean origin story?

**LR:** It's definitely an origin story. You look at *Iron Man* and the fact that he reveals his identity at the end of the film. *Bill* is the same, in the sense that the final scene is Shakespeare going up on stage, having almost decided on the title of his first comedy. He's not balding yet, but he looks a little bit more like Shakespeare. The film ends at the point where history picks up and it's similar to those superhero origin stories where everyone knows who, say, the Incredible Hulk is, but the film reveals how they got there. Around that time [the sixteenth century], there was a belief in magic, and also these spy networks which were interested in magic and alchemy. So, we thought 'let's make [Walsingham] slightly magical and come back from the dead. He doesn't just walk into scenes, he just appears!' And then, at the end of the film, he disappears again. I think it was in the pitch of the film, when we gave the character breakdown, that we said, 'Walsingham thinks he's Batman'. He thinks he's great but he's always one step behind Philip. He's constantly trampled by his own men, but there's no sense that he ever thinks 'am I good at this?' He always believes he's the best and then, even at the end, he gives a smug smile before he disappears, and you, the audience, think 'you did nothing!' Overall, I think it feels like an origin story and then within that, there are elements of the superhero in the Walsingham character.

**ES:** One of the starting points for our collection is *Shakespeare in Love*. Did you find that it was an influence or in the back of your mind? Were there call-backs to it, say in how *Bill* opens with Bill writing?

**LR:** The main reason we were aware of it was that when you've got to go out farming for finance, you point towards that Shakespeare film that did well! [. . .] One of the reasons there was such good feeling towards *Shakespeare in Love* was that it felt particularly rewarding for people who understood and were immersed in Shakespeare. If you have an audience who've never seen a Shakespeare play, they are getting slightly less out of that film than people who are versed in it, because there's so much crossover and reference. Quite early on, we said that we wanted there to be 'easter eggs' scattered throughout for the people who had that knowledge. However, we were looking at a broader, more family audience than *Shakespeare in Love*, so [we also thought] it should be a primer, that it could feel, to a large degree, like caperish, knockabout fun that you don't realize is, stealthily, encouraging a wider interest in Shakespeare. Because Shakespeare is trying to cram every idea he's got into one play, by the film's end the audience has been introduced to several themes that appear throughout his subsequent works.

**RH:** You create quite an endearing portrayal of the Shakespeare and Marlowe relationship for your audience, but there is a dark side, and I just wanted to learn more about how you drew them as this crime-fighting and writing duo.

**LR:** We knew that Shakespeare was coming to London, with all that burning enthusiasm of a young writer. Then you've got Marlowe, who's not the tired hack, but has seen fame and success. As soon as we started researching around 1593, we realized that they were both in London at that point, and that's when Marlowe's killed. And so that's two such exciting events that both happen around that magical year. We thought it would be a shame not to have Marlowe's death play a role in the story. At one point, Ben Jonson was going to be that character instead. Obviously, Shakespeare's got friendships right through to the end of his life (he was out drinking with some writer friends the day before he died), so, there were lots of people who we could pick, but it was the death of Marlowe in that year that made us settle on Marlowe. As a character, we picked what we needed from him for the story, rather than focusing too much on the historical facts, because there's a lot more history about him than there is about Shakespeare, besides the fact that there were these rumours about him being tied into Catholic plots. We thought that was perfect because we've got that plot thread running as well.

**RH:** It's interesting, in terms of their trajectory, that it starts with Marlowe being this practitioner of tragedy and Shakespeare being the purveyor of bum jokes and comedy. I'm interested in what you and Ben, as comic artists, were saying about the nebulous divide between comedy and tragedy by putting these two iconic artists on either side of that boundary.

**LR:** Well, I suppose, to a degree, there's always that outlook – which I don't agree with, as you can imagine – that comedy is that thing you do and then you progress to doing drama, then you're taken seriously, and you're considered good. We'd just come out of *Horrible Histories* into doing *Bill*, a family comedy and then into *Ghosts*, a primetime sitcom. We thought with Shakespeare, it's like he's been a kid in a band, who's done a bit of dancing, a bit of acting, he's had these quite puerile, kids-TV-type jokes, and now he's progressing into doing his sitcom, he's doing comedy. But what he will go on to do is drama. And he's got Marlowe, who's all about drama and doesn't get comedy, which in no way marries up to the history, but it worked for our story as he then is someone who helps Bill make that transition. Shakespeare did everything in a completely random order throughout and seemed to both start and end with comedy, but for our purposes, we said that it was comedy progressing towards drama!

**RH:** You couldn't really throw *Titus Andronicus* into this film!

**LR:** Exactly! *The Comedy of Errors* was obviously a tentpole for us and we just ignored *Richard III* and *Henry VI*, because they didn't really fit for us.

**ES:** Was it a deliberate choice to call Christopher Marlowe 'Chris'? In TNT's *Will*, 'Kit' is a sexy rebel type, but calling him 'Chris' makes him more of an everyman, more familiar.

**LR:** He in no way invites that, as he's sitting there brooding on his own in the pub! We've portrayed him as this tortured intellectual who's all about art and Bill immediately goes: 'so what I think you do, Chris is . . . ' You can see in Marlowe's reaction that it's the first time in his life that anyone's called him 'Chris'! It's a subtle thing, but in some ways, it felt like that moment distilled their relationship; one is this chirpy, plucky, wide-eyed kid and the other is this tortured, intellectual, serious soul. And he is immediately intellectually debased by Bill deciding that he's 'Chris'!

**RH:** Was naming Shakespeare and Marlowe 'Bill' and 'Chris' also to do with your audience not only being young but predominantly UK-based? Does this play into crafting the origin story of Shakespeare's life, not in superhero terms, but as a modern celebrity on an *X-Factor*-esque journey?

**LR:** It was two things. One, rather than it being in 'old English', we wanted to make it feel contemporary and relatable. Rather than them being 'William and Christopher', or 'Will and Kit', they're 'Bill and Chris', that's our version of them and it gives you a little bit of ownership. It was [also] a way of containing all the nonsense that we'd made up, by saying this is what happened to characters called Bill and Chris, not the historically verified stuff that happened to William Shakespeare and Christopher Marlowe. And obviously, also it's about the journey of Bill from young hopeful 'Bill from Stratford' to becoming 'William Shakespeare'. It's all of those things.

**RH:** In an episode of the podcast *Rule of Three*, Mat Baynton, who plays Bill, talks about the connection between comedy and music and the idea that comedians often dream of becoming musicians. Is there anything behind the fact that your Shakespeare begins *Bill* by dreaming of becoming an Elizabethan rock star in 'Mortal Coil'?

**LR:** When you meet almost any actor, they'll tell you that they play a bit, or are in a band; we loved the idea that Bill was one of those. But also, it was helpful for our story to have Bill have so many fads, that he's done a bit of dance, a bit of music, a bit of acting, and none of them have quite worked. That just helps audiences buy Anne's [unhappy] reaction to his announcement that he's a playwright; she doesn't seem unsympathetic, [rather it is] completely reasonable [that she thinks] 'stop messing around and get a job, we've got kids!' That is the correct response, rather than her trying to crush his dreams.

**ES:** Could you tell us a little bit about your idea of Anne? At one point, you have Bill and Anne appear like separated parents, but there's a redemptive arc as Anne helps save Bill's career and they patch things up.

**LR:** You completely see why, in story terms, *Shakespeare in Love* doesn't work if you acknowledge too much of the presence of Anne Hathaway. She doesn't exist for that film. And we always thought about how Shakespeare was with her from when he was eighteen. The degree to which that was under duress and dictated by circumstances has been argued; we just don't really know, but we felt that there was something in the fact that this is now a long-term relationship and, we were saying, a loving one. It meant that Anne was looking at their relationship in a different way. She was a little older than him, she is raising children while her eighteen-year old husband goes off to enjoy childlike pursuits. You know that there's genuine love and affection there, but also this huge frustration, which is then compounded by him going to London. Anne still supports Bill, and he doesn't always see it, but she does come to see him in London. It's only when she gets there and he's made false claims about how well he's doing that she thinks 'again, another thing that has failed, why did I believe in this?' and so they end up with a de facto trial separation.

**RH:** The ghostly appearance of Marlowe to Shakespeare in his cell is part-*Star Wars*, part-*Hamlet*. When Marlowe points to his heart, does he mean 'look to Anne', 'write what you know' or both?

LR: I think it's sort of both. Rather than reaching outwardly, which you do as a writer, there's an idea that it's always come from writing what you know. Marlowe's asking him, rather than looking to the outside world, to try and find something confined here in this room. Look to yourself, look to your heart, what are you thinking about? What are you feeling? And he realizes that it's Anne that he's thinking about and his feelings towards her, and that's what inspires him, but he needs a nudge in that direction.

RH: Were there any biographical depictions of Anne that influenced you and what were you trying to say to the audience about her relationship with Shakespeare?

LR: We wanted to make sure that people would be rooting for the relationship, rooting for them to find a way through. It starts early on, as we need our inciting incident, we need him to go to London. But it starts from a place of support that Bill's up there on stage, doing a gig with his band, and Anne turns up and brings the kids along to support him. Even later, when they're in the Globe, and he's accusing her of not really supporting him all that much, you're thinking 'No, stop right now! She really has!' And so, I think, we always felt like the divide was between love and security, family and ambition. And he'd always had ambition, but I think now he's going 'I've worked out the direction that's going to work for me'. And, as an audience, you know this is one that's going to work because of who Shakespeare is. We avoided the idea of it being sex or philandering, or anything like that, which was going to affect him in London because there were so many other big plots that he was going to be pulled into. We just avoided [complicating] Bill's love life, so the only person you're ever rooting for is Anne and for them to work it out and get back together.

RH: Where does the impulse to play multi-roles come from, for you as a company?

LR: It's enjoyable for us, particularly on an eight-week shoot. It also feels Shakespearean and that felt right when you've got this quite theatrical conceit. You only have to look at the *dramatis persona* at the beginning of a Shakespeare play and then look at the number of the Lord Chamberlain's Men and think 'that doesn't tie up! Everyone's going to have to be coming in and playing everyone!' And so it felt particularly right for this film. Also, Bill was an actor, as well as a writer, so we had him wearing a number of hats.

RH: Besides *The Comedy of Errors*, were there were any other Shakespearean plays or film adaptations that inspired specific moments in *Bill*?

LR: We were so keen for it to feel like there's too many ideas and too many references. Just when you go, 'oh, I think I get this reference, that's *King Lear*', it's actually Bill with the nascent ideas of twenty different things! In your early writing career, you think 'I've got a thousand ideas and I'm going to put them into a thing' and then as you get a bit more experience, you explore a single idea. That's where Bill gets to. As I say, ignoring the first history plays, Shakespeare's early work is comedies and we combine them all into one, and those are all the references that run through the song 'A Series of Funny Misunderstandings'. As the film progresses and becomes more dramatic, the references are more to the tragedies, and there are nods to the histories, but they're further and fewer between because we're in that blank spot in history. [. . .] We loved the idea of things happening to Bill and him taking those ideas and repurposing them in a completely different context. We went to the Shakespeare Birthplace Trust, and they were absolutely amazing. They were showing us one of the textbooks that was available [to Shakespeare], and then they placed that side-by-side with one of the plays in the First Folio, and it was basically the same, just with the words changed around. The overt plagiarizing was, one, commonplace, but two, necessary, if you're going to knock out a play in three weeks. You think 'he's like a magpie!' and so we said, 'a lot of this stuff, he should happen upon and get wrong', like he does at the start of the film when he's talking to Anne in half quotes. They're almost there, but not quite, and the quotes that *are* fully formed come from other people!

ES: How did you and Ben work together? Did you have similar or different points of focus and interests when you were writing?

LR: Well, I love plot, and trying to get the plot to work as a ninety-minute story. It was the first feature film that either of us had done and so a lot of the touchstones weren't Shakespearean at all. We were looking at the screenplay to *A Fish Called Wanda*, comedy capers, and Ealing films, and asking 'how do you structure a comedy caper that's multicharacter?' And then, as we started to get increasingly into the Shakespeare, it would be Ben, who would highlight an interesting point of character here, or, say 'that's actually a lot like that bit in that play', so maybe there's a reference in there that will also inform the shape of that scene.

ES: Do you think there is any part of you, or Ben either, in the writer characters of Chris and Bill, or in the characters you play in the film?

LR: Definitely. In almost every writing partnership, there's someone who sits down and does the typing, and someone else who walks around going, 'what if it's like this' and, within the writing montage, it was very much always Marlowe as the old sage sitting there doing the writing, and Bill wandering around, and suddenly leaning over his shoulder and saying 'do that, do that!' The assumption is that co-writers are two people who sit there with laptops and type a word each – it so rarely works like that. [. . .] Early on, there were certain bits of casting that came immediately from the writing; like, we didn't even have a conversation about who would be Croydon. When we were reading lines out to each other, we were doing them in Simon [Farnaby]'s voice, and the same with Philip. I think it was Rich, our director, who said 'clearly, you're Lopez' to me. Now I look at it and, of course, I am! Mat and Martha [Howe-Douglas] were going to be Bill and Anne but it was only those four that were set in stone from almost day one. Everything else was a combination of gradual realization of who fits which part and, also, production and availability on the day.

**RH:** It really speaks to your versatility, doesn't it? There's this ability in your troupe to play these various levels of emotion, like how the tragic moment of Marlowe's death is undercut by his body being dragged away. You punctuate one of the most touching moments in the film with a brilliant physical gag! How do you, as a writer, approach the balance between sincerity and irony?

**LR:** I've had to get my head around that. My innate instinct, particularly earlier in my career, was to always think of my job as making comedy and being a comedy person. I was always trying to find [laughs], and if there were two pages that didn't have one, I'd feel like I'd failed. I think it's actually from working with the others, through the years, that we've learnt the value of sincerity, and that there's a place for that in comedy. I think, in part, that's a fashion thing as well. When you look at *Blackadder* – with the famous exception of the end of *Blackadder Goes Forth* – they try to play for laughs insofar as they possibly can. Now, I look at a lot of the big 'hit' comedies, and they're comedy-drama and the sitcom doesn't have to be just laughs anymore. And the first time that I felt we'd really explored that balance was with *Bill*. So, that was a bit of an education. The tone of *Yonderland* was such that we didn't really take it through into that but in *Ghosts*, because you're dealing with pathos in the very concept of it – it's people who are dead and can't escape – there's lots of darkness within the conceit. It needed those moments of sincerity and so I've found that balance a little bit more in recent years.

**ES:** How interested were you in critiquing the authorship conspiracy theory?

**LR:** The closest thing to our release in terms of Shakespeare was *Anonymous*, and I struggled with that. Personally, I've never found anything particularly compelling about the authorship debate, apart from the late works, where I think it's widely accepted that there was collaboration. Also, with collaboration, when you are writing for a company, and you're doing a play in three weeks, everyone's looking at everyone else's stuff! We loved the idea that we were giving a little nod to the fact that perhaps, not everything that Shakespeare wrote, he wrote entirely on his own. But, at the same time, we say at the end that there was this play that was written in collaboration between Shakespeare and Marlowe, but it was left on a table in a pub and burnt! And the next thing that Shakespeare writes is the play that our audience knows and he did it on his own. Again, we then pick up where history is, but we put a nod to the authorship debate into that, that black hole, before we get there.

**RH:** Why do you think writers keep having the impulse to imagine Shakespeare's life?

**LR:** I think because it's fascinating. It never goes away. Everyone's always worried that there's going to be a generation which thinks 'Shakespeare is not that valid or relevant anymore' and the productions are going to stop. And yet, you ask a schoolchild today and, 400 years later, and thirty years later from when I was being introduced to Shakespeare, it's still there and it's still relevant. You want to give another audience an entry into it.

# 5

# 'The thing is, you're a douche'

# Fourth wave feminist representations of Shakespeare in *Emilia* and *& Juliet*

## *Gemma Kate Allred*

The last decade closed with two productions that, rather than being direct adaptations of Shakespeare plays, were influenced by both the Shakespearean canon and the early modern period. In Morgan Lloyd Malcolm's 2018 play *Emilia*, the historically fictionalized Emilia Lanier became every woman, embodying their collective anger. The 2019 West End show David West Read's *& Juliet* – neon pink, glitter-accented, and set to a soundtrack of Max Martin's teen-pop classics – is on first look an unlikely counterpart to *Emilia*. However, both productions raise questions about whose stories get told and by whom and about who controls the narrative. *Emilia* and *& Juliet* place early modern women in conversation with both a modern audience and Shakespeare himself.

This chapter explores what happens when Shakespeare is fictionalized for the modern stage and reaches out across time. These productions pitch Shakespeare as a selfish monstrous artist writing the status quo, against radical outspoken women who want to write and change the stories we are told and who would challenge his privileged position as an important playwright. Shakespeare here becomes a synecdoche for the male-centric nature of creation. Taking Rebecca Solnit's fourth wave feminist essays as a base, it argues that in *Emilia* and *& Juliet*, the historically fictionalized Shakespeare acts to silence early modern women. Further, I argue that these two productions can be read as a reaction to the silencing of women in modern society that Solnit claims is 'Violence' (2017: 19). These Shakespeares hold the white male privilege of being heard, of having their words afforded importance and respect. Mary Beard traces this privileged position back to 'very near the beginning of the tradition of Western literature' in Homer's *Odyssey* where Telemachus advises his mother, Penelope, that 'speech will be the business of men, all men' (2018: 3–4). In Beard's analysis, the role of being *a man* is 'learning to take control of public utterance and to silence the female of the species' (2018: 4). Our Shakespeares enthusiastically embrace this as they each navigate relationships with women who, unlike Homer's Penelope, refuse to be silenced. As Lloyd Malcom's Emilia takes as her battle cry: 'We are only as powerful as the stories we tell. We have not always been able to tell them. Time to listen!' (Lloyd Malcolm 2019: 2). This echoes the argument underpinning fourth wave feminism: 'if our voices are essential aspects of our humanity, to be rendered voiceless is to be dehumanized or excluded from one's humanity' (Solnit 2017: 18). These productions were devised and first performed within the maelstrom of the #MeToo movement, a reaction to allegations of sexual assault by Hollywood producer Harvey Weinstein, and other influential men, which saw women who had been subjected to sexual harassment or assault telling their stories using the hashtag '#MeToo'. They also followed in the wake of the 2017 Women's Marches that took place worldwide following Donald Trump's inauguration as President of the United States. Fuelled by this fourth wave of feminism, the early modern women of *Emilia* and *& Juliet* take on Shakespeare, here imagined as the poster boy for white male privilege, and demand that he and wider society acquiesce to 'the radical notion that women are people' (Marie Shear, quoted in Cameron 2019: 2).

These fictionalized Shakespeares draw heavily on the pop culture trope of Shakespeare as a troubled artist who laboured for his art, a portrayal that 'aligns with a broader myth of male genius unappreciated in its time' (Blackwell 2021: 129). Joseph Fiennes in *Shakespeare in Love* (1998) epitomizes this version of Shakespeare, who, faced with writer's block, takes inspiration from the women around him. However, there is a very different tone to this late 1990s Shakespeare – he acknowledges the women he leans on, and they are complicit in his process, with Shakespeare working to support his beloved Viola's dream of performing on the stage. Fiennes's flawed Shakespeare may have several failings but unlike the stage Shakespeares of *Emilia* and *& Juliet* he does not embody what Claire Dederer terms the 'selfishness' of 'monster geniuses':

> The selfishness of forgetting the real world to create a new one. The selfishness of stealing stories from real people. The selfishness of saving the best of yourself for that blank-faced anonymous paramour, the

reader. The selfishness that comes from simply saying what you have to say. (2017)

It is these character traits that lead *& Juliet*'s Anne Hathaway to call Shakespeare 'a douche' (*& Juliet* 2019) – to quote Urban Dictionary, 'someone who is more than a jerk, tends to think he's top notch, does stuff that is pretty brainless, thinks he is so much better than he really is' ('Douche', n.d.).

Although a 'douche' in *& Juliet*, Shakespeare is a popular celebrity. His amassed players announce his entrance as he enters rock-star fashion on an ascending platform clad in skin-tight jeans and a jacket emblazoned with a motif of a black (upstart) crow, to the refrains of the Backstreet Boys's 'Larger than Life'. This Shakespeare is arrogant and self-absorbed – an established and successful playwright certain of a successful opening night for *Romeo and Juliet*. In maintenance of patriarchal family roles, he is joined by an excitable Anne Hathaway, who has secured a babysitter and escaped for a night at the theatre. Her role is clearly set up as an enthusiastic wife there to support her artistic husband and these gendered roles are solidified in the opening moments of the production. Anne makes apologies and excuses for neglecting childcare responsibilities: she hasn't been out 'in ages', and she is so tired from her maternal duties that she hopes to 'stay awake' (*& Juliet* 2019). This echoes Solnit's observation that 'mothers are constantly found wanting [. . .] treated as a criminal for leaving [their] child alone for five minutes, even if that child's father has left it alone for several years' (2017: 5). Notably, Shakespeare can revel in his role as artist with no regard for his paternal role. Anne must justify her one night of leisure, while Shakespeare unapologetically indulges in what Dederer deems the brutalities of creation: 'The artist must be monster enough not just to start the work, but to complete it. And to commit all the little savageries that lie in between' (2017). It is not enough to create, to write. To be an artist your words need to find completion – they need to be heard. It is in this space that West Read's musical acts to challenge the status quo – disrupting Shakespeare's ability to complete his creative process and introducing an alternate means of effective creation through Anne's more collaborative approach.

*& Juliet* is promoted as the 'most famous love story of all time. Remixed', although the extent to which that is true for the core *Romeo and Juliet* story is debatable. Essentially, *& Juliet* only changes the end of Shakespeare's original. In the opening scene, Shakespeare offers his hastily written pages to the players dramatically recounting how 'Juliet plunges Romeo's dagger into her heart' (*& Juliet* 2019), only to be interrupted by a discontented Anne. 'What if Juliet didn't kill herself?', she asks, 'I mean, really that should almost be the start of the play' (*& Juliet* 2019). The start of the play-within-a-play (within a musical) it is, as, save for Juliet's ultimate death, the original still stands, albeit unperformed in this alternate timeline – a 'lost' prequel to the collaboratively written *& Juliet*. Tweaked elements of the underlying

original remain. For instance, Juliet finds a new husband at a ball. The refrain of Britney Spears's 'Oops! . . . I Did It Again' when sung by Juliet to acknowledge that, yet again, she has acted rashly is not only comic, it also simultaneously undermines the rewrite, moving us away from remixing history towards history repeating itself.

But whose history? Despite Juliet getting top billing as the eponymous heroine, I argue that this is not her story, but Anne's. Taken out of the domestic setting and placed within Shakespeare's creative domain, Anne actively challenges Shakespeare's authority as creator: 'the thing is, your ending's shit' (*& Juliet* 2019) she retorts, proposing collaboration. Shakespeare bristles at the criticism, the thought of collaborative writing is anathema. He claims to 'always write alone' (*& Juliet* 2019) complete with knowing look to the audience, a denial of the historical Shakespeare's co-written works. Bardophiles in the audience become complicit in Shakespeare's duplicity: he does collaborate, but only with men not women. Here Anne embodies Solnit's criticism of the *art monster* trope that: 'creative work is in conflict with personal life, and men who have epic creative lives are skipping other stuff that women can't' (2019: 100). Implicit in Anne's insistence that she influence the narrative is a push back against Shakespeare's and societal expectation that she acquiesces to superior male speech – to quote Solnit's mocking of the moral outrage surrounding outspoken women, 'How dare she consider the story to be about her or want to be the one who determines what the story is' (2019: 20). Anne is challenging the myth of the *art monster*. As a woman and mother she does not enjoy Shakespeare's privilege, she cannot commit 'savageries' required to be an artist (Dederer 2017) however, that should not act to silence her.

Using Shakespeare's golden quill, Anne and Shakespeare write themselves into Juliet's story, simultaneously performing both as themselves and in roles in their play-within-a-play. Anne creates for herself the role of April, Juliet's friend and confidante, and Shakespeare writes for himself a series of bit parts: bus driver, DJ, barman, etc. The joke is that Shakespeare is reduced to the status of spear-carrier in his own production as Anne takes the lead. The audience is supposed to laugh at the arrogant Shakespeare in a much-depleted role, but there is something else at play here. Will is effectively writing himself into Anne's narrative, undermining her self-expression. Alongside their self-penned fictional roles, they step out of the play and add wider context. Anne has a moving soliloquy, where she notes that Shakespeare was really wedded to his work and never wrote anything specifically for her or portrayed happy marriages. But this speech is itself undermined. Will interrupts his wife, denying her the opportunity to address the audience directly, downgrading her soliloquy to an aside and promising her that his next play will have a happy marriage, only to reveal its title: *Macbeth*. It is arguably Anne's story that she herself seeks to remix, cautioning Juliet against rushing into marriage.

There is a symmetry to *& Juliet*, which ends with Juliet asking for a 'new beginning for Juliet and her Romeo', (*& Juliet* 2019) placing their names in that order as that is how Juliet wants it. But those are not her words – it is not her decision, but rather a clear parallel to the final line of the original Shakespeare play. Anne's version of Juliet's story offers Juliet choice; however, Shakespeare brings Romeo back from the dead, removing that element of autonomy. The play ends essentially where it began, with Anne challenging Shakespeare's ending for a second time. The reincarnated Romeo is, to quote Anne, 'a douche' written in Shakespeare's image, 'both alike in dignity' (*& Juliet* 2019). The little he does to win back Juliet is controlled by Shakespeare, who is driven by his desire for his own narrative voice to overpower Anne's.

In a musical ostensibly about empowering women, Anne remains silenced, her efforts to rewrite Juliet's story undermined by Shakespeare every step of the way. In a final argument, Anne rebuts Shakespeare's declarations of love with, 'it's all words, words, words, with you Will' (*& Juliet* 2019), a line borrowed from *Hamlet* (2.2.189). Even in her anger she only has the words given to her by Shakespeare. In this Anne parallels our fictional characters, who can speak only through Shakespeare's golden quill. At the end of the play-within-a-play Juliet becomes the physical embodiment of Shakespeare's will. She takes control of the golden quill as it forms part of her costume when she returns to the stage for the only true balcony scene, declaring we will hear her 'Roar' through Katy Perry's girl power anthem. As she disappears into the stage (notably a parallel to Shakespeare's rock-star arrival at the start of the musical), Shakespeare laments that 'she's taken my play and she's taken my players', his complaint equally applicable to both Anne and Juliet (*& Juliet* 2019). But that is not the end of the musical, as Shakespeare reveals he still controls the golden quill. In a show of remorse, he allows Romeo to woo Juliet in his own inept words: 'I want to talk things to you from my mouth' (*& Juliet* 2019). Romeo remains Shakespeare's puppet, almost unintelligible without his author's script. It is at this moment that Shakespeare hands Anne the quill, as she writes for Romeo the romantic declarations of love Juliet wants. This consolatory gesture keeps the narrative control in Shakespeare's hands; Anne's speech is permitted only when it accords with his chosen ending.

In Lloyd Malcolm's *Emilia*, Shakespeare is similarly revealed to be, to borrow Anne's phrase, 'a douche' (*& Juliet* 2019). As with *& Juliet*, Charity Wakefield's Shakespeare in *Emilia* is shown in a battle of quills with a woman – in this case the historically fictionalized Aemilia Lanyer, Emilia. It is fitting that their first exchange is taken from *The Taming of the Shrew*, as Shakespeare and Emilia spar with the wasp's sting wordplay from Act 2 Scene 1. Framing Emilia and Shakespeare's first conversation as a parallel to that of Katherine and Petruchio instantly brings the uncomfortable gender politics of *Shrew* into *Emilia*. Much as a fiscally deficient Petruchio woos the wealthy Katherine, Emilia's creativity is framed as something to be tamed and controlled by a creatively deficient Shakespeare. Emilia in this scene is an equal, identifying herself as a poet comparable to Shakespeare:

> EMILIA1[1]: I hear you are a poet.
> SHAKESPEARE: I am.
> EMILIA1: Me too
> SHAKESPEARE: You write?
> EMILIA1: I do. (Lloyd Malcolm 2019: 25)

An exchange of poetry follows with Emilia offering Shakespeare lines from *Love's Labour's Lost* and *Romeo and Juliet*, and Shakespeare offering her Sonnet 128 and 130, meta-textually writing Emilia into the established canon from the outset. There is a sense of fatality in this scene because, as with *& Juliet*'s Anne, Emilia has what the audience knows as Shakespeare's words; thus, she woos with what appear to be borrowed expressions. However, within the timeline of *Emilia*, this Shakespeare is at the start of his career, and these lines are yet to be written. Opening the exchange with *Shrew* and closing with *Romeo and Juliet* suggests Emilia's fate is either to acquiesce to a man's – Shakespeare's – superiority or to be doomed to death.

As Shakespeare's fame rises, it is at the expense of Emilia and her work. There is a duality present: Emilia is increasingly seen in her role of mother, wife, and lover. Lloyd Malcolm's stage direction highlighting Emilia's difficulties is particularly poignant:

> EMILIA1 *tries to nurse her child but the* MIDWIFE *is constantly taking him from her. She is also desperately trying to write. She is also torn by her love of* SHAKESPEARE *and he distracts her from her mothering* AND *her work.* (Lloyd Malcolm 2019: 28)

This again echoes Dederer's 'selfishness' of creation. To create as a mother:

> you abandon some nurturing part of yourself [. . .] when women do what needs to be done in order to write or make art, we sometimes feel monstrous. And others are quick to describe us that way. (2017)

Emilia's writing is portrayed as domesticated, a private hobby for her enjoyment alone. Solnit's criticism of Dederer's 'selfish' framework points to its inherent acceptance of gendered roles, for Dederer, 'to be woman is to be a mother and daughter and wife [. . .] that the kindness part of women's lives is inevitably onerous' (2019: 100). Echoing Solnit, Lloyd Malcolm challenges gendered approaches to writing. She shows Shakespeare's work as protected and promoted. Henry Carey cautions Emilia against distracting Shakespeare: 'Young Will Shakespeare is making a real name for himself. You wouldn't want to ruin that for him, would you?' (Lloyd Malcolm 2019: 28-9). Emilia too is cautious of her impact on Shakespeare's work: 'I dare not be the reason your play is late' (Lloyd Malcolm 2019: 29). However, Emilia is not afforded the same respect. Carey belittles her writing as a 'hobby' and treats as a joke her suggestion that his men perform her work (Lloyd Malcolm 2019: 30). Similarly, Shakespeare readily accepts that society won't permit Emilia to be a playwright while acknowledging that she has the ability. He tells her 'You have your own talents my love. If you strive you can achieve the same as I' (Lloyd Malcolm 2019: 29). However, Emilia's creative expression is something that should be kept within the home – for private rather than public enjoyment. Shakespeare does not act to protect her work, refusing 'to be held at fault for the rules of our time' or to 'down tools [and] refuse to write unless women are given the same freedoms' (Lloyd Malcolm 2019: 39). Emilia can 'strive' as much as Shakespeare, and her work will still be restricted.

As Lloyd Malcolm's play develops, Shakespeare increasingly appropriates Emilia's words as his own. At first, he knowingly arrogates her genius; he invites Emilia to come and see *Love's Labour's Lost*, telling her: 'let me help your words find a stage. Let me pour you into my work' (Lloyd Malcolm 2019: 30–1). However, at the turning point of play – in the final scene before the interval – he denies Emilia's role in his writing. Emilia and Shakespeare's daughter has died. The two argue over expressions of grief, with Emilia responding to Shakespeare's insistence on female frailty with words from *Othello*, specifically the lines spoken by that play's Emilia to Desdemona before her death (5.1.94-102). In the next scene, Emilia is at the Globe Theatre watching Shakespeare's latest play, *Othello*. Shakespeare diminishes Emilia's role when challenged: 'you were happy to use my words' Emilia accuses. 'They aren't yours. No one owns words', Shakespeare retorts, 'I have the talent to recognise phrases or speeches that can be used, and I craft them' (Lloyd Malcolm 2019: 38). Shakespeare's 'art monster' acts to silence Emilia's voice through the 'selfishness of stealing stories' (Dederer 2017). As Hailey Bachrach notes:

> if writing is the way to enter history, to invisibly contribute to Shakespeare's plays must be read not as empowering, but rather as the ultimate form of historical exclusion. (2022: 169)

Shakespeare's Emilia in *Othello* assumes Aemilia Lanyer's name, identity and expression.

Emilia is 'monster enough' to 'complete' her work (Dederer 2017), but she suffers as her story cannot be heard. Rather, within early modern society, her gender means she lacks the liberty of being 'a valued person [. . .] in a society in which her story has a place' (Solnit 2017: 19). In Lloyd Malcolm's play, to be woman is to be mute and this silence is instilled from childhood: 'My voice feels too loud in here. I must try to whisper more', observes Emilia as a child, 'to hush my whole being' (2019: 5). Solnit notes that women's success feels like 'an awkwardly large thing that is assumed to be in other people's way and for which [women] might need to apologize periodically' (2019: 118–19). Emilia's silence is told in terms of space: both the space she physically occupies and that she intellectually inhabits: 'as I grow I must shrink. I must not take up too much space' (Lloyd Malcolm 2019: 5). Not only does Emilia strive not to take up metaphorical space – a male prerogative – she also lives her 'whole existence in [Shakespeare's] shadow' and suffers for it: without a voice she will 'never be at peace' (Lloyd Malcolm 2019: 35).

Dederer notes that 'finishing is the part that makes the artist' (2017) and within these plays Shakespeare's women render his creative climax imperfect. During *Emilia* Emilia interrupts Act 4 Scene 2 of *Othello*, storming the stage as

> *The person playing* [Shakespeare's] *EMILIA stops in shock and looks down towards EMILIA2 who continues the speech while battling her way through the Groundlings and to the stage.* (Lloyd Malcolm 2019: 42)

While she is ultimately subdued, Emilia's actions silence the male voice – her female voice reclaiming her words, silencing the male actor (in the world of the play) appropriating her words and denying Shakespeare his play's climax.

In *& Juliet*, Anne's desire is that Juliet be offered a choice – that Romeo's death does not automatically mean she too must die. While Shakespeare's selfishness ultimately ensures that his 'star-crossed' pairing prevails, the end is not without collaboration. Anne's accusation that Romeo is 'a douche' written in Shakespeare's image renders him 'obsolete', 'harmful and pointless' (McClouskey 2013). That is, until his restitution through her words. Relevant to Romeo is bell hooks's argument that:

> The first act of violence that patriarchy demands of males is not violence toward women. Instead patriarchy demands of all males that they engage in acts of psychic self-mutilation, that they kill off the emotional parts of themselves. If an individual is not successful in emotionally crippling himself, he can count on patriarchal men to enact rituals of power that will assault his self-esteem. (2004: 66)

Romeo, the 'sexy young man with a tight body and a lot of feelings' (*& Juliet* 2019) written in Shakespeare's image is initially killed off by his creator; this is a metaphorical 'psychic self-mutilation' of Shakespeare's 'emotional parts'. It is only when Shakespeare accepts that his conditions of artistic creation need not necessarily be exclusionary – that he need not embody the selfishness of the monstrous genius – that the play reaches a conclusion. By offering Anne a voice (however limited) her creative input allows both the play-within-a-play and the wider musical to end. Neither Anne nor Emilia is offered the complete freedom of expression they seek, their work incomplete, unfinished. However, each production can be seen as a call to arms, a call on the audience to finish the work. *Emilia* urges modern women to 'look how far we've come already. Don't stop now', commanding audience members to 'take the fire as [their] own' and 'burn the whole fucking house down' (Lloyd Malcolm 2019: 75), a suggestion that if we can kick Shakespeare's pedestal and question his authority maybe we can realize the overdue changes needed in modern society.

# Note

1 Within *Emilia* three actresses play Emilia as she ages, each identified within the play text as Emilia1, Emilia2 and Emilia3 respectively. For reader ease, I use 'Emilia' to refer to each interchangeably as I discuss the character in her entirety.

# References

*& Juliet* (2019), Book by D. West Read, Music and Lyrics by M. Martin. Directed by Luke Shepherd [Shaftesbury Theatre, London. November 2019].

Bachrach, H. (2022), 'Beyond the Record: *Emilia* and Feminist Historical Recovery', in J. Fitzmaurice, N. J. Miller, and S. J. Steen (eds), *Authorizing Early Modern European Women*, 165–78, Amsterdam: Amsterdam University Press.

Beard, M. (2018), *Women & Power: A Manifesto Updated*, London: Profile Books.

Blackwell, A. (2021), 'Sympathise with the Losers: Performing Intellectual Loserdom in Shakespearean Biopic', in V. M. Fazel and L. Geddes (eds), *Variable Objects: Shakespeare and Speculative Appropriation*, 127–50, Edinburgh: Edinburgh University Press.

Cameron, D. (2019), *Feminism: A Brief Introduction to the Ideas, Debates, & Politics of the Movement*, Chicago: University of Chicago Press.

Dederer, C. (2017), 'What Do We Do with the Art of Monstrous Men?', *The Paris Review*, 20 November. Available online: https://www.theparisreview.org/blog/2017/11/20/art-monstrous-men/ (accessed 13 July 2022).

'Douche' (n.d.), *Urban Dictionary*. Available online: https://www.urbandictionary.com/define.php?term=Douche (accessed 13 July 2022).

hooks, b. (2004), *The Will to Change: Men Masculinity, and Love*, New York: Atria Books.

Lloyd Malcolm, M. (2018), *Emilia*, Reprint with revisions, London: Oberon Books Ltd, 2019.

McClouskey, M. (2013), 'Could "Douchebag" Be a Feminist Insult?', *Everyday Feminism*, 30 December. Available online: https://everydayfeminism.com/2013/12/douchebag-is-a-feminist-insult/ (accessed 13 July 2022).

Solnit, R. (2017), *The Mother of All Questions*, London: Granta Books.

Solnit, R. (2019), *Whose Story is This?*, London: Granta Books.

# PART TWO

# Family

# 6

# Shakespeare's dead, long live his widow! One-woman plays about Anne Hathaway

## *Edel Semple*

In *Shakespeare in Love* (1998), the twentieth century's most popular Shakespeare biopic, Anne Hathaway is never seen and only mentioned a handful of times. As its title suggests, the film focuses on Will and on passion, romance and sex – all of which, it is implied, have nothing to do with the writer's wife. The film's scant references to Anne associate her with rural Stratford, a 'cold bed', and the oppressive obligation of family. In contrast to this side-lining of Anne as an inconvenient uxorial spectre, three twenty-first century one-woman plays foreground Anne:[1] Vern Thiessen's *Shakespeare's Will* (premiered 2005), Avril Rowlands's *The Second Best Bed* (premiered 2012), and Ger FitzGibbon's *The Bed* (premiered 2016).[2] Although the plays vary in their origins – written by Canadian, British and Irish dramatists respectively and premiering in their home countries – notably, they all depict Anne as newly widowed. For these dramatists at least, the death of the author is necessary to bring Anne to life.

The plays by Thiessen, Rowlands and FitzGibbon are by turns conventional and subversive in depicting their protagonist. These biodramas draw on biopics of women which, as Karen Hollinger compellingly argues, appeal to their audiences by showing 'their protagonists' triumph over or at least heroic survival of [. . .] victimization' (2020: 2). The three plays attend to Anne's suffering and her struggles within a repressive patriarchy, portraying her as both a victim and as an inspirational heroine who experiences trials and victories. As Katherine Scheil observes in her seminal study of Anne's afterlives, Anne 'has the potential to unleash, authorize, endorse, and promote a wide variety of conceptions of women, motherhood, and marriage' (2018: xv). In particular then, this chapter will explore how these twenty-first-century biodramas depict a very different Anne from the one imagined in *Shakespeare in Love* and propose they do so in order to meditate and authorize women's experiences of sexuality, family, grief and creativity.

Although each of the one-woman biodramas explored in this chapter decentres Shakespeare as a literary icon, their post-funeral setting and Anne's grief mean that her husband is a constant spectral presence. Her struggle to understand her identity with- and without-Shakespeare inevitably brings him on stage. She is spotlighted as the heroine, then, but through her remembrances Shakespeare is visible as a 'figure in the shadows' (Wilson 2007). The plays by Thiessen, Rowlands, and FitzGibbon all consider Shakespeare's legacy, and central to this is Anne's inheritance – the most infamous bequest in history: the second-best bed. While beds are the most cited household object in early modern wills (Cowen Orlin 2021: 194), and Shakespeare's 'family was well-off and his widow would have been comfortably provided for under English law, the connotations of "second-best," particularly when joined to an object so crucial to nuptial bliss as a bed, have long intrigued posterity' (Kehler 2009: 1). As stage properties, beds are freighted with meaning and in the three biodramas discussed in this chapter, the second-best bed is an especially fertile creative nucleus for a whole range of imagined narratives about William and Anne Shakespeare (Scheil 2018: 104).

Despite its title, *Shakespeare's Will* foregrounds Anne and her desires. In the opening lines, she sets out the preoccupations – the sea, sex and her husband – that have shaped her life: 'I long for the sea. . . . / Her white toothed smile. / Her roaring laugh. / Her salt spray on my lips. . . . / (*wry*) The sea was a far better lover than you, Bill' (2002: 1). This critical comparison of lovers, though jokey, foreshadows Anne's account of Bill's shortcomings in life and his post-mortem betrayal of her through his will. At Bill's funeral, Joan Shakespeare smugly foisted her brother's will on Anne, but reluctant to read it, she postpones the task by lapsing into reminiscence.

Thiessen imagines a queer life for Anne and Bill, one that eschews heteronormativity. The Shakespeares resist the binaries of 'chastity and lust, virtue and vice, Madonna and whore', as both spouses independently pursue 'queerer intermediate alternatives' (Freccero qtd. in Sanchez 2019: 87). Anne recalls how she first met Bill at a fair. With few words exchanged, the pair have sex and Anne speculates that this is Bill's first time with a woman, prompting her to ask 'do you [. . .] like boys?', to which he replies 'Don't know' (2002: 6). Anne then confides: 'It's fine [. . .] I like boys too, / men that is / I like the company of lots and lots of men' (2002: 7). When Anne discovers she is pregnant, the couple wed, but vow to make 'our own kind of marriage' (2002: 12). Later, as a wife and mother, Anne reflects how marriage allows her to avoid public censure; she has many lovers but rather than being called 'a whore', she is viewed as merely '"dissatisfied" / or "unfaithful" or / "adventurous"' (2002: 28–9). Anne takes pleasure in 'her own eroticism and so refuses to be contained by the social codes of "appropriate" femininity' (Wilson 2007).

Bill also deprivileges monogamous, procreative heterosexuality. He refuses to bring his family to London, apparently to ensure their wellbeing, but Anne knows it is because he has 'a companion / in the City. / A man' (Thiessen 2002: 34). When she protests the unfairness of Bill's absence – he may be the breadwinner but 'I give you decency, respect, lineage' – he insists on the fundamentality of their vow:

> You give me more than that:
> You give me my work.
> You give me my life, Anne.
> But my life.
> In the City. (Thiessen 2002: 35)

The couple's shared vow permits their freedom, but it also requires sacrifice, or at least a sacrifice by Anne that serves the patriarchy. The Shakespeares' marriage upholds then, but does not endorse, some gender inequalities. Bill gets to spend 'a lifetime away', while Anne must forgo his companionship – 'I miss my husband' – and face alone the struggles of childbirth, breastfeeding, and childrearing at home (2002: 49, 31).

Like Agnes in Maggie O'Farrell's *Hamnet* (2020), Thiessen's Anne is traumatized by the death of her mother. Having lost her to the pestilence, Anne quickly recognizes the disease's signs and flees with her children to the sea. In this Anne imitates the life-saving action taken by her own father who impressed upon her eight-year-old self that 'when the wind is up / you move on' (2002: 38). This memory suggests that for Anne, change and movement are salvatory. Moreover, Anne's childhood experience initiates the sea as variously a 'site of solace', transience, 'transformation and possibility' (Wilson 2007).

While Anne is happily reunited with the sea, her husband is present only in absentia. When the children question what he looks like, their mother guides them in creating a portrait. Thiessen's Anne literally makes her own Shakespeare; she produces his image in words and with the seaweed, stones and other found items on the shore. Ann Wilson convincingly argues that here Anne engages in a desire, shared by modern audiences, 'to know an unknowable' Shakespeare (2007). The portrait, moreover, literalizes the idea that Shakespeare is always made-up, 'a figure of myth' as Douglas Lanier asserts (2002: 118). This is especially true of Bill, whose increasingly rare visits to Stratford mean that he exists more in his family's collective memory and imagination than in their lived experience.

Fashioning her own Shakespeare, Anne demonstrates her creativity, a fact beautifully accentuated in the 2021 Shakespeare in the Ruins production of *Shakespeare's Will*.³ On a table lit from below, Anne (Debbie Patterson) used sand to shape a silhouette resembling the Chandos portrait, giving the audience a familiar, but still illusory and subjective, image of the iconic author. Anne tells the children that Bill's smile is 'Like the sun dancing on water', and since this is impossible to capture using the beach's flotsam, they 'will have to imagine [it]', (2002: 47). This response suggests that representations of Shakespeare are always limited; even when the portraitist knows the subject well, the ephemerality of life means that biographical gaps are fillable only by the imagination.

Anne's impromptu portrait of Bill is an expression of her faith in their bond; they are apart, but together. Anne believes so strongly that she knew her husband and they shared an understanding that it is almost pointless to read his will: 'No one knows the vow we kept, what we held most dear' (2002: 53–4). Learning that Bill has left her the second-best bed, Anne realizes that this bequest is a moral judgement.

Casting her mind back to the family's sojourn at the seaside, she recalls how it ended when Hamnet, aged eleven, drowned (as he does in Rowlands's play and in *All Is True* (2018)). Anne's son is lost, compounding her grief and repeating his father's abandonment: 'he / waving goodbye / like you / at the road's end / pack slung over your shoulder / waving' (2002: 57). Anne endures the tragic loss without her husband and, even when he returns to Stratford, she mourns alone. Bill's preoccupation with a male heir drives his bequest and Anne is incredulous at his cruelty: 'And with this / you blame me? / with this you punish me?' (2002: 58). Since Shakespeare's 'voice is heard only through his (indomitable) will' (Knowles 2009: vii), it appears as an attempt to assert his dominance over Anne. The bequest is thus intended as a coup de grace, but Anne withstands this bitter reprisal.

Wilson deems Thiessen's biodrama to be 'a discreetly poignant feminist work' (2007) and part of its female empowerment stems from Anne's refusal to be cast as the villain of the Shakespeares' life story: 'I will not suffer this, I will not!' (2002: 58). The Shakespeare in the Ruins production deftly captured the pathos of this scene. Patterson's Anne furiously buried the objects that symbolized her married life, rejecting the necrotizing hate of Bill's legacy. She then swept the sand smooth and placed the twig representing herself in the spotlight. As Patterson's Anne vowed 'I will go back to the sea', a golden light suffused the scene, signifying the dawning of a new day and a spiritual sanctification of her decision. To live, then, Anne must leave Shakespeare behind. In her rejection of her husband, she echoes the conclusiveness of Prospero ('I'll drown my book' (5.1.57)) and appropriates his potent magic:

> To hell with your words.
> Sink them in the sea
> drown them in the depths
> smash them on the shore
> let the waves carry them where they will.

(*smiles faintly*) For when the wind is up, you move on.
You always move on. (2002: 59)

Anne's alliteration from 'Sink' to 'shore' produces the effect of a ritualistic incantation that dispels Shakespeare's authority. Moreover, by repeating her father's precept (meaningfully, the play's final lines) she invokes in its stead a different power, which may be Anne's own experience, ancient wisdom, her father and/or the sea. If, as Ric Knowles argues, adaptations of Shakespeare's works and biography are a response to his cultural dominance in Canada, his position 'as a ghost that haunts the collectivity' (2009: vi), then Thiessen's Anne suggests it is time to lay this ghost to rest and move on.

Like Thiessen's, Rowlands's Anne is determined and independent. In *The Second Best Bed*, Rowlands has Anne 'take on Shakespeare, commandeering his plays, his genius' and, thus, his cultural prestige (Scheil 2018: xv). Amongst Anne's achievements are her wedding Will to conceal her pregnancy by a married man; writing the Shakespearean corpus and passing it off as her husband's; managing his career; securing the Earl of Southampton as his patron; all while raising a family, conducting secret love affairs and visiting London in disguise. Rowlands lionizes Anne when, recalling her trips to the playhouse, she claims: 'I could have played the men's parts as well as the women's. [. . .] I could have mended the costumes . . . held the book . . . and still cooked a fair meal at the end of the day' (2005: 25). This declaration of self-worth betrays Anne's irritation at the limitations imposed on her due to her sex. As a young woman, she had to conceal her writing to avoid accusations of being 'mad, bad' or a witch (2005: 16). The conspiracy means Anne has an outlet for her art, but her potential is still unfulfilled; she must remain in the shadows as mediocre men literally take centre stage in the playhouse. While Rowlands's biodrama is replete with fiction, then, it 'resonates with deeper emotional truths about women's exclusion from the worlds they wish to inhabit' (Şorop and Steele Brokaw 2019: 90).

On and off throughout her remembrances, Anne relates how she suffered for repressing her creativity. In her youth, she was tormented by her 'creations crying to [her] to set them free' from the papers under her bed (2005: 17). Here, the bed is 'a repository for Anne's literary achievements' (Scheil 2018: 197)[4] and Anne is a tortured romantic artist, an authorial type based on the template provided by *Shakespeare in Love* (Shachar 2019: 23–63). Celebrating Anne as the true creative genius, Rowlands simultaneously playfully capitalizes on the Shakespeare Authorship Question and diminishes Will as his wife's puppet, her beloved but 'playing a part of [her] devising' (2005: 35). Handsome and with only a vague ambition 'to be famous' for 'something' (2005: 13), Will, like Thiessen's Bill, has a partnership with his wife, but it is distinctly hierarchical. Anne's superiority is evident when she recalls her spouse's comical nickname of 'Wandering Willy', his public shaming for lewd behaviour, his contraction of the pox, and how she caught him with two whores, who he left unpaid (2005: 11, 17, 37). Like the

Shakespeare of *Anonymous* (2011), this Will is a cypher, a tool and shield for a virtuoso mastermind, a mere bit-player in another's story.

In contrast to Will's extramarital affairs, which carry an air of the ridiculous, Anne's are presented as meaningful. Anne enjoys sex with her husband – they had 'good times' in the second-best bed (2005: 14) – and with many other people. She recalls a youthful relationship with a grammar school teacher where she exchanged her body for his knowledge, and long-term affairs with the Earl of Southampton, who she secured as Shakespeare's patron, and with Alice, her own Dark Lady (2005: 15, 21, 27–8). Like Thiessen's heroine, Rowlands's Anne is a vivacious, agentic figure who enjoys disrupting heteronormativity. She remembers fondly, for instance, how she and Alice often cross-dressed as men and visited London, its theatres, and taverns: 'The freedom of doublet and hose!' (2005: 29). For all her queer unconventionality and feminism though, Anne's final act shores up the status quo by preserving Shakespeare's image as an immortal bard.

At the end of Rowlands's biodrama, Anne destroys Will's confession of their conspiracy. History will deem her 'the shrew from Stratford who drove her genius husband away', but she regards this as part of her grand scheme: 'We had such sport my sweet, sweet lad! For thirty years we threw dust and moonshine in all their eyes. And for the rest? (*She reaches for the candle.*) Why, it's silence. *She burns the manuscript and blows out the candle*' (2005: 40). In this moment, Anne is reminiscent of Hamlet, whose dying words she quotes (5.2.342), and her actions may bring to mind Macbeth's 'Out, out, brief candle!' speech (5.2.22). In evoking these tragic heroes, Anne boldly claims them and their cultural prestige. The moment is more bittersweet than triumphant however, as Anne sacrifices the truth, out of love for Will, meaning she remains 'a poor player' whose time on stage ends with her husband's death, in silence and darkness, the 'greatest playwright that never was' (2005: 40).

Ger FitzGibbon's *The Bed* (2016) is set a week after Shakespeare's burial and the setting and inclusion of sounds and voices offstage mean that Anne, in contrast to Thiessen's and Rowlands's protagonists, is identifiably a traditional housewife. The play opens with Anne sequestering herself in the marital bedchamber, a lived-in domestic space which is dominated by a large four-poster bed. Upset at inheriting only this bed, Anne apostrophizes her dead husband in an address that is by turns comic and poignant. While this Anne is a conventional 'good wife', she also succeeds in placing her needs first – solitude, a jug of ale (cleverly preprepared and hidden in her room!), warmth, marital mementoes and security – and, by the close of the play, she gets what she wants.

Ostensibly Anne locks herself away 'to get on with [her] grief' (2016), but she really acts in response to Will's will. While Thiessen's Anne immediately understands that the bequest of the bed is an indictment and Rowlands's knows it is a memento of happy times, FitzGibbon's Anne is confused and hurt: 'I DON'T UNDERSTAND IT, WILL! [...] YOU'LL HAVE TO COME

BACK AND EXPLAIN [. . .] I can read INSULT when it smacks me in the face!' (2016). Will is a beloved husband, especially missed because Anne is beleaguered (her daughter Susanna has 'deposed' her and taken over the house). Susanna, her zealot husband, and Shakespeare's sister greedily focus on the financial value of his possessions, but Anne sees in the room only proof of their affectionate partnership and intimate vestiges of the man himself: 'The clothes [. . .] seem . . . so empty. As if your shape is leaving them'; *She holds [Shakespeare's] doublet to her. Hugs it. Fights the tears*' (2016). 'Sorrow implies value' (Eagleton 2003: 2) and it can confer it too; Anne's grief invests Shakespeare's death with personal significance for the audience. In her speech, actions, and use of props, Anne is a domestic heroine and her husband is a family man. Shakespeare's death threatens his wife's identity and, literally, her place within the home. Where once 'This – house, furniture, everything – was mine. MINE', Anne realizes that she is now isolated, in danger of being treated 'like some feeble-headed wretch', thrown only crusts and relegated to the boxroom (2016). However, she knows her worth and resists such treatment: 'I WILL NOT SETTLE FOR THAT' (2016).

Of the three plays, FitzGibbon's is the only one that details Shakespeare's death. Surrounded by his family, including his dogs and little granddaughter, Will lay in bed when, Anne recounts: '[you gave] the longest sigh I ever heard, on and on, as if you were releasing into the air everything ever said, or written, or thought . . . giving it all back to the room, and the house, and the wide, wide world' (2016). Through Anne's eyes, the audience sees Shakespeare's death as both mundane and momentous. She witnesses the passing of her mortal husband and of immortal genius, gifted now to the world. Anne defies humanity's transience, instead viewing her husband's words as a benefaction that will sustain humanity long after his death: 'I won't give up. I'll clutch you here as long as I can. I'll tell little Elizabeth about your poetry. Those sun-filled showers of words, tumbling out of you, all generosity and lavishness. Falling from your hand like the richest corn' (2016). Elsewhere in the play Anne is repeatedly linked to Shakespeare's Cleopatra, and here she echoes the queen's description of Antony's magnificence and munificence (*Antony and Cleopatra*, 5.2.81–91). As Cleopatra deifies her lover, so too does Anne glorify her husband, their marriage and its conjugal pleasures: 'Eternity was in our lips [. . .] We were a race of heaven' (2016) (1.3.36–8). Anne is a familiar and domestic figure, but through this association with tragic celebrated lovers, FitzGibbon glamourizes the Shakespeares; they are everyman figures *and* they are exceptional.

The second-best bed is a metaphor for the significance of the Shakespeares' marriage and, as the play's climatic finale reveals, the guarantee of Anne's centrality within the home. Will has bequeathed Anne the leviathan-sized bed because it buttresses the house, as she gleefully realizes: 'Haha – they can't move this without the ceiling coming down. And where the bed is, I have to be' (2016). Will is not simply a literary genius; he is a practical and caring husband who ensures his widow's comfort. Comically, Will helps again, indirectly, when Anne uses the script of one of his failed plays to rekindle the fire. Asking who will keep her bed warm now, Anne ends the play by answering: 'You will, Will. You will' (2016). Pensive and yearning for her lost love, Anne is reminiscent of her counterpart in Rowlands's finale but, contrastingly, she looks to the future with quiet confidence. Unbowed, Anne's spirit is bolstered by the evidence of her husband's love. As darkness falls on the room, Anne's expression of faith seems validated as she is lit and warmed by the firelight from Shakespeare's papers.

It is striking that all three biodramas about Anne end with her discarding her husband's words. Thiessen's denouement sees Anne tossing Shakespeare's will aside, and Rowlands's and FitzGibbon's plays both conclude with his papers burning. Considering the cultural, social and economic power of Shakespeare in the modern era, this is a powerful image. For twenty-first-century dramatists and their audiences, this destructive act may represent a cathartic release from the weight of Shakespeare's influence, a ritualistic farewell to his genius, a recognition of the unknowability of the author, or a desire to 'move on' and phoenix-like begin anew. For these Annes, the destruction of Shakespeare's papers is a self-affirming, and even liberatory, act. The final movement of each play is Anne enacting *her* will, suiting and asserting *her* self, needs and desires. Thiessen's Anne affirms her autonomy by dooming Shakespeare's words to the depths and returning to her spiritual sanctuary. Rowlands's Anne, in burning her husband's confession, eternally links herself to Shakespeare as 'the poet's wife', sacrificing the recognition and rewards owed to her genius (2005: 27). 'But I don't regret it' she says, as she chooses to maintain her role forevermore in the 'play for the world's stage' that she herself has written (2005: 40, 13). FitzGibbon's Anne is displaced by her husband's death, but his bequest secures her position in the home and, crucially, her sense of identity. Tending to the fire made by his rough papers, Anne exudes a steadfast belief in her husband's love and continuing presence in her life. The parish register of the Holy Trinity Church, Stratford, reveals that the historical Anne outlived William Shakespeare by seven years. Perhaps influenced by this fact, the biodramas I have discussed all offer a comforting message that life goes on; each Anne survives the loss of her husband. The death of the author occasions these plays, but they make clear that Anne's life continues, and they all prove that her afterlife is as rich and varied as her husband's.

# Notes

1  As the longest-running solo show about Anne – *Mrs Shakespeare, Will's first & last love*, written and performed by Yvonne Hudson – has been in performance since the late 1980s, and my focus is the twenty-first century, I have omitted this play from my discussion.

2   All further references to Thiessen's and Rowland's plays are to the printed editions. References to FitzGibbon's play, as yet unpublished, are to the script he kindly shared with me – thank you Ger!
3   With special thanks to Sara Malabar of Shakespeare in the Ruins for granting me access to this production. The company's 'This is how we cripped it' video goes into further detail on the production's use of object theatre.
4   Scheil discusses *Mrs Shakespeare . . . the Poet's Wife*, Rowlands's extended, multi-actor version of the play, but the point is applicable to *The Second Best Bed*.

# References

Cowen Orlin, L. (2021), *The Private Life of William Shakespeare*, Oxford: Oxford University Press.
Eagleton, T. (2003), *Sweet Violence: The Idea of the Tragic*, Cornwall: Blackwell.
FitzGibbon, G. (2016), *The Bed*, Cork, Ireland: Unpublished Playscript.
Hollinger, K. (2020), *Biopics of Women*, Oxford: Routledge.
Kehler, D. (2009), *Shakespeare's Widows*, New York: Palgrave.
Knowles, R. (2009), 'Introduction: Adapting to Shakespeare', in *The Shakespeare's Mine: Adapting Shakespeare in Anglophone Canada*, iii–ix, Toronto: Playwrights Canada Press.
Lanier, D. (2002), *Shakespeare and Modern Popular Culture*, Oxford: Oxford University Press.
Rowlands, A. (2005), *The Second Best Bed*, Malvern: Kenyon-Deane.
Sanchez, M. E. (2019), *Shakespeare and Queer Theory*, London: Bloomsbury Arden Shakespeare.
Scheil, K. (2018), *Imagining Shakespeare's Wife: The Afterlife of Anne Hathaway*, Cambridge: Cambridge University Press.
Shachar, H. (2019), *Screening the Author: The Literary Biopic*, Cham, Switzerland: Palgrave.
*Shakespeare in Love* (1998), [Film] Dir. John Madden, USA: Miramax.
*Shakespeare's Will by V. Thiessen* (2021), Directed by Rory Runnells [Shakespeare in the Ruins, Digital Theatre Production. 19 November–12 December].
Şorop, A. and K. Steele Brokaw (2019), 'Play Review: *The Second Best Bed*', *Cahiers Élisabéthains: A Journal of English Renaissance Studies*, 100 (1): 89–91.
Thiessen, V. (2002), *Shakespeare's Will*, Toronto: Playwrights Canada Press.
'This is How We Cripped it (*Shakespeare's Will*), with Debbie Patterson' (2021), *Shakespeare in the Ruins*, 18 November. Available online: https://www.youtube.com/watch?v=Tnv_mdVYGGM (accessed 24 June 2022).
Wilson, A. (2007), 'Waves and Wills: Van Thiessen's *Shakespeare's Will*', *Borrowers and Lenders: The Journal of Shakespeare and Appropriation*, 3 (1).SHAKESPEAREAN BIOFICTION ON THE CONTEMPORARY STAGE AND SCREENONE-WOMAN PLAYS ABOUT ANNE HATHAWAY

# 7

# Interview on playing Sue Shakespeare in *Upstart Crow* (BBC, 2016–21) *Helen Monks in conversation with Ronan Hatfull and Edel Semple*

**Helen Monks** is a writer, actor and comedian. Since 2016, she has played Sue Shakespeare in the BBC sitcom *Upstart Crow*, scripted by Ben Elton, and later in the stage production, *The Upstart Crow*. Monks has also appeared in television shows such as *This England*, *Raised by Wolves* and *Inside No. 9*. She is co-artistic director of LUNG, Britain's leading campaign-led verbatim theatre company.

**Ronan Hatfull:** You deliver the opening words to the first series of *Upstart Crow*: 'Romeo, Romeo, wherefore art thou Romeo?' These words are instantly recognizable. Were you conscious of that when filming? Did that have any impact on what you then carried forward with Sue as a character?

**Helen Monks:** It establishes the world of *Upstart Crow*, which takes all the most recognizable, famous and eloquent bits of Shakespeare and puts them in a completely new context and demystifies them. The idea that you've got this stroppy Midlands teenage girl absolutely butchering his poetry is about establishing what *Upstart Crow* goes on to do throughout each series: to demystify it. It was always my aim to make Sue as ugly and earthy as possible. I think it's changed a bit, but the traditions of Shakespeare are that it's quite floaty and RP. So, I was aware of the need to demystify it, but what's great as an actor is being told to do something as badly as possible! What a gift! It takes the pressure off in a way.

**RH:** Do you think the overall purpose of the show, was to make Shakespeare earthy again and to make it accessible for the audience?

**HM:** What it felt like for me, when I read those scripts, was that someone had translated Shakespeare so that I could understand what was happening. And the other thing that it did – and maybe this is because I have got a theatre background – it made me feel clever. I do know more than I think I do, because to get the jokes, you must have some knowledge of Shakespeare. I think everybody is always surprised when they watch it that Shakespeare has subconsciously gone into your brain. I have teacher friends who play it to their students in schools because it demystifies [Shakespeare] in a sense that it helps people to dissect the plots, and understand, also, that 'this is a play about fathers and daughters' or 'this is a play about twins getting mixed up'. When I've seen Shakespeare productions since, it has brought me a new understanding when I'm watching the *actual* Shakespeare and I'm incredibly grateful for that.

**Edel Semple:** Just off the back of that I was listening to your episode on the podcast *Mad Women in the Attic*, and you said that you often find that your characters can shape how you are in the rehearsal room, that you bring something from your characters to the outside world. Is there anything of Sue that you've brought along with you or kept?

**HM:** I definitely accessed a lot of my inner grumpy teenage side when playing the part. That was built in, but it really grew throughout. Ben [Elton] was clear that this was about [Shakespeare's] difficult relationship with his stroppy teenage daughter, and we really pushed it to its limits. I remember, when I was doing some research into the character, reading the words on her gravestone and it just describes her as the daughter of Shakespeare, and I just wondered 'who would she have been if she'd lived now, with the education that she had, and with the status and cultural capital that she had? What would her gravestone have read if she was a modern contemporary woman?' Reading that definitely fed into the character, in terms of how frustrating it must be when you're really smart and capable, and you're surrounded by all these stupid grownups. She does have superiority, I think, and she's clearly incredibly intelligent. That's where her grumpiness comes from. It's not just hormones. It's also being trapped in this house and in this system and the structure of the unfairness of just being a woman at that time.

**ES:** Sue is so vitally important to the show, not just because you open the entire thing, but because there's this lovely development: she grows from being a sullen teen telling everyone to 'shut up' to some maturity and thoughtfully critiquing Shakespeare. Do you have a favourite thing about her?

HM: When we first meet her, she's thirteen. And I think she's angry and frustrated, but she doesn't yet have the knowledge or a way of articulating that. And then, throughout the series, her intelligence surpasses her anger, and she's able to have a reason, and a way of putting into words, why she feels frustrated at everybody and how she can make use of that feeling. Someone once said to me that anger is the most useful emotion and I always thought of that when I played Sue because it all comes from love. It comes from a sense of injustice and unfairness. Also, I think Sue does maybe soften [across the three series] because there is an extent to which you have to accept your place in the world, and you can't fight it all the time. So Sue educates herself, develops and becomes smart. It was so fun, throughout the three series, to play that. It's quite a subtle shift and change. I absolutely love the scene with David Mitchell, where Hamnet has died, because it was the one moment where we didn't have a punchline. I remember there were a lot of conversations around how they would have felt. At the beginning, we were saying that everyone died in those days, so they probably were fine about it. It was David who said 'I don't think that we feel any differently. If it was 500 years ago, or 200 years ago. I think human emotions haven't changed. It's only context that's changed.' So, we just played everything like we would play it now. We didn't try to think about how they would respond, we just responded as we would. That's why Shakespeare transcends the ages because those human essences always remain the same.

RH: The reaction to Hamnet's death is one of the most remarkable moments across all three series. *Upstart Crow*'s overall tone walks an interesting tightrope between irony and sincerity. There's cringe comedy and things like the 'Will Kempe as Ricky Gervais' joke, for instance, threaded throughout every series, but then we're hit with the Hamnet-focused episode in series 3. The fact that there's no punchline in this episode and you, as a team, leaned into the seriousness of the loss – was there discussion with Ben Elton and the director about how you were going to go about that? Was there any awareness in the cast of this being an atmospheric call back to the end of *Blackadder Goes Forth*, when the heroes go over the top to their doom?

HM: It was actually the same director [Richard Boden] who directed that final scene in *Blackadder* and the Hamnet episode, and the connection was very much recognized within the room. In terms of the line between comedy and irony, it all just came from Ben Elton loving Shakespeare and having a real expertise with Shakespeare. It's never a mockery, rather, to even understand the jokes you have to possess an affinity for Shakespeare, I think. The way that the episodes are structured mirrors a Shakespeare play, and I remember people saying that this is the kind of thing which Shakespeare would have approved. He would have liked to come and watch himself because it mirrors a lot of his writing methods and structures. There are a lot of jokes about the fact that Shakespeare's comedies aren't funny, but I remember always thinking that they would have been *at the time*. Comedy is all about context. In terms of that tipping point between sincerity and irony, it also comes from the character of Shakespeare being the most lovable idiot ever and having a really good heart. His mistakes aren't born from meanness, jealousy or arrogance. My favourite part of every episode is when Shakespeare and Anne are sitting by the fireplace, as husband and wife. I think that really sums it up, because that's about love, isn't it? There's a secret bond between them and a realization that they are in a good, loving, committed relationship.

**RH:** Do you think that Elton and yourselves as actors are sometimes trying to rehabilitate Shakespeare?

**HM:** I think that there's an exploration of how something could have come about. The joke is often that it was by accident, or that someone else gave [Shakespeare] the idea. Not only does that demystify Shakespeare, but it also demystifies the process of writing in general, and suggests that all creative ideas are stolen and unoriginal! I do think there's something interesting in exploring the parallel lives of Shakespeare and the texts, and in examining the context of the time with a knowingness of now. I think what it does really well is nod to the fact that lots of these injustices still happen today. That comes in the character of Kate with what she's fighting for. There's often a bit of overlap with contemporary issues for modern female actors. So, the show does an excellent job of not being superior, [it avoids] looking back and suggesting that these are problems of the past. There is also a nod to issues that are discussed within Shakespeare's plays themselves and how these still exist in contemporary culture.

**ES:** While playing Sue, you also get to play versions of other great Shakespearean women like Juliet, Katherine from *The Taming of the Shrew* and Beatrice from *Much Ado About Nothing*. Do you think that by playing these characters, you're able to rewrite, or maybe even 'correct', some of Shakespeare's plays?

**HM:** In the recent stage play [*The Upstart Crow*], I got to deliver a speech by one of King Lear's daughters and, again, there was a sense of putting a new twist on them. Having permission to do that is really fun. As I said earlier, it's probably every actor's dream that you get the permission to do those speeches in an 'un-Shakespearean' way! More and more, I think, when people do Shakespeare, they are deconstructing it and trying to make it truthful. I guess this is a bit of a cop out, but we were always playing immediate circumstances with all the scenes. So, although we would do a lot of research and try to understand how 'this bit is a homage to this play', it was always about playing Sue in those contexts. Like in the *Much Ado* episode, it was about playing Sue's reaction to Claude and the awkwardness, rather than playing a version of Beatrice. I didn't really think of it in those terms because Sue rolls her eyes so much at the plays! So, I adopted that attitude into my methodology of how to play the character. I wasn't necessarily hyperaware of all the different characters that I was getting to play within the show, because Sue isn't bothered about her dad's plays!

ES: It's the other way around, isn't it? So much of Sue's life influences her dad Shakespeare's life and his plays.

HM: Yeah, that's so true. It's that way round, isn't it? He is unconsciously and sometimes consciously stealing other people's perceptions and perspectives on things. But there definitely is a camaraderie between everyone that isn't Shakespeare. They all have that 'eye roll' at him, to different extents and in their own way for different reasons. And that was always really fun, because we do hold Shakespeare up on a pedestal and for good reason, but it was always enjoyable to play out the idea that he's an idiot! If he was alive now, he would be more complicated than just being a hero and a genius, I'm sure.

RH: Do you think that exploring Shakespeare's relationships with his friends and family is an effective way of extrapolating why he was able to portray such vivid interpersonal relationships?

HM: We were always thinking about our immediate circumstances because it's about how you're feeling now and modern life. I always think of Kate and Sue's relationship, how Kate wants to be best mates with Sue and that's really cringy and embarrassing. Sue thinks she's really lame! That is such a modern concept that we can all relate to, [but] those little intricacies of how humans relate to each other [were probably the same in Shakespeare's day]. Its why Shakespeare's plays have lasted so long; how humans interact with each other will always be the same. It's why this needs to be a comedy and why I really stand by the idea that Shakespeare, in his day, would have been an absolute riot because the funniest things ever are those human complexities and interconnected relationships.

RH: Did you look at any other portrayals of Susannah or model your portrayal on other strong woman in modern fiction and sitcoms?

HM: I didn't, to be truthful. We just tried to make the show funny and original. However, I've grown up watching so many sitcoms – David Mitchell's work to start with! – so it was really easy to know how he would perform and how to respond to him. Also, just being aware that comedy does have many different forms and distinctive styles. The history of watching *Blackadder* was helpful in finding [the show's] tone and knowing what they were looking for. I guess shows like *Harry and Paul*, and knowing Harry Enfield's work as well and how he brings his quirkiness and eccentricity to the sitcom form, [was helpful too]. That was the thing about *Upstart Crow* that was so bizarre; it was this room full of people who I already knew so well from growing up watching them! There wasn't necessarily an extensive research period, we just explored in the room and, actually, it was a really quick turnaround. We would do a readthrough on Wednesday mornings, rehearse Wednesday, Thursday and Friday, do some pre-recorded scenes on a Monday and then do the live studio recording on the Tuesday night. And then on the following Wednesday – that next day – we'd do the readthrough for the next episode! It was like being in rep [repertory theatre]. A lot of it was about the practicalities of getting the episode on its feet, working out what was funny and what wasn't. What was brilliant about performing it in front of a live audience was that people would try new things and surprise the cast members by throwing things in. You've got that first go to get the genuine laugh and then if you need to do a retake, sometimes it can feel a bit disheartening, so Ben would sometimes throw in an extra line. [. . .] When we did the stage version of the show, I was curious to see how it translated to the stage because it's so clearly built for television. It actually worked well, and it made me realize for the first time that Ben had written the episodes as plays in their form and structure. The liveness of that studio audience was always electric, and it was almost like being in a Shakespearean theatre, where the audience is really responsive, and they get a lot of the in-jokes. It felt like we were on the same page, and the same thing happened with the live show. Ben's managed to capture what a Shakespeare play would have been like in terms of the audience being so involved, so noisy and responsive. The liveness is definitely what I think makes it makes it feel really Shakespearean.

**RH:** Do you think some of those actors, and David Mitchell in particular, brought any element of their previous roles to *Upstart Crow*, such as Mitchell's Mark Corrigan in *Peep Show*?

**HM:** Definitely, everybody brought their own context. David Mitchell has traditionally played slightly lame, weird, socially awkward men who are trying to fit in. They're clever but slightly social outsiders. You project that onto the fact he's playing this hero. That itself is a funny casting choice, [added to by] the context of knowing David Mitchell from panel shows and knowing that he is smart. He's a brilliant actor, and every character feels truthful and different, but you do also project onto him the person that you know he is. So, I think the casting choices in themselves were really funny, like Harry Enfield as John Shakespeare. The context for him is that he's outrageous, rogue and leftfield, and that fed into the character he's then playing within the series.

**RH:** What was it like being part of the central female trio of Sue, Kate and Anne? What do you think those women's roles are in relation to Shakespeare in the show?

**HM:** It was brilliant because I think we all came with the same aim, which was that they were different from each other, and that's how they were written. We are all quite different as people anyway and as performers. It just immediately fell into place. Every choice Liza Tarbuck makes as Anne is really smart and deliberate. Gemma Whelan's Kate is the Everywoman, and you can't help but relate to all the situations that she's in, where she's so smart, so enthusiastic and just as nerdy as Shakespeare is. And then you've got the sort of antithesis of that which is Sue, who's so downtrodden by everything. What I really like as well is that their relationships with each other are really complicated. Like I said, Kate is trying to be best friends with Sue and following her around, and Sue thinks she's incredibly lame. Me and Gemma would always look forward to those scenes. She would, even when we weren't recording, be like 'hello, be my friend!' I really liked the relationship between mum and daughter too, because it felt truthful and realistic. We weren't necessarily super smushy, but there was a deep love there [between Anne and Sue].

**RH:** Having discussed how Mitchell and Enfield brought their own experiences to *Upstart Crow*, it would be remiss not to discuss your own work as a theatremaker with LUNG on community activism, audience engagement and political issues. Do you think your work as a theatremaker has informed anything about your work on screen or, specifically, the way that Sue is an agitator in some ways?

**HM:** I always have my writer's hat on. It mostly makes me think about Shakespeare in terms of the idea that he was just this normal man from the Midlands. Personally, I think that is such a political act - to be able to imagine that Shakespeare was just a normal person. I feel like that should be me, I should just be cracking on with it, but in an inspiring way where you think he's just an everyman, really. In terms of Sue, when I began the role, I was twenty. I was annoyed about the world and everything, and I remember being so satisfied that I had this role where I could just be really annoyed at everybody! That was brilliant and I could really relate to how frustrated Sue must have felt in youth, when I have all of the privileges of being a woman in 2016. I guess there's added elements with the show where you maybe get an extra kick out of it if you work within theatre. My favourite line in *Upstart Crow* is about Shakespeare doing all the work and the writing, then he tries to go to a restaurant and all the actors get the best tables, and he's not even on the list! I think there's elements of that where you can tell that it's Ben Elton writing that line, rather than being based on research he's done on Shakespeare. So, I guess, as an audience member, I've always enjoyed that aspect of it. I think

I've really grown with Sue as well, because I'm now twenty-eight, so we've been doing the sitcom such a long time. We all have had big life things happen and the theatre company grew alongside it. In fact, we were naming the theatre company while I was doing the first series of *Upstart Crow*. I remember asking everybody for ideas and what they thought of 'LUNG' as a name. I don't think they thought it was that good, but we went with it anyway! Everyone's always been really supportive within the room, and it's definitely been very inspiring. So, it's probably worked the other way, in that work with everyone within the *Upstart Crow* company has informed LUNG, more than the other way around. Everyone is incredibly supportive and to be in a room of people who have been that successful, it feels a bit more attainable and it's demystified the creative process for me.

# 8

# Father Shakespeare

# Grieving for Hamnet on stage and screen

## *Katherine Scheil*

The 1999 Hollywood film *Shakespeare in Love* depicts a fictional scenario of Shakespeare's romantic life through his illicit love affair with the upper-class woman Viola de Lesseps. The film only mentions Shakespeare's family very briefly, when the character Dr Moth questions him, 'You have a wife, children . . . ' Shakespeare dismisses his family as an impediment to his ability to write, remarking that he has experienced 'a cold bed too, since the twins were born'. In contrast to *Shakespeare in Love*'s libertine Shakespeare, several more recent works of biofiction imagine a Shakespeare who is a flawed family man. This chapter explores recent texts that focus on Shakespeare as a father, particularly through his relationship with his only son Hamnet.

Hamnet Shakespeare is primarily a biographical blank slate. As Graham Holderness remarks, 'Everything we know about Hamnet Shakespeare is that he was baptised 2 February 1585, Stratford-upon-Avon, one of a pair of twins; and buried, 11 August 1596. He was eleven years old. He was born; he lived; he died. And one more thing: he happened to be the only son of the most famous writer in history' (2016: 101). Since Hamnet died at age eleven, he didn't marry well or poorly, he caused no social scandals in Stratford, and he had no romantic life or career. 'I did nothing', as the character Hamnet declares in Dead Centre's play *Hamnet* (2017: 37). He was 'boy eternal', as *The Winter's Tale*'s Polixenes would put it, and thus innocently available for biofictional use, and his 'short life is lost in the lost years of Shakespeare's biographical record' (Wheeler 2000: 136). The gaps that constitute Hamnet's life have been filled in by biofiction, most often to provide an emotional component to Shakespeare's character, underlining the tragic nature of his fatherhood and providing imaginary scenes of grief and loss. The untimely death and 'biographical blank slate' of Hamnet have been marshalled by what Stephen O'Neill describes as Hamnet's 'many literary fathers and mothers' (2021: 2) in order to fashion a sympathetic but criticizable 'Father Shakespeare'. These biofictional Hamnets help explain one of the enduring mysteries of Shakespeare's life story: the source of his creative inspiration, locating it in his grief for his only son.

As attractive as Hamnet's story has been to the many writers discussed in this chapter, Hamnet has not always been part of Shakespeare's biographical story. In Nicholas Rowe's 1709 biography, Shakespeare was the father of 'three Daughters' but no sons. Edmond Malone was the first to remark that it would be difficult to imagine that 'a man of such sensibility, and so amiable a disposition, should have lost his only son, who had attained the age of twelve years, without being greatly affected by it' (1790: 353). Malone's construction of a grieving paternal Shakespeare has appealed to biographers, novelists and other writers for over 200 years.

The imagined circumstances of Hamnet's death have offered multiple options for constructing biofictional 'Father Shakespeares'. Was Hamnet ill for an extended period of time, probably from the plague, what Stephen Greenblatt calls a 'reasonable hypothesis' (2021), offering his father the opportunity to visit him before his death, or even to be present for his last hours? Or did Hamnet die suddenly and accidentally, as he does in Vern Thiessen's 2005 play *Shakespeare's Will*, resulting in a vengeful Shakespeare, who takes out his anger on his wife Anne? While no evidence survives about Hamnet's life, biofictional accounts of Shakespeare's reaction to the loss of his only son underpin both biography and literary criticism.

The search for some sort of 'truth' about Shakespeare's relationship with his only son has occupied a variety of literary critics. Psychoanalyst Eugene J. Mahon contends that Shakespeare's *Hamlet* was inspired by grief for his dead son. The 'uncanny connection' between Hamlet and Hamnet is thus evidence that 'the deepest sorrow can be transformed into beauty when indomitable genius insists on transcending its own suffering' (2009: 425–6, 443). Keverne Smith likewise argues that 'this most extraordinary writer was indeed an ordinary father when it came to bereavement – searching, not necessarily consciously, for ways to place his loss in perspective with his life' (2011: vii). Smith uses research on grief to argue that for Shakespeare, 'writing after Hamnet dies is therapeutic' (2011: 1). Shakespeare did not forget about his family back in Stratford, but instead, hid his feelings, and thus his 'reactions to the loss of his young boy are in his plays, but [they] are buried like fossils and require an understanding of grief processes to unearth them' (2011: 1). Peter Bray sees a more overt working out of Shakespeare's grief in *Hamlet*. Bray maintains that Shakespeare wrote *Hamlet* 'to reconceive and externalize an inner representation of his dead son', and that the loss of Hamnet put Shakespeare into a 'crisis of consciousness' and a 'spiritual emergency' (2008: 95).

Not everyone agrees that Hamnet's death produced tragic works. R. W. Chambers describes Hamnet's death as 'the cruelest blow which I can imagine falling upon any man', but surprisingly speculates that this tragic event inspired Shakespeare to write 'his happiest works' (1937: 138). In Richard P. Wheeler's version, Shakespeare's grief is expressed not in *Hamlet*, but instead in the history plays, where 'the beloved son's or a young boy's death produces a volatile mix of parental grief, guilt, distraction, helplessness, recrimination, rage' (2000: 145). Manfred Draudt even uses Hamnet's death to interpret Shakespeare's will, arguing that Shakespeare shows an 'extraordinary obsession with a male heir and the male line of inheritance, an obsession which must be grounded in the traumatic experience of the death of his beloved son in August 1596' (2001: 305). In the absence of any factual details, these works nevertheless imagine Shakespeare's fatherly grief as a connection to his literary works. As Edel Semple argues, representations of Hamnet 'use Shakespeare's body of work to suggest that art aids in understanding and coping with loss' (2023).

Biographers likewise have keyed in on Hamnet's death as a way to sketch out an emotional life for Shakespeare that fuels his literary works. In a chapter called 'Speaking with the Dead' in *Will in the World*, Stephen Greenblatt offers a highly speculative fantasy of Hamnet's death (italics mine throughout): '*Sometime* in the spring or summer of 1596 Shakespeare *may have* received word that his only son, Hamnet, eleven years old, was ill. *It is possible* he understood and responded at once, or he *may have been* distracted by affairs in London' (2004: 288). Building on this tale of Hamnet experiencing an extended illness, Greenblatt's story shifts from conditional language to definitive statements:

> at some point in the summer he *must have* learned that Hamnet's condition had worsened and that *it was* necessary to drop everything and hurry home. By the time he reached Stratford the eleven-year-old boy – whom, apart from brief returns, Shakespeare had in effect abandoned in his infancy - may already have died. (2004: 289)

Greenblatt continues to create a grieving paternal Shakespeare, noting that there is 'no reason to think that Shakespeare simply buried his son and moved on unscathed'. In writing his most famous play, Shakespeare 'may well have reopened a deep wound, a wound that had never properly healed'. Insistent that Shakespeare would have attended Hamnet's funeral, Greenblatt claims that 'Shakespeare *undoubtedly* returned to Stratford in 1596 for his son's funeral' and that 'Shakespeare *must have* stood there and listened to the words of the prescribed Protestant burial service' (2004: 288–9).

But why *undoubtedly must* he have? There's no evidence that Shakespeare attended his son's funeral. Later in his biography, Greenblatt's motives become clear; this industrious 'Shakespeare', who 'stood in the churchyard, watching the dirt fall on the body of his son' channels Hamnet's death into artistic inspiration and 'managed even to transform his grief and perplexity at the death of his son into an aesthetic resource, the brilliant practice of strategic opacity' (2004: 315, 377). Thus, the death of Hamnet is necessary in order to inspire Shakespeare's aesthetic sensibility.

Shakespeare's son Hamnet, and the 'bitter and terrible loss' that his story inevitably invokes, as Park Honan puts it (1988: 236), have recently emerged as a more prominent component of Shakespearean biofiction. The bardcom *Upstart Crow* (2016–18), the stage play *Hamnet* (2017) and the film *All is True* (2018) all feature Hamnet's story to varying degrees, and the runaway bestselling novel *Hamnet* by Maggie O'Farrell offers an extended story with Hamnet as the tragic denouement of the narrative. These texts all work to displace the 'Shakespeare in Love' model of an unhappily married man with alternate urban love interests, in favour of designing Shakespeare as a flawed paternal figure who atones for his mistakes and advocates forgiveness.

## Tragedy in Bardcom: *Upstart Crow* (2016–18)

Ben Elton's *Upstart Crow* (2016–18) uses Hamnet's story for an uncharacteristically dark and sombre episode, to criticize Shakespeare's fatherhood and failure to prioritize his family. Hamnet is first introduced in episode three of season one, as a pudgy young boy begging for sweets from his father when he returns from a 'business' trip to London. In this show, Shakespeare is very much 'the sitcom dad', whose teenage daughter Susanna delivers characteristic eye-rolls, who has a 'dad job list', and who ends each episode with his stay-at-home wife at their fireside. Shakespeare is frequently seen in the domestic setting of his Stratford home, and throughout the series he often returns to consult his wife about professional and domestic matters. Thus, the narrative regularly casts Shakespeare as a father figure, not as an urban romantic lover, as he is in *Shakespeare in Love*.

Within this comic framework, Elton's choice to include the death of Hamnet (the final episode of season three) is a curious one. In 'Go On and I Will Follow', Hamnet is preparing for his confirmation as Shakespeare gets notice of the London theatre awards, which are on the same date as Hamnet's confirmation. Anne calls him a 'horrible selfish man' for choosing to attend the awards rather than the confirmation, underlining Edel Semple's argument that Hamnet 'represents familial responsibilities' (2023). When Shakespeare returns to his Stratford home unaware of the tragedy, he finds a sullen and silent family. As Ronan Hatfull describes it, Shakespeare is 'met not with the usual mix of paternal smut and daughterly disgruntlement but, instead, a wall of silence' (2019: 303).

A distraught Anne challenges him to find words of comfort to explain Hamnet's sudden death. 'You're the clever one, you always know the answers', she tells him. At the end of the episode, Shakespeare recites in a voiceover his 'grief fills up the room of my absent child' speech (from *King John*) as he and Anne repose quietly by the household fire. The absence of laughter from the studio audience is jarring, seeming out of place in this usually delightful and witty sitcom, and the episode ends with a black screen showing the details of Hamnet's death. Hatfull describes this as 'the most audacious moment in *Upstart Crow* to date, when the program pierces the membrane between tragedy and comedy to produce a moment that utterly represents Shakespeare's private life on a human scale, made the more tragic by the closing credits of the season', which he aptly describes as 'appearing in the manner of an obituary' (2019: 303). One does have to wonder why Elton was motivated to call attention to this component of Shakespeare's biography, particularly when it is so disruptive to the comic tone of the series. Even so, numerous viewers on the show's Twitter feed have praised this episode, describing it as 'genuinely moving' and 'not afraid to deal with tragedies'. Viewers seem appreciative of the tragic ending and the injection of pathos into the otherwise comic narrative. These representative reactions (just a few of many) suggest that contemporary audiences welcome a Shakespeare who is less genius, more human; less the *Shakespeare in Love* and *Will in the World* libertine-philanderer and more the caring but flawed, grieving and relatable father.

## *Hamnet* on stage (2017)

The 2017 stage play *Hamnet*, by the Irish theatre company Dead Centre, portrays the afterlife of eleven-year-old Hamnet, allowing him to engage with the ghostly presence of his famous father, involving both characters in an isolated reverie of loss, punctuated by occasional bursts of humour. Hamnet is a typical tween – witty, tech-savvy with his cell phone and Google searches, and unafraid to accost his father with straightforward and difficult questions. Hamnet frequently quotes from *Hamlet*, as he wrestles with the missed opportunity of connecting with his father. 'He went away after I was born', he remarks, 'I don't even really know what he looks like. I'm not actually sure if I've ever seen him. Except in my imagination, in my mind's eye' (2017: 14). Mid-way through the play, the two characters meet. Shakespeare tells his son:

> Don't you recognise me?
> I suppose you haven't seen me in a long time.
> Have you never seen a picture of me?
> You've grown.
> How's your mother?
> Why don't you speak?
> You look like you've seen a ghost.
> Give your father a hug. (2017: 23–4)

Later, Shakespeare wrestles with his grief and asks for Hamnet's forgiveness: 'I was going to come back, Hamnet. I was always coming back. It's you that went away. Forgive me. I'm living in the past. I haven't done anything wrong. I've done nothing! Really, I've done nothing. But that's the problem. You needed me. And I did nothing' (2017: 37).

In the climactic scene of the play, Shakespeare and his son come together briefly. Shakespeare exclaims, 'I'm sorry. I love you. Stand up. My son. My shadow. I'm sorry' (2017: 38). The stage direction reads, '*SHAKESPEARE holds HAMNET in his arms. In the projection they are connected, son in the arms of his father, but on stage, alone, HAMNET is leaning impossibly far forward, leaning in the air by himself for a moment, and then levels again, as his father rights him*' (2017: 38). In this moment, the clever use of technology generates unity and separation so that Shakespeare and his son are both together and apart. Later in the play, Shakespeare urges his son to 'stop haunting me', and to 'let me rest'. He pleads, 'You have to let me work. I've grieved long enough' (2017: 42). In this version, Shakespeare's grief causes writer's block rather than creative inspiration. Hamnet even mocks the artificial nature of writing, as he asks, 'And who will write me? Some grown up who's completely forgotten what it's like to be 11. They'll make me say things I'd never say'. He continues, invoking the lines from his namesake Hamlet:

And in this harsh world draw thy breath in pain
To tell my story.
Don't worry. It isn't very long.
I didn't do much.
I did nothing.
In this harsh world.
We did nothing. (2017: 47–8)

The 'we' of the final line encapsulates the play's indictment of both father and son, one for dying young and inducing writer's block, and the other for doing nothing but writing.

## Shakespeare's interminable grief: *All is True* (2018)

In Kenneth Branagh's 2018 film *All is True*, also written by *Upstart Crow*'s Ben Elton, a similarly repentant Shakespeare is possessed by grief over the death of Hamnet, nearly twenty years before the film is set, and critiqued for prioritizing career over family. The story centres on Shakespeare as a middle-aged father, returning home to his family in Stratford. He faces up to the grief of losing his only son and is reunited with his two daughters, Susanna and Judith, and his wife Anne. In the opening scenes, the 1613 burning of the Globe is one of two traumatic events that result in Shakespeare's return to

Stratford. En route from London, Shakespeare stops in the countryside, and is joined by a nameless young boy who tells him, 'I had a story, but it was never finished. Would you finish it for me?' The boy (likely Hamnet, though never identified as such) returns throughout the film to haunt Shakespeare's thoughts, as a representative of loss. Shakespeare has several altercations with his wife and daughters related to his relentless grief for Hamnet; at one point Judith proclaims, 'the golden boy is gone' and her father is left with a 'useless, pointless girl'. Later she critiques him for returning home only to 'mourn Hamnet'. 'We've already mourned him', she says, but must revisit this painful episode because 'suddenly you've found the time to mourn him too'. Like Leontes in *The Winter's Tale*, this Shakespeare is repentant and remorseful, conceding that 'Hamnet died and I wasn't here, I know that'. He tells Anne, 'We lost our boy and I know that, I wasn't here'. Anne adds acridly, 'you were hardly here'. Later, Shakespeare learns the truth about Hamnet's death, which was suicide at his desperation to please his father. At the end of the film, he sees the ghostly Hamnet, who tells him, 'My story's done. I can rest. . . We are such stuff as dreams are made on, and our little life is rounded with a sleep'. The film concludes with an ailing Shakespeare finding peace for his grief, but only after he has apologized to his family and has been castigated by Judith.

Isaac Butler describes this version of Shakespeare as 'befitting our present moment, one in which we are trying to renegotiate our relationship to powerful men, the work they produce, and their misdeeds' (2018). This Shakespeare is 'a crap husband and father' who repents and 'comes to understand the cost of his greatness, and how that cost has been borne on the backs of those he claimed to love'. Shakespeare's unreconciled grief for his son is the motivation for his character in this latter period of life, and he is often tearful, contemplative, mournful and solemn. While Butler argues 'it is also absurd to depict a man as so paralyzed by grief 20 years after his son's demise' (2018), Branagh remarked that 'The loss of the child was key, and it was (screenwriter) Ben (Elton) who, with the closeness of the names, said what if we don't have father haunting son, but son haunting father in the form of young Hamnet?' (Riefe 2019). Thus, Hamnet serves to bring Shakespeare to justice and redeem him for neglecting his family. The Shakespeare of *All is True* is a contrite and remorseful father, whose belated 'penitence comes after all' and whose son haunted him until his last days.

## Conclusion: O'Farrell's *Hamnet* (2020)

Maggie O'Farrell's highly acclaimed novel *Hamnet* (published as *Hamnet and Judith* in Canada) moves beyond using the death of Hamnet to either justify or critique Shakespeare's literary career. O'Farrell rewrites the now-familiar scene of Hamnet's burial to foreground Hamnet's mother, here named Agnes (as in her father's will), 'recuperat[ing] the Shakespearean family as a site of maternal agency', as Stephen O'Neill puts it (2021: 4). In striking contrast to the exclusive focus on the father–son angle in Greenblatt's biography and in the 2017 stage play *Hamnet*, O'Farrell refuses to even name Shakespeare in her novel, staging Hamnet's funeral with Shakespeare 'behind' Agnes, and narrating the scene solely through her point of view. Here Agnes insists that her maternal role and her grief are just as important as her husband's: 'They made him together; they buried him together', and they 'cleaved together in that bed to create the twins' (O'Farrell 2020: 286–7). Unlike Anne in *Upstart Crow*, who urges Shakespeare to find words of comfort for Hamnet's death, this Anne/Agnes 'doesn't want the words, has no need of them' (O'Farrell 2020: 287), suggesting that they 'do nothing', as the 2017 stage Hamnet puts it.

In the novel's final scene, Agnes goes to see *Hamlet* and discovers that Shakespeare has instructed the actor playing Hamlet to mimic Hamnet's exact mannerisms. Shakespeare himself, playing the ghost, has 'taken his son's death and made it his own; he has put himself in death's clutches, resurrecting the boy in his place' (O'Farrell 2020: 304). This act of sacrificing himself for his son, rather than productively channelling his grief into his art, wins the respect of Agnes at the end of the novel. She realizes that Shakespeare has 'done what any father would wish to do, to exchange his child's suffering for his own, to take his place, to offer himself up in his child's stead so that the boy might live' (O'Farrell 2020: 304). As Jo Eldridge Carney notes, in the finale of the novel, 'seeing the two Hamlets on stage, father and son, helps [Shakespeare's wife] understand how her husband's grief and her son's legacy have been transformed through art' (2021: 166). The resolution of O'Farrell's novel hinges on Agnes's understanding and acceptance of her husband's use of their son's death in his most famous play. O'Farrell thus dilutes the frequently exclusive focus on father–son, and instead empowers Agnes as an equal partner in determining Hamnet's legacy. As the product of both father and mother, this Hamnet is not just an inspiration or hindrance for his father's art; his death brings about both paternal and maternal grief. Likewise, O'Farrell refuses to use Hamnet's death to expiate Shakespeare as a 'crap husband and father' or to enhance a portrait of a grieving paternal Shakespeare. Her insistence on the value of Agnes's experience and judgement foregrounds Shakespeare's wife as an equal partner in suffering the loss of Hamnet, as Agnes imagines that she can 'feel the air between the three of them' (2020: 305) – father, son and mother.

# References

*All Is True* (2018), [Film] Dir. Kenneth Branagh, UK: Columbia.
Bray, P. (2008), 'Men, Loss and Spiritual Emergency: Shakespeare, the Death of Hamnet and the Making of *Hamlet*', *Journal of Men, Masculinities, and Spirituality*, 2 (2): 95–115.

Butler, I. (2018), '*All Is True* Is a Shakespeare Biopic for the #MeToo Generation', *Slate*, 21 December. Available online: https://slate.com/culture/2018/12/all-is-true-shakespeare-movie-accuracy-kenneth-branagh-hamnet.html (accessed 13 July 2022).

Carney, J. (2021), *Women Talk Back to Shakespeare: Contemporary Adaptations and Appropriations*, London: Routledge.

Chambers, R. W. (1937), 'The Jacobean Shakespeare and *Measure for Measure*', *Proceedings of the British Academy*, 23: 135–92.

Dead Centre (2017), *Hamnet*, London: Oberon Books.

Draudt, M. (2001), 'Shakespeare's Marriage and Hamnet's Death', *Notes and Queries*, 246: 303–5.

Greenblatt, S. (2004), *Will in the World*, New York: W.W. Norton.

Greenblatt, S. (2021), 'A Wise Woman in Stratford', *New York Review of Books*, 14 January. Available online: https://www.nybooks.com/articles/2021/01/14/hamnet-shakespeare-wisewoman-stratford/ (accessed 13 July 2022).

Hatfull, R. (2019), 'Review of *Upstart Crow* Season Three', *Shakespeare Bulletin*, 37 (2): 300–3.

Holderness, G. (2016), 'His son Hamnet Shakespeare', in P. Edmondson and S. Wells (eds), *The Shakespeare Circle: An Alternative Biography*, 101–9, Cambridge: Cambridge University Press.

Honan, P. (1988), *Shakespeare: A Life*, Oxford: Oxford University Press.

Mahon, E. (2009), 'The Death of Hamnet: An Essay on Grief and Creativity', *The Psychoanalytic Quarterly*, 788 (2): 425–44.

Malone, E. (1790), *The Plays and Poems of William Shakespeare*, London: H. Baldwin.

O'Farrell, M. (2020), *Hamnet*, London: Tinder Press.

O'Neill, S. (2021), '"And Who Will Write Me?": Maternalizing Networks of Remembrance in Maggie O'Farrell's *Hamnet*', *Shakespeare*, 17 (2): 210–29.

Riefe, J. (2019), 'Q&A: Kenneth Branagh on Finding Shakespeare's Vulnerable Side as Star and Director of *All Is True*', *The Observer*, 11 May. Available online: https://observer.com/2019/05/kenneth-branagh-all-is-true-shakespeare-vulnerable-side-interview/ (accessed 13 July 2022).

Semple, E. (2023), 'Hamnet Shakespeare: A Difficult Dead Celebrity Child', in S. Coleclough, R. Visser, and B. Michael-Fox (eds), *Difficult Death, Dying, and the Dead in Media and Culture*, London: Palgrave.

Smith, K. (2011), *Shakespeare and Son: A Journey in Writing and Grieving*, Santa Barbara, CA: Praeger.

*Upstart Crow* (2018), [TV programme] 'Go On and I Will Follow', BBC, 3 October.

Wheeler, R. (2000), 'Deaths in the Family: The Loss of a Son and the Rise of Shakespearean Comedy', *Shakespeare Quarterly*, 51 (2): 127–53.

# 9

# Shakespeare and son in *All Is True* and O'Farrell's *Hamnet*

## Paul Franssen

As I have argued elsewhere, fictions of Shakespeare's life, whether prose narratives, drama or film, are subject to ideological fashions (Franssen 2016). One element in Shakespeare's biography that has featured in several recent fictions is the death of his son Hamnet, aged eleven, in 1596. Hamnet's death is amongst many facts in Shakespeare's life about which we know very little as there are no surviving records. The cause of death is unknown, as are Shakespeare's whereabouts at the time. Nevertheless, as in archaeological research, so in biofiction it is often the least documented biographical events that invite most fictional treatment, allowing the scarce facts to be bent to current ideological fashions: in this case, that of critiquing the patriarchy.

There is a tradition of seeing Hamnet's death as a judgement on Shakespeare: as a punishment for his supposed sexual adventures in London, as the price he is made to pay for his talent or for pursuing his career, or as the impact of his absenteeism and neglect of his family. For example, in John Mortimer's TV series *Will Shakespeare*, also made into a novel, Hamnet's death is connected to Shakespeare's philandering with the Dark Lady (episode 4). When Shakespeare takes his son with him to London, they quarrel over his extramarital adventures; consequently, Hamnet runs away, and contracts a cold of which he dies soon after (Mortimer 1977: 167–71). Neglect rather than philandering is the point of Neil Gaiman's *Sandman* series of graphic novels (1989–96), where Shakespeare strikes a Faustian bargain with the Shaper (the eponymous Sandman), the personification of the artistic imagination. Shakespeare will receive outstanding writing talent, for a price (1990a); a later issue (1996: 33) suggests that this price is his only son's untimely death. Hamnet plays the changeling boy in a command performance of *A Midsummer Night's Dream*, for the real-life elves Auberon and Titania. He attracts Titania's attention and dies shortly afterwards. What this supernatural fiction symbolizes becomes clear when Hamnet complains of having been neglected by his father, who only cares about his art (1990b: 13).

In William Boyd's TV-drama *A Waste of Shame* (2005), Shakespeare is also an absent father, but here the gender debate becomes more prominent. When Shakespeare comes home for Hamnet's funeral, Anne scolds him for neglecting his family. She is very bitter, but in view of Shakespeare's way with women throughout the film, her anger is understandable. Shakespeare exploits the Dark Lady, a half-Moorish, half-French sex-worker whom he uses but also despises while reserving his ideal love for the Fair Friend, an effeminate aristocrat. Social snobbery, misogyny and racism come together in a very unflattering picture of 'ungentle' Shakespeare: Katherine Duncan-Jones was an adviser to the film, and it shows (cf. Franssen 2016: 152–6).

As in this last example, Hamnet's death has often featured in debates on gender roles and differential opportunities for men and women. In this chapter, I will focus on two recent Shakespeare fictions with a clear gender perspective, revolving around Hamnet's death. The Kenneth Branagh film *All Is True* (2018) presents Shakespeare as ultimately responsible for his son's death, because of his gender bias. In Maggie O'Farrell's novel *Hamnet* (2020), by contrast, the attribution of guilt to Shakespeare is mitigated by an apotheosis of his art as a way of working through his sorrow. Thus, what seems to begin as a feminist indictment of male egotism, as in *All Is True*, ends up reconciling traditional and radical views of gender roles and of art.

## Absent Shakespeare in *All Is True*

In *All Is True*, Shakespeare is guilty of parental absence combined with gender prejudice. The film begins with the marital crisis between Anne and Will Shakespeare after the latter's retirement in 1613. On his return home, Shakespeare is denied entry to the marital bedroom by Anne and relegated instead to the guest bedroom: 'We've seen you less and less. To us you are a guest', she tells him. The issue is not Shakespeare's adultery, though the scandal of the sonnets is mentioned, but his absence from home and the resulting familial neglect. When, after his retirement, he belatedly starts mourning for Hamnet and planting a garden in his memory, Anne and Judith are uncomprehending: 'You scarcely knew him', Anne tells him, and Judith feels offended by her father's focus on his son: 'Why did the wrong twin die?', she correctly summarizes his thoughts. This sibling rivalry is compounded by the father's sexist attitude to his children. Throughout, Shakespeare longs for a grandson to replace his lost son, and as Susanna has only brought forth a daughter, he cajoles Judith to marry. 'I know what you think is the purpose of a woman's life', Judith tells him, meaning it is to bear male children. Judith is the film's feminist spokesperson: to men, she says, 'A daughter is nothing – destined only to become the property of another man'.

The film's plot builds up to two revelations concerning Hamnet and his twin sister Judith, which reveal Shakespeare's sexism. Shakespeare had never seen Judith's talents, because she was a mere girl, but had exaggerated hopes of Hamnet, who had recited poems for him. The first revelation is that illiterate Judith, not Hamnet, had composed these verses, which Hamnet had then written down and appropriated to impress his father. The second discovery is that Hamnet had not died of the plague, as Anne had given out, but of suicide by drowning. This plot twist builds on the controversy over Ophelia's burial in *Hamlet*. The reason for Hamnet's suicide was his inability to live up to his father's expectations. Judith, jealous of Shakespeare's affection for his supposedly brilliant son, had threatened to reveal the truth about the poems' authorship. Therefore, what Shakespeare stands accused of is his exaggerated expectations of the male heir, partly caused by a lack of awareness in relation to his children, due to frequent absences from the homestead. Once more, the dead Hamnet personifies Shakespeare's guilt as an absentee father and a sexist.

The film ends on a note of reconciliation: some time later, Shakespeare is happy to see Anne at last signing the marriage licence with her name, replacing the cross she had used on their wedding day. Judith, too, has learned to write, so Shakespeare gives her the penknife originally meant as a gift for Hamnet, showing his belated acceptance of his daughter as his heir. After Shakespeare's death, Anne and her daughters each read aloud a stanza from 'Fear no more the heat of the sun'. Women's literacy has been achieved at last.

The plot element of Hamnet stealing Judith's lines recalls the feminist topos of the female Shakespeare, derived from Virginia Woolf's *A Room of One's Own* (1929). In a fiction interpolated in this argumentative essay about women's neglected potential, Woolf traces the hypothetical adventures of Shakespeare's sister Judith, gifted with her brother's talent, yet held back by the patriarchal society. She ends up committing suicide when pregnant, without having had her work acknowledged (Woolf 2015: 35–6). In later fictions, it is Shakespeare's wife, Anne Hathaway, who is credited with having written (some of) Shakespeare's works, which were passed off as his. Examples include Arliss Ryan's novel *The Secret Confessions of Anne Shakespeare* (2010) and Avril Rowlands' one-woman play *The Second Best Bed* (2013), and its expanded version, *Mrs. Shakespeare . . . The Poet's Wife* (2005) (see Semple's chapter in this volume). These are prime examples of modern texts that 'update Anne as a figure of female empowerment by allowing her to voice ideas about independence [. . .] women's education, and the power relations between husband and wife' (Scheil 2018: 194). Such plots illustrate the feminist claim that men thrive because of the undervalued or unacknowledged work done by women. *All Is True* transfers this topos to the next generation of Shakespeares, without thereby exculpating

Shakespeare: it is his gender prejudice rather than that of society at large that forms the obstacle to Judith's success. The price for overrating the son and underrating the daughter is that son's death.

## Gendered mourning in O'Farrell's *Hamnet*

The marital crisis caused by Hamnet's death was revisited in Maggie O'Farrell's novel *Hamnet* (2020). It is largely narrated from the perspective of Anne Hathaway, here called Agnes, and that of her children. Shakespeare's name is not mentioned: he is just 'her husband' or 'the father'. As the plot is clearly that of the Shakespeare family, I will use their actual names throughout.

The novel's opening pages foreshadow Hamnet's death and raise the reader's expectation that this will be another indictment of Shakespeare, in a feminist attack on the patriarchy. Hamnet seeks an adult to help him when his sister Judith has contracted a disease which is later revealed to be the plague. No one can be found, least of all Shakespeare himself: 'For a moment, it crosses [Hamnet's] mind to call his father's name, to shout for him, but his father is miles and hours and days away, in London, where the boy has never been' (O'Farrell 2020: 5). The reader might assume that this will be the novel's thematic centre: the absent father's responsibility for his son's death.

Yet, the novel quickly takes away this impression. Shakespeare's absence is justified by his troubled relationship with his abusive father, John. Having to work for him and live close to him demoralizes Shakespeare. This answers that perennial question in Shakespeare biographies: Why did Shakespeare leave Stratford for London, so soon after marrying Anne? Scholars and creative artists alike have speculated whether it is a sign of an unhappy marriage, also suggested by the infamous bequest of the second-best bed in Shakespeare's will. Here, a bad marriage is not at issue, at least before Hamnet's death. It is Anne herself who urges her husband to leave, as she recognizes his unhappiness in Stratford. She colludes with her brother to persuade John to send his son to London, to sell the family business's gloves there. She proudly sees herself as the 'puppeteer, hidden behind a screen, gently pulling on the strings of her wooden people, easing and guiding them on where to go' (2020: 208–9). Hamnet's death is simply bad luck, as suggested by a remarkable chapter, describing the string of coincidences that brought the plague from Alexandria to Stratford (2020: 166–80).

Yet this leaves a second biographical question: Why did Shakespeare never bring his wife and children to live with him in London, once he could afford to buy a house there? From this charge, too, he is exonerated. He repeatedly offers to take them there, but Anne will not hear of it, because of Judith's weak health: 'Judith would never survive [the city]' (2020: 316; cf. 242). Her care is understandable: early modern cities were unwholesome places, where life expectancy was far lower than in the countryside. Shakespeare therefore accepts the inevitable; and, as the book adds, in a rare factual error: 'He will never buy a house [in London]' (2020: 241).

This does not mean that Shakespeare is wholly blameless. After hurrying home for Hamlet's funeral, he soon leaves for London again against Anne's wishes, making her feel deserted (2020: 282–6). Things are compounded when, on his return after a year's absence, she suspects that he has sought the solace of other women in London (2020: 310–14). As this phase of the novel is mostly presented from Anne's perspective and that of her daughters, we have no confirmation of this infidelity. Readers do catch glimpses of Shakespeare in London as a steady worker: always writing new plays, on tour with his company and pained whenever he is reminded of Hamnet by seeing a boy actor (2020: 304). He keeps his mourning under control by working it off. Unlike John Mortimer's TV series and book *Will Shakespeare* (1977, 1978), *Shakespeare in Love* (1998), or *Waste of Shame* (2005), O'Farrell offers no scenes of Shakespeare revelling with his colleagues or chasing women; rather, he has a reputation for being tight-fisted, saving up all his money for his family (O'Farrell 2020: 26). Anne's ceaseless mourning does make him feel constricted whenever he comes home to Stratford, as does his father's proximity. To alleviate both of these problems, Shakespeare buys New Place, to get Anne out of the house next door to the parental home in Henley Street where Hamnet died, away from troublesome in-laws and hopefully from the memories, too.

As a reader, one is torn between two perspectives: Shakespeare's desire to return to his old life, to sublimate his sorrow in his work (2020: 281–2); and, more powerfully because the perspective is usually hers, Anne's anger at her husband for deserting her in the midst of her grief. When her husband returns, Anne is so furious that she is tempted to stab a knife into his feet (2020: 311). Judith, too, vents her rage at him for his absence (2020: 308).

Yet, the impression that Shakespeare is just a weak and egotistical male who deserts his family when they most need him, is qualified by the book's ending. Anne's anger with Shakespeare's absenteeism comes to a climax when she learns that he has written a play named after their lost son: *Hamlet*, a common variant on the name Hamnet. How can he use their private grief for a spectacle in London, for people who have never known her son? What she interprets as his exploitation of their private sorrow makes her decide to travel to London, to see what her husband is up to and to confront him. Gradually, however, her rage is transmuted into a greater understanding. She first visits his lodging, while he is away at the theatre, and sees how modest it is: just a bed, a chair and a writing desk, with the beginning of a letter to her still sitting on it. It is not what she had expected: 'Such austerity, such plainness. It is a monk's cell, a scholar's study. [. . .] no one else ever comes here, [. . .] no one else ever sees this room. How can the man who owns the largest house in Stratford [. . .] be living here?' (2020: 351–2). No sign therefore of luxury, feasting or womanizing, just of honest hard work.

Yet the real epiphany is still to come. In a moving scene, Anne attends a performance of *Hamlet*, as one of the anonymous spectators; and although she is furious at first, and has come to confront her husband, she gradually realizes that she has misjudged him. Not unlike a D. H. Lawrence heroine, she suddenly has a flash of insight into her husband's life and imagination, which up to that moment had been closed off to her. She recognizes that it is he who is playing the ghost. Here O'Farrell alludes to the old tradition that Shakespeare himself had played Old Hamlet (cf. Franssen 2016: 13). The stage Hamlet is a young boy, whose movements and tone of voice resemble her dead son's. Her husband, she concludes, must have trained up the actor to behave like that. Most importantly, in playing the ghost, himself also called Hamlet, the father has given a new lease of life to his son:

> As the ghost talks, she sees that her husband, in writing this, in taking the role of the ghost, has changed places with his son. He has taken his son's death and made it his own; he has put himself in death's clutches, resurrecting the boy in his place. [. . .] He has, Agnes sees, done what any father would wish to do, to exchange his child's suffering for his own, to take his place, to offer himself up in his child's stead so that the boy might live. (O'Farrell 2020: 366)

This insight makes Anne change her mind: rather than callously exploiting their loss, her husband has used his art to sublimate it. She resolves to be reconciled to him, after the performance. The book ends here, suggesting that all will be well.

Thus, ultimately the novel acknowledges the power of art to transmute human experience to provide solace. In this way, Shakespeare has overcome the trauma of losing his son, and given Anne relief; even the theatre audience, unaware of the author's personal background, is mesmerized by the drama's intensity. So, in the end, Shakespeare, the feckless immature husband, is revealed as a great artist.

As Stephen O'Neill has observed, at first glance this lays O'Farrell open to the charge of replicating the dichotomy between male transcendent art and the female investment in the body and nature – a binary often deplored by feminists (2021: 218). For O'Farrell's Anne is close to nature: born from a woman from the wild forest, she is herself a benign witch, who cures her neighbours with herbs and flies a kestrel. She gives birth to Susanna in the woods, alone, rather than at home with her meddlesome in-laws. She has intimations of the dead, such as the presence of her mother's ghost on her wedding day, and can see into the future: she knows Susanna's sex during pregnancy, and foresees people's deaths, even her own, though not Hamnet's. Anne, in other words, is a mystic, intuitive, nurturing woman, close to nature, semi-literate; while her husband makes a career in the city and sublimates life in art, precisely as gender stereotypes will have it. As O'Neill observes, however, in this way, O'Farrell reflects 'early modern gender roles', and even 'the gendered division of emotional labour in the period' (2021: 222). Besides, many minor characters break through such patterns: unlike her mother, O'Farrell's Susanna is business-like and hates plants; Mary Arden dislikes her daughter-in-law for being so close to nature. If John Shakespeare is a brute who cannot control his anger, Anne's stepmother Joan is no better.

## Shakespearean intertext in *Hamnet*

The way O'Farrell's Shakespeare processes his own past into his play is typical of much Shakespearean biofiction. If Anne does not know that *Hamlet* was based on an old Danish chronicle, by way of intermediary sources, O'Farrell does: her Shakespeare ruminates about histories of 'long-dead king[s]' as suitable plots for his plays, to make him forget his grief over Hamnet (O'Farrell 2020: 303). Yet his works are also based on his own experiences rather than on his reading and imagination alone. This notion seems fundamental to the genre; it is what makes the writer's life a worthwhile subject to begin with. Thus, elements from an author's works are projected back into his life and treated as the biographical origins of these works (see Franssen 2016: 83–5). Yet O'Farrell does this in a subtle way, as the relation between the author's real-life and his works is not a literal replication of plot elements, but chiefly a symbolic working through of trauma.

There are faint intertextual echoes from *Hamlet* throughout the book. When Hamnet asks, 'where is everyone?', 'Where can they be?' (2020: 8), this recalls *Hamlet*'s opening: 'Who is there?' Later, there are sightings of Hamnet's ghost by the midwife and Judith (2020: 336–9). In addition, there is the suggestion that Shakespeare's obsession with twins in his work came from his real-life twins. Of course, twins of different sexes can never be identical twins; apart from age, there is no more resemblance between them than between other siblings. Yet in *Twelfth Night*, dated around 1600, Viola resembles her twin brother Sebastian so much that they are mistaken for each other, particularly after she has dressed up as Cesario. Sebastian, as a consequence, unwittingly protects her by fighting Sir Andrew Aguecheek on her behalf, because Sir Andrew mistakes him for her (4.1). O'Farrell projects this back into Shakespeare's life in the novel, as Hamnet and Judith are so alike that they are mistaken for each other. This inspires Hamnet to try to fool death:

> It occurs to Hamnet [. . .] that it might be possible to hoodwink Death, to pull off the trick he and Judith have been playing on people since they were young: to exchange places and clothes, leading people to believe that each was the other. Their faces are the same. (O'Farrell 2020: 200)

So, when Judith is in her sickbed, he lies down close to her, as if he were taking her place, hoping to fool death into carrying him away rather than his weaker sibling, offering his life for hers. This act of self-sacrifice points forward to Shakespeare's own symbolic switching of places with his son in the book's climax, himself becoming the ghost that Hamlet might live.

## Conclusion

O'Farrell's novel paints a credible picture of life in Shakespeare's age, at least one that seems credible to our gender-aware era. It has won the Women's Prize for Fiction, foregrounds gender roles and prioritizes the female voices in Shakespeare's family. Chiefly, it is a tribute to Anne Hathaway, sketched as a strong woman in her own right. Yet it also valorizes the greatness of the man who, for most of the novel, is kind and protective, yet sometimes appears selfish and immature. O'Farrell's Agnes sees his potential from the start, when she holds his hand in a particular way, like a fortune teller, and there reads some of his inner life (2020: 43–4, 57–8). Later, when she comes to doubt her husband, the reader may come to doubt him as well. He makes a sweeping come back near the end, however, when it is revealed that in his absence, he was mourning his son in his own way, creating a classic tragedy in the process, and a work of great consolation for Anne, too.

As O'Neill suggests, the idea of Shakespeare playing Old Hamlet to immortalize his son Hamnet is a reworking of Stephen Dedalus's theory in the Library scene of James Joyce's *Ulysses* (O'Neill 2021: 217). When Shakespeare enters the stage as the Ghost of Old Hamlet,

> To a son he speaks, the son of his soul, the prince, young Hamlet and to the son of his body, Hamnet Shakespeare, who has died in Stratford that his namesake may live for ever. (Joyce 2016: 178)

Yet, whereas Stephen's theory ends up showing Shakespeare's feet of clay, and blaming Anne for many of his weaknesses, O'Farrell reworks this idea into a celebration of the art that may overcome grief, giving both Anne and her husband their due. Thus, rather than polarizing, O'Farrell's novel works to reconcile traditional and radical views of gender roles and of art. She sets right what she has called the 'jaw-dropping vilification and downright barefaced misogyny' often reserved for Anne (quoted in O'Neill 2021: 213), but without making 'Shakespeare [. . .] the scapegoat for all the sins of the white patriarchy' (Franssen 2016: 160). In that sense, *Hamnet* provides a welcome corrective to fictions like *All Is True*, which, in the name of gender equality, sketch a somewhat stereotypical picture of Shakespeare as the absent and patriarchal father.

# References

*All Is True* (2018), [Film] Dir. Kenneth Branagh, UK: Sony Pictures.
Franssen, P. (2016), *Shakespeare's Literary Lives: The Author as Character in Fiction and Film*, Cambridge: Cambridge University Press.
Gaiman, N. (w), M. Zulli (i) (1990a), 'Men of Good Fortune', in *The Sandman: 13: The Doll's House*, New York: DC Comics.
Gaiman, N. (w), C. Vess (i) (1990b), 'A Midsummer Night's Dream', in *The Sandman: 19: Dream Country*, New York: DC Comics.
Gaiman, N. (w), C. Vess, B. Talbot, J. Ridgway, M. Zulli (i) (1996), 'The Tempest', in *The Sandman: 75: The Wake*, New York: DC Comics.
Joyce, J. (2016), *Ulysses*, Minneapolis: Lerner Publishing.
Mortimer, J. (1977), *Will Shakespeare: The Untold Story*, New York: Dell.
O'Farrell, M. (2020), *Hamnet*, London: Tinder Press.
O'Neill, S. (2021), '"And Who Will Write Me?": Maternalizing Networks of Remembrance in Maggie O'Farrell's *Hamnet*', *Shakespeare*, 17 (2): 210–29.
Rowlands, A. (2005), *Mrs. Shakespeare . . . The Poet's Wife*, Malvern, PA: Miller.
Rowlands, A. (2013), *The Second Best Bed*, Worcester: Worcester Repertory Company.
Ryan, A. (2010), *The Secret Confessions of Anne Shakespeare*, New York: Penguin.
Scheil, K. W. (2018), *Imagining Shakespeare's Wife: The Afterlife of Anne Hathaway*, Cambridge: Cambridge University Press.
*A Waste of Shame* (2005), [Film] Dir. John Mackay, UK: BBC/Open University.
*Will Shakespeare* (1978), [TV series] Dir. Mark Cullingham, Robert Knights and Peter Wood, UK: Granada.
Woolf, V. (2015), *A Room of One's Own*, edited by D. Bradshaw and S. N Clarke, Oxford: Blackwell.

# 10

# Interview on writing the play *Shakespeare's Sister* (2015)

## *Emma Whipday in conversation with Ronan Hatfull and Edel Semple*

**Emma Whipday:** is Senior Lecturer in Renaissance Literature at Newcastle University, UK, and author of *Shakespeare's Domestic Tragedies* (2019). She is also a playwright: her plays include *Shakespeare's Sister* (2016) and *The Defamation of Cicely Lee* (winner of the American Shakespeare Center's 'Shakespeare's New Contemporaries' prize in 2019).

**Edel Semple:** What was the inception of *Shakespeare's Sister*?

**Emma Whipday:** So, there's a practical answer and there's a theoretical answer. I was a student at Oxford and I'd been doing adaptations of classic novels as summer garden shows. We'd done *Dracula*, *Emma* and *Sense and Sensibility*. I was looking for adaptation projects, but I wanted to move into original work, and I happened to have read Virginia Woolf's *A Room of One's Own* for the first time. It's such a short story about Shakespeare's sister, but it's a tantalizing snippet. I thought, 'oh, that would be a beautiful bridge between adapting other people's work and creating something myself', but that was the more practical element. *A Room of One's Own* was dramatic for me in terms of my thinking and my feminism. Up to that point, I'd mainly read dead, white, male authors and I'd got through Oxford wanting to see myself in a lineage with them, almost speaking back to them, because that was the canon and I wanted to engage with it. Reading *A Room of One's Own* completely transformed the way I looked at literary history. I was really excited by that story of Shakespeare's sister, but I also had issues with the way that Woolf told a story that implied that the reasons that she couldn't be a playwright were inherently to do with being a woman or not having Shakespeare's ability to live and succeed in his world. It seemed that if a woman was sexual then she had to die, which, of course, has a real lineage in terms of early modern culture and drama. I think, while being very inspired by Woolf, I wanted to show how it was the systemic, societal barriers that made it impossible for a woman with Shakespeare's genius to write the plays of Shakespeare in that time. So that was my starting point.

ES: Your Author's Note begins with the quote from Woolf, on imagining what would have happened to Shakespeare's genius sister Judith, and then you explain that 'this is not a true story'. Why did you choose to open with that blunt statement?

EW: I wanted to show that I knew Shakespeare's biography – that his daughter was Judith, and his sister was Joan – so this was a warning, it let the reader know that I wasn't writing inaccurate biofiction! I think it was also because I was situating myself with Woolf in terms of saying that there are reasons that this story doesn't exist. I wanted to flag up the same thing as Woolf; there's a reason we don't have these stories about these female writers. Since writing this, I feel like I could have done more to refer to other female playwrights of the period and engage with the fact that there were elite and, probably, non-elite women, making theatre. I think a lot of feminist scholars have noticed that in some ways, Woolf's idea of Shakespeare's sister is problematic for the way it erases female creativity from literary history while drawing attention to the difficulties of female creativity and literary history.

ES: Yes, you've got a tension there. What's the relationship between truth, or facts and history, and imagining the past in your play?

EW: I wanted to give my imagination free rein in terms of the storytelling, but I wanted to root it enough in lived experience by drawing on historical characters. It was quite important to me that the minor characters all have the names of real people, even if I was moving them slightly in plot or in time. So, Dorothy Clayton was from a couple of decades earlier and was arrested for cross-dressing and prostitution. I moved her in time so that she could be in the play. Introducing Augustine Phillips as my semi-villain was obviously deeply unfair, but at the same time, I wanted someone who was a member of the playing company. I suppose there are all these huge gaps in Shakespeare's biography, especially around the 'lost years' and about how particular theatre companies formed. So, I wanted to write into those gaps imaginatively, but within the architecture of the world that we do know about and the world that does exist. I know that Richard Burbidge didn't create his company the way I described it happening, but it felt like there was enough of a gap in theatre history that I could play with that a bit.

ES: You mentioned Dorothy, who was a real person and is mentioned in Jean Howard's work [*The Stage and Social Struggle in Early Modern England*]. Did you feel that you had a responsibility either to your play's audiences, and/or to the real-life historical figures, like Dorothy Clayton, Shakespeare and Shakespeare's real sister Joan?

EW: I could argue that I ought to have had more of a moral responsibility to these figures from history. I think in terms of Shakespeare, I didn't feel any responsibility, in that he can take it, you know? His reputation is not going to be affected by anything I write. And Shakespeare-the-character is almost entirely separate from Shakespeare-the-playwright by this point, because he's been so repeatedly staged, reiterated and reimagined. I was doing my MA while I was working on this play, and one of the modules we did was 'Shakespeare's Afterlives', and I was looking at Shaw's puppet play about Shakespeare where it's himself – the character of Shaw – arguing with Shakespeare as a puppet about the weight of his literary reputation, and how hard it is to do anything when this figure exists. It's quite funny, I recommend it. But I think that was helpful because it reminded me of the fact that when you're writing against this force of gravity – and I think I'd also read Gary Taylor's *Reinventing Shakespeare*, where he talks about Shakespeare as a black hole – any writer writing to or against Shakespeare, you have the right to push back as much as you want, because he's so big that it's not an equal contest. His reputation has become this whole other thing separate from the work itself; so for Shakespeare, I didn't feel any responsibility. I felt more responsibility for the female characters, but it wasn't a responsibility to be accurate. I wanted to create a world that seemed true to life, but I didn't feel like I had to tell anyone's stories accurately. What I felt responsibility for was the kind of story I was telling, rather than whether it was true or not, and whether I was enabling the female characters to have the same creativity, egos, messiness and fights that male characters would get to have in a world like this. I was really influenced by *Shakespeare in Love*, but at the same time it presents such an intensely masculine world; it takes the all-male stage idea and runs with it. You get a cross-dressing female heroine, Elizabeth I, a seamstress, and you get some sex-workers in the audience. But the fact that [*Shakespeare in Love* presents] such a male world and all the women exist to enable male creativity or appreciate male genius, I was writing against that. I felt I had a responsibility to tell a story where women were getting to do the things, make the mistakes and have the conflicts, that the men got to have in that world.

**ES:** Katherine Scheil, author of *Imagining Shakespeare's Wife: The Afterlives of Anne Hathaway*, has written about how there was a substantial female community in Stratford. However, we never see that in, say, *Upstart Crow* or *Shakespeare in Love*. And, when watching *All Is True*, I wondered where all the women were; well they were in Emma's play!

**EW:** Even in my play, if I wrote it now, it's still a very male world with a few women on the edge of it. I'd been reading a lot of Shakespeare; I was being influenced by those plays and by *Shakespeare in Love*. I think now, I would try to make that more equal, but it's quite telling that the men get a lot of stage time, though *Shakespeare's Sister* still feels like a female-centred play, compared to most art about Shakespeare. That tells you a lot about the existing Shakespearean tradition! Another thing I was interested in with this play was class. I get frustrated by Shakespeare conspiracy theories because they're so often classist, suggesting someone who's non-elite couldn't have written these plays. I was keen to show a world where there was male creativity and female creativity in this non-elite sphere, rather than the elite spheres where a lot of our records of female creativity come from. I was writing the play, quite self-consciously, during the economic depression and the aftermath. I was graduating into a world where a lot of the graduate schemes and publishing opportunities were disappearing; this economic instability made me think about class. And so, I suppose that was something I was wanting to write in as well. I feel that Shakespeare, in general, does not need defending, but he does need some defending against films like *Anonymous* because of the kind of prejudices that it embeds about who can be a genius and the assumption that only someone with a particular kind of education from a particular kind of family could have been a genius.

**ES:** In your play, Judith has a love affair with Ned Alleyn and then things start to fall apart, there's heartbreak and sacrifice. I was wondering whether that was a turning point or a defining moment for her? I then started to think about how Shakespearean biofictions often depict the hero being inspired by his personal experience – like in *Shakespeare in Love*, Will's falling in love informs his writing of *Romeo and Juliet* – but in your play Judith writes from her imagination and is inspired by reading the Bible. Was Judith's creativity and inspiration something that you thought a lot about?

**EW:** I'm glad that you picked up on that because at the time I was writing, I was reading a lot of writers' advice, trying to think about myself as potentially a playwright or a screenwriter. Lots of them said 'write what you know'. Ironically, I did end up writing what I know in that I ended up doing a Masters and a PhD in Early Modern Studies. But, at that point when I started working on the play, it was something I didn't know. I really resisted the idea that people could only write out of their own experience. I think, also, that there are an awful lot of literary works and plays that come out of Greek drama and the classical tradition, and as someone who went to a state school and didn't have any classical education, I sympathized with the idea that Judith wouldn't have had the same classical education as her brother, so she wouldn't have had those sources for the stories that were the root of Humanism and the Renaissance. I liked the idea that she could go back to Biblical stories as a world she could have had which was also a rich, story-filled, complex world.

**ES:** Did you think it was important to show Judith in the act of writing?

**EW:** Absolutely. I was aware that it was a coming-of-age play, that it was a tragic love story, that it had all these other elements, but I wanted it to be, primarily, about Judith as a writer. I wanted to foreground the materiality of writing; the ink spilling, the messiness of the papers, to have the writing be as present as possible. As I said, I had problems with *Shakespeare in Love*, but I saw it at a very formative age and I think it did shape my imagination and the fact that it begins with Shakespeare writing – of course, he's working on his autograph – and the film's continual imagery of the inkpot, quill and pages all reinforce 'this is Shakespeare'. I wanted Judith to have a similar opportunity for that writerly-ness to be visible.

**Ronan Hatfull:** Linking to your formative experiences with *Shakespeare in Love*, were there any Shakespearean moments, tropes, images or relationships that you consciously used as models or frames in *Shakespeare's Sister*? What was the role of intertextuality in what you were writing?

**EW:** Ending with the words 'remember me' was a very purposeful calling up of the ghost in *Hamlet*. I wanted to, at that moment, bring the two together in the audience's minds, or at least those audience members who are familiar with *Hamlet*, to have that clash, because it would give it extra power to have that canonical moment being echoed by the woman [Judith] whose voice we haven't heard in history. He's asking us to pay attention to her. In quite early drafts, I tried to have Judith just casually say things that Shakespeare then scribbles down [a situation often depicted in plays, films and TV]. I didn't want to do that; at one point I decided, this is more interesting if it's about Judith and *her* play. It's about *her* art completely distinct from her brother's. She doesn't need to influence him for her art to have meaning. So, I decided to work against that quite firmly. There probably are lots of echoes, that are almost accidental, because I was reading a lot of Shakespeare at the time when I was writing, and I didn't mind that. But I had to get Shakespeare out of the way of my plot. In the initial drafts, there was a love affair with Southampton as part of the story. I then realized that if Judith's plot was going to sing at all, he [Shakespeare] just had to be gone, he had to be off the stage and couldn't appear until the end. And that's because he's replacing her at that point and coming back into the world she can't inhabit. I felt like I was doing something similar with [Shakespeare's] language in that I had to push it out to make room for what I was doing.

**ES:** How did it come about that the audience is prepared to see Shakespeare, in Stratford, and you then choose not to stage him until Act 5? And even then he's barely visible in moonlight and powerless to help his imprisoned sister. Was that about keeping Judith central or were you humanizing Shakespeare?

**EW:** I was attempting to humanize him, to decentre and demystify him. Staging him [early on] just became another kind of mythologizing; it was so hard to not have him be 'Shakespeare'. I wanted to play on expectations as well because it is a play called *Shakespeare's Sister* and I like the idea that the audience shows up and they think 'oh great, Shakespeare's coming', but it's sort of endlessly deferred, you want to see what he's like in the flesh and you're not sure if you quite believe in him. I wanted to reflect all of that in the audience experience. I felt the only way to humanize him and allow Judith to have a kind of equality on stage with him was to have the lighting dark, have him be powerless and have no choices to make; to put him in that passive feminized position within the power dynamics of that period.

**RH:** In the development and writing process, how were you thinking of your audience? I'm thinking here of what Tom Stoppard said in *Rosencrantz and Guildenstern are Dead* about 'every exit being an entrance somewhere else'. What were you thinking in terms of taking Shakespeare away, or nodding to the potential of a relationship between him and the Earl of Southampton? That's quite a well-worn myth within the Shakespeare mythos; why gesture to that? What did you intend your audience to be, in terms of their knowledgeability?

**EW:** The original first draft I wrote was as a screenplay rather than as a play. And for that, I was imagining the audience of *Shakespeare in Love*. In my daydreams, I was imagining a massive, mainstream audience who wouldn't necessarily have the Shakespeare knowledge that I had, and I really wanted it to function for that audience. But as I was writing it, I got more interested in early modern playing conditions. I couldn't not have the conversations about Shakespeare's biography and the lost years; the things we know, and we don't know. So, I think I was always writing with the potential for a specialist knowledge in the audience and the things they might know, but I was always keen for it to function as a story [where an audience wouldn't need] any knowledge of that world. It's then interesting that the life that this play has had in being performed in the reconstructed Blackfriars Theatre at the American Shakespeare Center has brought it to a well-informed Shakespearean audience. But it's also been performed in drama schools, which bring the Shakespeare knowledge but not the theatre history necessarily, depending on the drama school, which is a different context. The play did have one staged reading at King's [College London] as part of the Shakespeare 400 celebrations, where it was entirely an academic audience, and that was bizarre, because there was an awful lot of laughter, because they got every single one of the tiny nods [to a fact]. It was recognition laughter rather than funny laughter, if you know what I mean? It created a completely different mood because of all that knowledge.

**ES:** You mentioned that when you initially conceived the play, you were aged about twenty-one and you were thinking of working within a tradition. Did you think about yourself as a woman dramatist writing about a woman dramatist? Did you find opportunities to think about your situation, aspirations, anxieties and the female theatrical community?

**EW:** I think I was trying to work through what it meant to be a woman writer by writing *Shakespeare's Sister*. My university experience had been quite masculine in that Magdalen [College] when I was there was 70 per cent male, and compared to a lot of other English departments, there was a substantial proportion of male English students. It felt like quite a masculine world. I was taught by Laurie Maguire in my third year, and it was quite a shock, a shift, an exciting thing to suddenly have this feminist Shakespearean teaching me. I was looking for models, for a sense of lineage. Again, to come back to the fact that a lot of my favourite authors up to that point had been men – Oscar Wilde, E. M. Forster, C. S. Lewis – I wanted to be androgynous in my mind and then I sort of suddenly discovered writers like Doris Lessing, and I found in writers like Elizabeth Jane Howard and Margaret Drabble a particular generation of professional female authors who were finding their own way, working out what it was to be a woman writer. I was thinking about those questions and trying to think through them in writing the character of Judith. It was embarrassingly autobiographical! I was just trying to work out 'what do I do to become a playwright? How do I run away to London to join the players?' I was writing that through her, as well. I was, at that point, almost fantasizing about the idea of this female community of theatre-makers, all together, because I had not, at that point, experienced anything like that. It was like a talisman to write this play and write this sort of feminist world.

**ES:** On your Author's Note you say you wanted 'to challenge the isolation of Woolf's female playwright'. Why did you situate the female community in the theatre, rather than in, say, a domestic space in Stratford?

**EW:** My impulse in writing the play was quite anti-domestic. I did not want Judith to be stuck in the domestic space, I wanted to get her out. I was really fighting against the relationship between femininity and domesticity. And I have since worked a lot on domesticity, and now could frame the domestic as a radical space, a space of resistance. But at the time, I was feeling like 'I want to get her out of there' and the theatre felt like the exciting space where things are happening, and I wanted her to be in it. The play itself is almost telling the story of what I was working through, which was initially when I pictured Judith being in the theatre – to come back to *Shakespeare in Love* – it was like Viola getting to be in the theatre company, a woman getting to be in the male space.

**ES:** Was Judith's end always tragic and did you think of the play as a tragedy? Or do you think of it as a kind of positive tragedy? I ask as it reminds me of *The Duchess of Malfi* and *The Tragedy of Mariam* where the heroines die, but die for their beliefs. Do you think of Judith as a martyr for her art?

**EW:** Originally, the play that Judith was writing wasn't *The King's Second Concubine*, it was originally about a saint – I think it was St. Lucy – and I'd picked a saint who died for her beliefs because I wanted Judith to be a martyr figure. Then I thought it was too on the nose and I also wanted to explore different things in the play-within-the-play. Bizarrely, I'd written the entire *The King's Second Concubine* – it was my first attempt at a semi-original play – so I was like 'hang on, here's one I made earlier!' so I just smuggled it in. So yes, I was thinking in terms of martyrdom, I wanted the ending to be tragic, because I agreed with Woolf that [Shakespeare's genius sister] would have died, though I didn't agree with *how* she died. I didn't like the suicide, obviously. It's very Woolf, sadly, to have that as a choice, but I didn't want that to be the thing that killed Judith. I did feel like the whole argument is that she couldn't live that life and so her death was the clearest way to show that.

**RH:** To place your work in a contemporary context, was there any desire to reflect on potential LGBTQ+ relationships and connotations? For example, in the scene where the character Lucy Morgan (a teenage sex worker) notices that Judith looks like Will and then kisses her.

**EW:** I did want the potential for queer desire and a queer relationship. The actors in the Theatre Royal Haymarket version felt that they discovered a whole relationship between Lucy and Dorothy. I hadn't explicitly written that, but I could see why they found that there and I liked it as a choice. In terms of the body language and of Dorothy stepping in to protect Lucy, it was all written for them with that subtext that they brought out. With the feminist intentions of the play, I had an explicit framework for what I was doing and made every choice in relation to this. I feel like the potential LGBTQ+ resonances of the play were more submerged and less conscious to me, but I did want them to be there. You know, that was a conscious choice around Lucy in that moment, but I guess it's never developed in terms of a plot. It remains a subtext.

**ES:** Have you found that writing *Shakespeare's Sister* influenced your later work?

**EW:** It's had a huge influence on my playwriting. *The Defamation of Cicely Lee* is responding to *Cymbeline*, but it's also responding to my own work in what I said about the world in *Shakespeare's Sister* still being quite male. I wanted *Cicely Lee* to be more equally male and female, and to have, again, female friendships and conversations and conflicts between women to be at the centre of it. I think, in *Shakespeare's Sister*, female friendship becomes important by the end, but the primary one-on-one intimacy happens between women and men. And interestingly, in *Cicely Lee* the central relationship is between two friends, and they have their breakup, as it were, and an ambiguous reconciliation at the end. I wanted to use the romance plot to plot a relationship between women and I think the seeds of that came from looking to *Shakespeare's Sister* and seeing how Judith is still, in some ways, a lone woman in a man's world, rather than having the kind of female friendships that I know from my own life have been a huge part of my emotional landscape. So, I wanted to explore that. It's also interesting that as an academic, a lot of the thinking I did through writing the play has then informed my academic projects. I've gradually realized the extent to which, for me, creative work is inextricable from academic work. The research on one informs the other.

**ES:** It's a critical commonplace that every generation reinvents Shakespeare and, in your play, Shakespeare is reinvented as Judith Shakespeare. What might twenty-first-century audiences find in your Judith Shakespeare? What have you found from seeing the play performed for audiences?

**EW:** I think, from seeing the play performed, and talking to audiences, people do tend to respond quite directly to my feminist project. It's not a subtle play, in terms of what it's trying to do. It's explicitly political and I think people do respond to that. I tried to include some humour in it and the director of the American Shakespeare Center, Jim Warren, kept saying that it was unexpectedly funny. I hadn't necessarily thought through the interesting ways that audiences would respond to being with Judith and believe in the politics of the play. In the current climate in relation to nostalgia and the past, and the politics of that, I feel like there is this desire in a twenty-first-century audience to step into these past worlds. In some representations of Elizabethan England we see burgeoning creativity, a looking to the future, there's a sort of escape to hope, from the perspective of a twenty-first-century audience. The version of Shakespeare we're getting is one that on the one hand, lets us acknowledge his canonicity and his genius, and on the other hand, is trying to decentre this version. We can use Shakespeare to look at the things that we've lost and forgotten in the past and join them with Woolf in her project of creating this feminist lineage of female writers that I think there's still a hunger for; that's also what I'm trying to do.

# PART THREE

# Theatre

# 11

## 'Not the fashion'

## Imagining the formative presence of early modern women in Shakespeare's circle

### *Naomi J. Miller*

At the conclusion to *As You Like It*, Rosalind observes famously that 'It is not the fashion to see the lady the epilogue' (Epilogue, 1–2). With more lines than any other female character in Shakespeare's plays, Rosalind's shrewd caution about what is 'not the fashion' for women's voices was at once seemingly contradicted and actually reinforced by the delivery of these lines by a boy actor playing a girl on Shakespeare's stage – signalling a matter of what an audience 'likes' to see. When considering biofictions about Shakespeare and early modern women, Rosalind's caution can be applied outside the frame of a single speech to acknowledge a gap between appearance and reality, aspiration and consequence.

Contemporary biofictions about Shakespeare have entertained multiple possibilities for early modern women who might have influenced the playwright in his female characterizations, fulfilling what one might take to be the modern authors' implicit aspirations to celebrate little-known women's voices. And yet the majority of these women are represented in the roles of lover and/or muse, often with little regard for the women's own voices and roles in the historical record. Playwrights and novelists have found irresistible the temptation to put a name to Shakespeare's 'Dark Lady', perpetuating a modern 'fashion' for casting various historical or fictional women in that role, while emphasizing their importance primarily in the passive positions of inspiration or influence. In contrast, in this chapter, I consider biofictional representations of Mary Sidney Herbert, Aemilia Lanyer and Mary Wroth on both page and stage, and explore the differential consequences of the fashion for claiming women's fictionalized influence over Shakespeare, by attending to their own historical voices.

Playing with multiple possibilities associated with the Shakespeare authorship debate, actor and theatre director Mark Rylance's play *I Am Shakespeare* entertains a range of candidates for the position, including 'Mary Sidney Herbert, the Countess of Pembroke, to whose sons the First Folio was dedicated' (2012: 68). Rylance's very modern Countess links her relationship with her 'hidden lover, Dr Lister', to the 'forbidden relations across class boundaries [in] so many of the love affairs in Shakespeare works' (2012: 71). The Countess's formative role as an influence upon Shakespeare becomes visible in the reference to her adaptative translation of Garnier's tragedy *Marc Antoine* (the first play about Antony and Cleopatra in English blank verse), in which she claims that she 'used the idea of translated historical drama as a veiling device to tell the truth' (2012: 73). And indeed, Rylance uses his own play as a veiling device to suggest, in her voice, that 'it would certainly be refreshing to hear the opinions of some other women' (2012: 84), particularly where Shakespeare is concerned. Rylance gives credit to Robin Williams's argument in *Sweet Swan of Avon* that Mary Sidney Herbert was the author of Shakespeare's plays in convincing him that 'the brilliant Mary Sidney [. . .] may throw important light on the mysterious authorship of the Shakespeare plays and poems' (Williams 2012: back cover). Yet he takes a detour in making the creative choice, as playwright, to represent the Countess of Pembroke in a surprise reveal as not a Sidney after all, but the love child of Queen Elizabeth, and as the lover rather than sister of Philip Sidney. So despite his inclusion of the Countess in his theatrical roster of Shakespeare authorship candidates, Rylance nonetheless replicates the pattern of representing a woman author as the lover of a more famous man.

Before the publication of my own novel, *Imperfect Alchemist* (2020), Mary Sidney Herbert had not yet received extensive treatment in biofictions, whether on the page or the stage. She does have a walk-on role in the second novel of Deborah Harkness's All Souls trilogy, *Shadow of Night* (2012), where she's introduced to the reader as 'the foremost woman of letters in the country, and Sir Philip Sidney's sister' (223). However, the Countess of Pembroke's role in this novel, and in series 2 of the television series spinoff (*A Discovery of Witches* (2021)), is not that of the eloquent author of her own play and poems but a figure connected to magic. At her first meeting with Diana Bishop, for instance, an embroidered bee and snake magically detach themselves from Mary Sidney's slippers and escape of their own accord. Along those lines, the television series represents her on-screen as a woman whose alchemical expertise connects her to other magical figures in that fantasy world, rather than to other authors, whether male or female.

I was encouraged by a trade editor to pitch my novel about Mary Sidney Herbert, *Imperfect Alchemist*, by referencing Harkness's novels and the television series because the Countess had popular 'name recognition' through that series that might appeal to publishers. However, because I was interested in featuring the Countess in my own biofiction as a female scientist and published author who mentored other women authors, rather than as a magician, I composed my novel with primary reference to Mary Sidney Herbert's own voice – in her Psalms, her play *Antonius* and her completion of Philip Sidney's *Arcadia*.

In *Imperfect Alchemist*, Shakespeare is moved and inspired by reading Mary Sidney Herbert's play, *Antonius*, and by meeting her when he brings his players to perform *As You Like It* at Wilton House, where he accepts a commission from her to produce a play about Antony and Cleopatra for the public stage. The following passage illustrates Shakespeare's point of view:

> *Antonius* had infused his consciousness from its opening speech, a paean to a goddess in the voice of a general willing to risk all for love. While her adept verse drew him in from the start, it is her characterization of the indomitable Queen that still holds him in thrall. A Cleopatra of head-turning complexity – lover and mother, seeker and ruler, coward and hero, flawed and yet complete. He has mulled over the tragedy and wrestled with its contradictions ever since, tempted to take on the story himself.
>
> No such character has ever appeared on the English stage.... Even as her play captured his attention, so must his own transmutation of the story capture hers. He's convinced that any celebration of this queen's *infinite variety* must commence with dark before light, shadows before bright possibility. It remains to be seen how she will treat a playwright who aspires not to contradict his patron's vision, but to complicate it. This Countess makes hungry where most she satisfies. (Miller 2020: 331–2)

Subsequently, the Countess collaborates with Shakespeare on the play that becomes his *Antony and Cleopatra*. These passages include excerpts from her *Antonius* as well as Shakespeare's play. An accomplished alchemist as well as author, she inspires Shakespeare to envision both their collaborative partnership and the relationship between Antony and Cleopatra in terms of the hermaphroditic ideal of alchemy, which brings together spirit and matter, male and female, Sol and Luna.

Constructing a biofictional frame that extends far beyond Mary Sidney Herbert's authorial collaboration with Shakespeare, I include the voices of other women authors in my narrative. As I explain in the author's note: 'Responding to her known patronage of women authors such as Aemilia

Lanyer and her goddaughter, Mary Wroth, I have imagined some of these women into the Countess's writers' circle, their interaction with the male authors inspiring visions of new possibilities', while 'my account of Mary's collaboration with Shakespeare is another fiction that is not beyond the realm of possibility' (Miller 2020: 440). Again, placing women authors centre stage, I include an imagined performance of *Antonius* at Wilton House, where Mary Wroth plays Cleopatra and Aemilia Lanyer plays Charmian.

At the close of their collaboration, Shakespeare tells the Countess, 'Together we have crafted a play unlike any I have written before – a play of communion across boundaries.' Which also, Mary reflects, 'expanded the boundaries of her own vision while connecting with his. A worthwhile experiment' (Miller 2020: 361). Unlike Mark Rylance, I'm concerned to bring Mary Sidney Herbert's published words, as a dramatist in particular, to modern audiences, framed with fictional dialogue that conveys her compelling influence upon writers ranging from Shakespeare to Aemilia Lanyer, Ben Jonson to Mary Wroth.

In *A Room of One's Own*, Virginia Woolf imagined that if Shakespeare had had a sister, equal in talent, she would have been 'so thwarted and hindered' that she could not have written her own poems and plays, let alone seen them published or performed (2004: 57). We now know that Woolf was wrong. Defying the era's constricting morals and mores, some women authors in Renaissance England found space and recognition – and with it, scandal and censure. Woolf didn't know about them, because over the years they had been erased from the 'canon' of accepted classics.

My projected biofiction series *Shakespeare's Sisters*, which commences with *Imperfect Alchemist*, presents an array of early modern women authors as autonomous peers of Shakespeare, rather than simply as passive objects of desire or figures of inspiration. In six interrelated biofictional novels, the series aims to restore attention to these remarkable female figures – Mary Sidney Herbert, Mary Wroth, Amelia Lanyer, Anne Clifford, Elizabeth Cary and Queen Anna of Denmark – by capturing their stories from their own perspectives. *Shakespeare's Sisters* centres on women whose lives and voices both shape and are shaped by women, many of whom play a part not simply in Shakespeare's circle, but in each other's stories.

The only woman author from this group who has been treated in multiple biofictions is Amelia Lanyer, again most consistently represented as Shakespeare's 'dark lady'.[1] The title of Mary Sharratt's novel *The Dark Lady's Mask: A Novel of Shakespeare's Muse* (2016) says it all. While a passionate and eloquent character in her own right, Sharratt's Lanier receives the most attention for her identity as the instrument of Shakespeare's invention. Nonetheless, in refreshing contrast to the handful of other novels that include Mary Sidney Herbert in a supporting role, Sharratt gives the Countess her due as the translator of Robert Garnier's *Marc Antoine* through a masque performance drawn from that translation in which Sharratt's

Lanier performs (2016: 81). And towards the end of the novel, Mary Sidney Herbert sends Lanier her Psalms and affirms her admiration for Lanier's *Salve Deus Rex Judaeorum* (2016: 371).

Sharratt opens her historical afterword to the novel by affirming that 'this is a work of fiction. There is no historical evidence to prove that Aemilia Bassano Lanier was the Dark Lady of Shakespeare's sonnets' (2016: 394). She admits, however, that 'as a *novelist* I could not resist the allure of the Dark Lady mythos' (2016: 394). In this compelling fictional narrative, Sharratt's Lanier inspires and empowers Shakespeare's success, only to be abandoned and effectively repudiated by the playwright. And yet, after Shakespeare's death, Lanier receives a box of papers, densely packed, with a missive saying only '*For my eternal Muse*'. Enclosed are all of Shakespeare's plays, including 'the early comedies that they had written together and that he had gone on to revise and make wholly his own, as if to erase her' (2016: 388). Reading the later plays, Lanier finds herself in Shakespeare's *Othello* as Emilia, who speaks 'lines so passionate, they might have come from her own *Salve Deus*', and recognizes her lost daughter, conceived with Will, in *The Winter's Tale*, where 'Odilia live[s] again in Perdita' (2016: 390). Although resolved to see these plays published with a preface by Ben Jonson 'to insure Will's posterity', she reflects that 'once more, men would be her mask and she would be erased. Yet she was the indelible thread woven into Will's great tapestry' (2016: 392). While Lanier's great religious poem, *Salve Deus Rex Judaeorum*, is described in the novel, the culmination of the narrative represents her central achievement as being Shakespeare's 'eternal Muse', the vital thread in *his* 'great tapestry'.[2]

Another Shakespearean biofiction that sets out to celebrate Aemilia Lanyer is Morgan Lloyd Malcolm's play *Emilia*, which premiered to glowing reviews at Shakespeare's Globe in 2019 before transferring to the West End. This eloquent and bold transmutation of Aemilia Lanyer's voice offers much to admire, including its focus on Lanyer's identity as a poet, as well as its central attention, through casting preferences, to gender and colour as explicit topics. Once again, however, the focus on women's voices serves more to celebrate the brilliance of Shakespeare's characterizations of women, by attributing his genius to the formative influence of a woman such as Lanyer in his circle, than to celebrate the brilliance of the women themselves.

Here again, Mary Sidney Herbert appears as a supporting character who serves as an intermittent mentor to Emilia. Dismissing Shakespeare's writing as 'bilge', Malcolm's Countess introduces Emilia to Shakespeare, with the caveat that 'she's not your type' (2018: 20–1). The Countess declares that she will see her own poems published one day and encourages Emilia to do the same, advising her to 'play the game well Emilia and you will succeed' (2018: 20). That brief interaction marks the extent of the play's acknowledgement that Mary Sidney Herbert was a published author. What's more, Malcolm includes only one example of Aemilia Lanyer's actual published voice.

Malcolm shows Emilia constantly writing and asserting when discouraged that 'I will write my way out of this. No one can take my words from me. At least I have that' (2018: 45). And yet the majority of her speeches consist primarily of language adapted from Shakespeare's Emilia in *Othello* – most notably in complaining, 'have not we affections, desires for sport and frailty, as men have?' – so that the audience can accept Malcolm's fiction that Shakespeare stole such speeches from Emilia for his plays. When Emilia discovers that she has become known as the 'dark lady' of Shakespeare's sonnets, she laments that this is how she'll be remembered, exclaiming, 'Is there anything more violating?' (2018: 72). In Malcolm's play, Emilia's other writing is reduced to a reference to short poems with 'subtle warnings and instruction to women on how to approach marriage' (2018: 60), a fictional invention. The single moment when Malcolm accords Emilia her legitimate historical voice occurs near the end of the play, in the blistering language of Aemilia Lanyer's dedication of *Salve Deus Rex Judaeorum*, 'To the Vertuous Reader', excoriating men who 'do like Vipers deface the wombes wherein they were bred' (2018: 76).

Malcolm's play achieves an effective and moving dramatization of feminism, interleaving historical with modern women's voices onstage. However, the play perpetuates the practice of many modern biofictions, whether on page or stage, that represent female figures in Shakespeare's circle in the role of lover and/or muse. When biofictions choose to feature these women not through their own words but as figures imagined to have challenged, inspired and deepened Shakespeare's characterizations of women, their own voices and perspectives are lost.[3]

In *Strange Labyrinth*, my own sequel to *Imperfect Alchemist*, I focus on the story of Mary Wroth, England's first female fiction writer, struggling to create a place of her own in a world where most women's roles were scripted by men. Recognizing connections between the early modern and modern worlds, *Strange Labyrinth* delves into complex issues of race, gender and sexual orientation in Jacobean England. My novel explores how Wroth, in her prose romance *Urania*, drew on her own experiences – as wife and widow, mother and lover, author and friend – to depict characters pursuing paths never previously represented by a woman in print.

My biofictional representation imagines a historically likely interaction between Wroth and Shakespeare on the grounds of Wilton House at the performance of *As You Like It* that is documented in the archival papers of the Countess of Pembroke and also occurs in *Imperfect Alchemist*. In *Strange Labyrinth*, a conversation with the playwright after the performance includes Mary's observation that 'breeches are only the start of liberty for women [. . .] and allowing Rosalind the last word was a nice gesture of possibility' (Miller forthcoming). Shakespeare then tells Mary, 'I've written something for you and your cousin', and hands her the sonnet 'Let me not to the marriage of true minds', adding that 'the poem speaks for itself, and for those readers who may find their own truth within it' (Miller forthcoming).

Later that evening Mary Wroth pens her own poem, 'As these drops fall', in response to Shakespeare's sonnet, which rings changes on the phrase 'love is not love' (Miller forthcoming).

My biofictional reconstruction of the interaction between Mary Wroth and William Shakespeare takes inspiration from Wroth scholars who have traced the formative presence of early modern women in Shakespeare's circle. Jane Kingsley-Smith advances a compelling argument that Shakespeare composed Sonnet 116 for 'the unique historical situation of the marriages of William Herbert, 3rd Earl of Pembroke and his cousin (who was also his mistress), Lady Mary Sidney', who became Mary Wroth upon her marriage (2016: 292).[4] Considering the further possibility that Wroth might have served as a patron to Shakespeare, Kingsley-Smith suggests that Wroth can be seen to function 'not as a Dark Lady but as a "Begetter"' (2016: 300). Advancing our modern awareness that early modern women such as Mary Sidney Herbert and Mary Wroth authored works that both engage with and diverge from the works of Shakespeare, *Strange Labyrinth* represents Mary Wroth performing the part of Cleopatra in her aunt's *Antonius* and subsequently staging a production of her own play at Penshurst Place. *Love's Victory* reconfigures Shakespeare's examples of same-sex friendship and heterosexual romantic love in a play such as *As You Like It* into an affirmation of a woman's right to choose, whether a male lover or the 'liberty' of 'chastity'.[5]

I offer these examples of my own biofictional treatment of Mary Sidney Herbert's and Mary Wroth's interactions with Shakespeare because, unlike stage plays such as Mark Rylance's *I Am Shakespeare* and Morgan Lloyd Malcolm's *Emilia*, I am committed to bringing the actual voices of early modern women authors in Shakespeare's circle to the attention of modern audiences.

Interestingly, in many of the examples discussed in this essay, Shakespearean biofictions can be seen not so much as narrative explorations of the historical figure of Shakespeare as speculative inventions regarding how other historical figures, including women in his circle, might have shaped his plays. In some sense, then, recent Shakespearean biofictions that feature early modern women seem concerned less to celebrate these women's voices than to admire Shakespeare's female characters, whose creation they fictionally credit to the formative presence of women in Shakespeare's circle. An implicit assumption underlying these works is that Shakespeare *must* have had a female 'muse', or even collaborator, in order to be able to conceive such complex and convincing women characters. This notion serves as an adjunct to the authorship question.

Mark Rylance's play *I Am Shakespeare* revolves around that very question. It climaxes in an overlapping chorus of voices that includes Shakespeare scholars as well as Shakespeare's characters exploring 'who Shakespeare is' and 'who am I?'. The chorus culminates in an original sonnet about an oak tree, spoken in alternating lines by the four 'authors' represented in the play – the historical 'William Shakspar', Francis Bacon, Edward de Vere and Lady Mary Sidney – that concludes that everyone owns the tree. The modern protagonist of the play, Frank Charlton, 'a Shakespearean authorship researcher who was once a star Shakespeare academic', asks, 'What's in a name? Suppose we all agreed upon the name, we'd still imagine many different Shakespeares.' In the final scene in the film *Spartacus*, where all the slaves stand up and claim to be Spartacus in order to hide and protect him (2012: 95), Frank finds his answer to the authorship controversy: 'He hid himself so that we could each be him. Our own author. Our own authority.' Thus when the constable who has been investigating the true identity of Shakespeare throughout the play returns to the stage, Frank, and his neighbour Barry – and, ideally, members of the audience – all rise to affirm 'I am Shakespeare' (2012: 93–7). As Rylance explains in his introduction, he is 'more concerned with the search for identity, our own identity, than the search for the identity of the author of the Shakespeare works' (2012: 7).

Indeed, I propose that many Shakespearean biofictions on page and stage are more concerned with enhancing audience appreciation of Shakespeare's plays through engagement with other historical figures than with exploring Shakespeare's 'true' identity. Thus the 'bio' in these biofictions finally turns out to reflect not simply the biographical details of historical figures but also the lives and identities of modern playwrights and audiences, novelists and readers, who may find themselves appreciating Shakespeare anew, not as an icon so much as a participant in our quests to make sense of our own worlds.

# Notes

1. For a compelling consideration of the range of existing biofictions about Lanyer, see Susanne Woods (2022). Because different biofictions about Lanyer use different versions of her name, I employ the historically accurate spelling, Aemilia Lanyer, when referring to the historical figure, and the biofictional spellings when referring respectively to Sharratt's (Lanier) and Lloyd Morgan's (Emilia) biofictions.

2. Relatedly, see Douglas Lanier's analysis of Shakespeare in popular culture which points out that 'the kind of empowerment' offered by variations on the authorship controversy is 'deeply ambivalent', particularly where 'the heroine' who appears as 'lover-muse [. . .] becomes the secret source of Shakespeare's artistic powers [. . .] but does not herself become an artist of Shakespeare's stature' (2002: 118).

3. For more on Malcolm's play, see Woods.

4. A central crux of Kingsley-Smith's argument is that both William Herbert and Mary Wroth reuse the phrase 'love is not love' in their original verse, while a search of the Chadwyck-Healy database for all phrases beginning 'love/love is

not' between 1580 and 1640 produces only three examples of that phrase in poetry: Shakespeare, Herbert, and Wroth (2016: 298–99). For more on 'love is not love', Pembroke, and Shakespeare, see Lamb (2019).

5   See my extended analysis (Miller 2014) of the dynamics of same-sex friendship and heterosexual romantic love in Wroth's *Love's Victory* by comparison with those in Shakespeare's plays across genres that feature heterosexual romance.

# References

*A Discovery of Witches* (2018–2022), [TV series] SkyOne.
Harkness, D. (2012), *Shadow of Night*, New York: Viking Penguin.
Kingsley-Smith, J. (2016), '"Let Me Not to the Marriage of True Minds": Shakespeare's Sonnet for Lady Mary Wroth', *Shakespeare Survey*, 69: 292–301.
Lamb, M. (2019), '"Love Is Not Love": Shakespeare's Sonnet 116, Pembroke, and the Inns of Court', *Shakespeare Quarterly*, 70 (2): 101–28.
Lanier, D. (2002), *Shakespeare and Modern Popular Culture*, Oxford: Oxford University Press.
Lloyd Malcolm, M. (2018), *Emilia*, London: Oberon Books.
Miller, N. (2014), 'As She Likes It: Same-Sex Friendship and Romantic Love in Wroth and Shakespeare', in P. Salzman and M. Wynne-Davies (eds), *Mary Wroth and Shakespeare*, 137–50, London: Routledge.
Miller, N. (2020), *Imperfect Alchemist*, London: Allison & Busby Books.
Miller, N. (2022), *Strange Labyrinth*, Unpublished manuscript [publication forthcoming].
Rylance, M. (2012), *I Am Shakespeare*, London: Nick Hern Books.
Sharratt, M. (2016), *The Dark Lady's Mask: A Novel of Shakespeare's Muse*, Boston: Houghton Mifflin.
Williams, R. (2012), *Sweet Swan of Avon: Did a Woman Write Shakespeare?*, Santa Fe, New Mexico: Wilton Circle Press.
Woods, S. (2022), 'Lanyer: The Dark Lady and the Shades of Fiction', in J. Fitzmaurice, N. J. Miller, and S. J. Steen (eds), *Authorizing Early Modern European Women: From Biography to Biofiction*, 57–69, Amsterdam: Amsterdam University Press.
Woolf, V. ([1929] 2004), *A Room of One's Own*, London: Penguin.

# 12

## 'That's power'

## Representations of performance in Shakespearean biofiction

*Stephen Purcell*

Shakespearean biofiction on screen often involves a depiction of Shakespeare's plays in performance. Narratives of this sort inevitably make a number of assertions about what early modern Shakespearean performance was like; as such, they are valuable insights into what popular audiences imagine Shakespearean performance is, or could be, today. In my 2009 book *Popular Shakespeare*, I considered *Shakespeare in Love* (1998) and the *Doctor Who* episode 'The Shakespeare Code' (2007) as expressions of 'the Globe myth' before analysing them alongside depictions of Shakespearean performance in other historical periods (2009: 157–64). These were, I argued, links in an intertextual chain of screen depictions of Shakespearean performance going back to Olivier's *Henry V* (1944). All three construct early modern Shakespearean performance as essentially democratic, breaking down the barriers of social class as the audience is transformed and unified by the performance. This chapter provides an update of sorts to my analysis, considering the more recent films *Anonymous* (2011) and *Bill* (2015). It also returns to *Shakespeare in Love* and 'The Shakespeare Code' to examine some of the aspects of these depictions unexplored in my 2009 book, and to consider the intertextual relationships between all four narratives.

## Court performances

One such aspect appears early on in *Shakespeare in Love*: the presentation of a court performance of *The Two Gentlemen of Verona*. This sequence provides an important counterpoint to the public performance of *Romeo and Juliet* at the Curtain theatre that will structure the film's climax. Where Shakespeare and Viola's performances in the latter will transfix and deeply affect the popular audience they perform before, the court performance is shown to be largely limp and unaffecting, only Will Kempe's extratextual comic business with a dog really achieving its desired effect. As the performance begins, the Queen is eating snacks and coughing, clearly unengaged. The actor playing Valentine holds his hands up in declamatory style, a stark contrast to the more naturalistic acting we will see in the final *Romeo and Juliet*. Kempe's performance of Launce's leave-taking monologue (2.3) livens things up a bit; the Queen cackles as the dog misbehaves, and most of the audience laughs along with her. As Valentine delivers the lines beginning 'What light is light, if Silvia be not seen?' (3.1.174), we see close-ups of contrasting reactions: where the Queen is falling asleep, Viola is mouthing along with the poetry, entranced. This double effect allows the film to make a key statement about the potential effects of Shakespearean performance, as director John Madden notes in the DVD commentary: it signifies to mass audiences who might not have been engaged by Shakespeare in the past that 'this is alright, because even the Queen of England can find Shakespeare boring', while also suggesting that Shakespearean performance can have a hypnotic and transformative effect when it strikes the right chord with the spectator. Indeed, where most of the shots of the actors and audience in the *Two Gentlemen* sequence are static, Madden begins to employ more movement as the camera closes in on Viola, and orchestral strings start to play on the accompanying soundtrack; a moving camera and an orchestral score will be used throughout the film whenever Shakespeare's dramatic poetry takes effect.

Where the court performance in *Shakespeare in Love* is shown to be largely uninspiring, comparable sequences in the authorship conspiracy movie *Anonymous* take a very different line. Here, the drama achieves its strongest emotional effects on the Queen herself. Early in the film, the elderly Elizabeth watches an outdoor performance of *A Midsummer Night's Dream*; a close-up on her enchanted face leads into a flashback in which, forty years earlier, a young Elizabeth watches the same play. The play is, according to the film, the juvenile work of Edward de Vere, Earl of Oxford. Perhaps because the film wishes to assert the play's powerful effect on the Queen, it is staged with the totalized aesthetic of a Victorian painting. Where *Shakespeare in Love*'s court performance was enacted on a bare stage before a plain curtain, *Anonymous*'s court performances of *Dream* both play out in front of painted backdrops and realistic trees, amongst which clusters of lighted candles flicker prettily. The fairies wear wings and horns, and Bottom a realistic donkey head. In the later version of the performance, Oxford himself lurks in what looks like the wings of a Victorian stage, partially hidden by scenery and a curtain. The actor who appears to be playing Puck looks up at Oxford as he observes the moment in which Titania wakes up and falls in love with Bottom, suggesting Oxford as an Oberon-like figure, manipulating the Queen with the 'magic' of drama.

We return to a rather more impervious version of Elizabeth in the court performance that forms the climax to the family comedy *Bill*. The performance is part of a summit between Elizabeth and Philip II of Spain, but Philip's men have infiltrated the palace under the guise of 'The Cockerney Players of Bow', and Shakespeare's play, written under duress as a front for an assassination attempt on the Queen, is to be passed off as the work of the treacherous and conceited Earl of Croydon. The central joke is that the young Shakespeare is trying to fit all of his ideas into a single play: an earlier rehearsal sequence showed him packing plot elements from numerous plays into the Gilbert-and-Sullivan-style musical number 'A Series of Funny Misunderstandings', and when he is forced by the villains to rewrite his play, he comes up with a drama that weaves together parts of *Henry V*, *Macbeth*, and (unbeknownst to the conspirators) *Hamlet*'s encounter with the ghost. The performance begins in the mode of the court performance in *Shakespeare in Love*, with the unimpressed Queen slumped in her chair. The Earl of Croydon plays the lead Macbeth-like role himself, and his acting style is comically mannered. The performance improves as it continues, though, the court audience becoming more engaged: in another nod to *Shakespeare in Love*, the spectators gasp when a spurt of 'blood', represented by a crimson handkerchief, seems to burst from a player's chest. By this point, the Queen is starting to look more interested in the drama. Several barrels of gunpowder are stacked behind the stage, ready to be ignited upon a particular cue line. However, Shakespeare foils the assassination attempt, and intervenes by appearing in a puff of smoke with the words of *Hamlet*'s Ghost to accuse the Earl of complicity in the plot. A melee ensues, and the audience appear confused as to whether or not the fighting is real, until Shakespeare tears down a tapestry, which functions here as a sort of discovery space, to reveal the barrels of gunpowder. Impressed more by Shakespeare's loyalty than by his drama, the Queen orders the Earl of Southampton to finance Shakespeare's future writing, and when Shakespeare tells her that he has 'a few ideas', she replies, 'Excellent. Though maybe one at a time, eh? 'Cos that was a bit dense.' *Bill* thus serves as a parodic origin story. As Wardle notes, in this film, Shakespeare's plays 'are always fragmented, and never experienced on the public stage', so that 'there is no celebration of the power of theatre itself' (2018). Such power is hinted at, however, in a brief epilogue scene set backstage at the Rose theatre which shows Shakespeare getting ready to go onstage and perform in his new play, provisionally titled *A Series of Comedy Errors*. His wife Anne enters excitedly, telling him 'It's a full house', and as the film ends, he walks out onto the stage to applause. Much like *Shakespeare in Love*, then, *Bill*'s final moments cast Shakespeare's court performance as a prelude to the real fulfilment of his potential in the public playhouse.

## Public performances

The depictions of performances in public playhouses in *Shakespeare in Love* and 'The Shakespeare Code' were the focus of my analysis in *Popular Shakespeare*, so I will not re-tread them here. Some points, however, bear reiterating in order to set some context for my discussion of *Anonymous*. The performance in *Shakespeare in Love* takes place in a specially built reconstruction of the Curtain theatre on a bare thrust stage. The play's spectators are visible in the background of nearly all the footage of the stage actors, while shots of group reactions – gasps and cries especially – are intercut with close-ups on individual spectators looking moved and transfixed. Madden employs a moving camera and orchestral soundtrack through much of the sequence, both of which the film has firmly established by this point as signifiers of Shakespeare's dramatic poetry casting its spell over the listener. At the end of the performance, the audience is stunned into silence, before ecstatic applause breaks out, the spectators in the galleries rising to their feet.

Spells of a more literal kind form the basis of the plot of 'The Shakespeare Code'. The Doctor and his human companion Martha Jones arrive in 1599 London to discover that a trio of witch-like aliens called Carrionites are manipulating Shakespeare to create a portal that will allow more of their kind to invade the Earth. Shakespeare has been picked because of his facility with words, which, for the Carrionites, carry a quasi-supernatural power. Near the start of the episode, we see the Doctor and Martha at the newly built Globe Theatre, having just watched a performance of *Love's Labour's Lost*. As in *Shakespeare in Love*, the audience is united in a standing ovation, and Martha, the television audience's on-screen representative in the episode, affirms that the performance was 'amazing, just amazing!'. As Shakespeare gives a post-show speech from the stage, the Carrionite Lilith, who sits alone in a gallery box, magically seizes control over him causing him to suddenly promise the crowd that his as-yet-unfinished sequel to *Love's Labour's Lost* will be performed 'tomorrow night', to looks of surprise from the actors. The following day, the Doctor articulates the 'magic' of the Shakespearean theatre, realizing as he does so the nature of the Carrionites' plan: 'you can change people's minds just with words in this place'. When *Love's Labour's Won* is performed at the episode's climax, we see only snippets of the performance, but it seems to be well-received, Will Kempe's Costard entering to applause and cheering. The Carrionites watch from a box, awaiting the lines they have inserted into Shakespeare's play which will summon more of their kind to Earth. When the portal opens, however, Shakespeare improvises a speech to close it up again, and the Carrionites are sucked back into the portal, along with hundreds of fluttering pages of Shakespeare's now-lost play.

I am hesitant to claim that there was any conscious borrowing from *Doctor Who* in *Anonymous*, but there are similarities. As Douglas Lanier has argued, *Anonymous* seems to 'double down' on the classist assumptions of the Oxfordian authorship theory, reimagining 'the author of Shakespeare's plays as an aristocratic pseudo-populist, his popular audience as puppets useful to his schemes' (2013: 222, 224). Like the Carrionites, Oxford is enthralled by theatre's capacity to reach so many people with 'the writings of one man, the ideas of one man', concluding, 'That's power'. Oxford gives Ben Jonson a play to stage on Bankside, hoping that Jonson will pass it off as his own; Jonson refuses, but Shakespeare, portrayed in this film as a shallow and vainglorious actor, is only too willing to take the money and public adulation. When Oxford watches his work in performance at the Rose theatre, he looks on from a box in the galleries, an isolated figure like Lilith, twiddling his inky fingers almost as though they contained the 'magic' of his writing. A chorus of three playwrights, Marlowe, Dekker and Nashe, are present alongside Jonson at almost every public performance depicted in the film, and these characters serve as audience avatars in the same way that spectator-characters like the Nurse and Henslowe do in *Shakespeare in Love*. But where such characters in *Shakespeare in Love* are emotionally absorbed in the drama, *Anonymous*'s on-screen chorus are, with the exception of the enthusiastic Dekker, detached and sceptical, even as the rest of the audience get whipped up into a frenzy.[1] During the 'St Crispin's Day' speech, the actor playing Henry V moves into the yard as many groundlings rush to take his hands, and when he roars the final line, the crowd cheer wildly. The chorus of playwrights look stunned; this is intercut with several shots of Oxford gazing fixedly at the stage and accompanied by a swelling orchestral score. The implication is clear: 'magic' is at work here, but the playwrights' troubled glances hint that it is far from benevolent. Indeed, the performance of *Henry V* climaxes with an eruption of genuine crowd violence, as the groundlings become dangerously caught up in the fictional war. Oxford loses his composure, laughing maniacally and shouting to his servant, 'Do you see? Do you see?', before goading the mob on.

*Anonymous*'s public playhouse performance sequences share much in common with earlier depictions. As in *Shakespeare in Love*, the camera is often positioned so that the spectators are visible behind and around the onstage actors, their transfixed faces and emotional reactions becoming the focus. Like both *Shakespeare in Love* and 'The Shakespeare Code', *Anonymous* shows the spectators laughing loudly at comedy and responding with gasps to violence and special effects.[2] The influence of the real-life reconstruction of Shakespeare's Globe is evident, with Globe actors such as Mark Rylance, Alex Hassell, James Garnon, Jasper Britton and Michael Brown playing their early modern counterparts and erstwhile Globe director Tamara Harvey directing the theatre scenes, while the costumes for the film's *Twelfth Night* recall Jenny Tiramani's designs for the Globe's celebrated 2002 production. The performance style is more interactive than the largely (and anachronistically) naturalistic acting we see in *Shakespeare in Love*; Hassell's Henry V and Romeo both descend into the yard to make physical contact with spectators in a practice that has no recorded precedent in the Elizabethan theatre, but which has been common at the reconstructed Globe. Oddly, the stage is depicted throughout the film as filled with painted, perspective-effect scenery, despite such scenery being a clear anachronism. Many of the public playhouse sequences also appear to depict night-time performances, lit by flaming torches. A possible explanation for these anachronisms is that they are present to assert some continuity with the proscenium-arch theatre performance styles with which modern popular audiences are assumed to be more familiar.[3]

The film's most telling anachronism is in its presentation of the Essex Rebellion. Historically, the Lord Chamberlain's Men were commissioned to play *Richard II* on the eve of Essex's ill-fated attempt at a coup, presumably because its controversial deposition scene was seen by Essex's supporters as useful propaganda for their cause. *Anonymous*, however, presents the same events through a performance of *Richard III*, whose title character is constructed in the film as a highly provocative caricature of Robert Cecil, Essex and Oxford's enemy. William Cecil has told his son, who has severe curvature of the spine, that he must compensate for his 'malformations' with 'cunning' and 'ruthlessness'; the film thus invites us to believe that a popular audience would have understood *Richard III* as a direct attack on the younger Cecil. In Shakespeare's play, the actor playing Richard is usually able to use the character's early soliloquies to forge a playful complicity with the audience;[4] *Anonymous*, however, ignores this aspect of the play's dramaturgy, and has the spectators start to boo and hiss the character over his opening soliloquy when they recognize him as Cecil. By the end of the play's second scene, the actor playing Richard/Cecil is being pelted with vegetables, his lines virtually inaudible amidst the booing and heckling. Oxford's servant Francesco is in amongst the groundlings and helps to spur them on with chants of 'down with Cecil!', shepherding them towards a confrontation with the armed authorities that will result in several of their deaths. Throughout *Anonymous*, then, Oxford is portrayed as a sort of caster of spells, controlling the writing from afar, more like *Doctor Who*'s malevolent Carrionites than *Shakespeare in Love*'s inspirational poet. This construction of the plays as a kind of political 'dark art' is all the more obvious for the film's unconvincing misrepresentation of *Richard III*'s dramaturgy.

## Inclusion and exclusion

These films are all about the unifying power of Shakespearean theatre, so it is worth asking who is included in the group being united, who is excluded, and to what ends. As we have seen, *Shakespeare in Love* and *Doctor Who* follow Olivier in presenting Shakespearean performance as, in Lanier's words, 'the site of an idealised, democratic popular culture' (2002: 144). *Bill*'s plot confines it largely to the elite audience of the court, but it suggests by implication that Shakespeare's true artistic home was in the public theatre; indeed, an awkwardly justified scene between Shakespeare and Anne at the Rose theatre (filmed at the modern Shakespeare's Globe) presents performance for a popular audience here, rather than for the Queen at court, as Shakespeare's ultimate ambition. *Anonymous*, by contrast, reasserts class difference, in keeping with a film whose prologue insists that 'the son of a glovemaker [. . .] armed but with a grammar school education' is unlikely to have written the works of Shakespeare; here, the depiction is of an elite class who use popular culture to control an easily manipulated plebian public. In all four films, audiences represent a mix of ages and genders, but only in *Doctor Who* are they also racially diverse – the episode commendably attempts to correct the widespread misconception that early modern London was monocultural, with Martha, who is Black, pleasantly surprised to see two other Black women walk past, as the Doctor assures her that Elizabethan London is 'not so different from your time'.[5]

Most of the films tend to reassert heteronormative gender roles in their depictions of performance. *Doctor Who* mentions 'men dressed as women' as a feature of early modern performance, but the only speaking roles we ever see are men playing men.[6] Likewise, the snippets of performance seen throughout *Anonymous* are almost entirely of male characters speaking, the main exception being a scene between the androgynous witches in *Macbeth*; the queer potentiality of cross-dressed Shakespearean performance is thus consistently downplayed.[7] *Shakespeare in Love* goes even further in this respect. Immediately after the court performance at the start of the film, Viola insists that boy players will never be able to represent true love, and indeed the film's climax rests on the premise that a boy actor with a broken voice could not plausibly play Juliet, since this is what prompts Viola to step in at the last minute (this is despite the fact that mature men are playing the roles of the Nurse and Lady Capulet). Thus, the homoerotic charge that must have been present on some level in early modern performance is downgraded into a historical flaw in need of correction by the heteronormative casting of a woman in the only female role that is the object of male desire in the play. There are subtle hints of a queer identity in the film's presentation of Sam, the boy actor: he smiles fixedly at Shakespeare when the latter touches him lightly on the chin and asks him 'Are you ready to fall in love again?'. But even Sam is heterosexualized as the film progresses, when, along with the rest of the cast, the character is treated to a night in a brothel by the play's financial backer, Mr Fennyman: we see him briefly being kissed by a female sex-worker and confessing, somewhat ambivalently, 'I quite liked it . . . .'

Surprisingly, *Bill* is the outlier here. *Bill*'s main queer-coded character is the Spanish 'master of disguise' Gabriel Montoya, whom the film initially sets up as a one-joke character who is constantly on the lookout for opportunities to wear women's clothing. As the film progresses, though, Montoya finds his calling as a cross-dressed actor in Shakespeare's plays, playing female roles in both the rehearsal of Shakespeare's first script and the performance of his final one. When, at the film's climax, it becomes apparent that his fellow assassins/actors do not value the commitment he is bringing to his female roles, he defects and releases the kidnapped Shakespeare from his bonds. 'You set me free', says Shakespeare, surprised; 'No, you set me free', Montoya replies. In the epilogue scene, Montoya can be seen adjusting Shakespeare's costume and now appears to be presenting as a woman in earnest. The film thus springs something of a surprise on its audience, moving from a series of simple heteronormative jokes about cross-dressing to a sympathetic portrayal of a character who seems to be embracing a queer/trans identity.[8]

As we have seen, all of these films employ anachronism to assert various sorts of continuities between modern audiences and their early modern counterparts. Some of these are what I have called 'assimilative' anachronisms (Purcell 2009: 30–3): covert anachronisms that attempt to hide or downplay their departure from the historical record. The presentations of night-time performances and painted backdrops in *Doctor Who* and *Anonymous* could be considered examples of these, as could Kempe's Grimaldi-style clown wig in *Shakespeare in Love*, or indeed the emergence of naturalistic acting in the film's performance of *Romeo and Juliet*. *Anonymous*'s earnest tone makes it the most susceptible of the four films to this sort of anachronism, and its many historical errors have been widely critiqued. The other three films, however, also make use of what I have called 'disjunctive' anachronisms (Purcell 2009: 33–6): self-advertising anachronisms that the audience is invited to notice and enjoy, lending a degree of irony to the film's presentation of the past. Thus, for example, in *Doctor Who*, Shakespeare wearily insists, 'No autographs. No, you can't have yourself sketched with me', while in *Shakespeare in Love* he visits a Freudian psychoanalyst, and in *Bill*, he gets fired from the band *Mortal Coil* for a rock-n-roll lute solo. Much like the TV show *Horrible Histories* for which its cast and writers are most famous, *Bill*, in particular, is filled with disjunctive anachronisms, from Marlowe and Shakespeare dressing up as vegetables as part of an advertising campaign, to the burst of disco-style dancing that rounds off the film's climactic scene. These films thus implicitly acknowledge that what is being presented is not only, or even primarily, a depiction of the historical past, but rather, a commentary on the present.

# Notes

1. See Kirwan for a detailed analysis of the film's depiction of these playwrights (2014).
2. Rain starts to fall during Hamlet's 'To be or not to be' speech, perhaps in a nod to the sudden downpour that affects the performance of *Henry V* in Olivier's film. Notably, despite the weather, the crowd remain totally entranced.
3. Semple points out that the film is framed by sequences set in a modern Broadway theatre, which imply a continuity between the early modern audience, the Broadway audience, and the film's audience (2023).
4. Mark Rylance, who plays the character performing Richard in the film, certainly did so when he played the role himself at the Globe in 2012.
5. Lindy A. Orthia has criticized *Doctor Who* for its 'whitewashed' depiction of the past as 'harmoniously multi-racial' (2010: 207).
6. As Wardle remarks, the episode 'is less conservative in its representation of Shakespeare's sexuality than *Shakespeare in Love*' (2018), in that it suggests a bisexual identity for Shakespeare when he flirts very briefly with the Doctor; however, the character's amorous attention is mostly focused on Martha.
7. Semple observes that the film also removes any suggestion of homoeroticism between Shakespeare/Oxford and the Earl of Southampton, since 'Oxford's interest in Southampton derives from paternal concern, not queer desire' (2023).
8. The film does not make the nature of this identity clear in its final moments; I am thus using he/him pronouns to refer to the character in the absence of any clear steer otherwise.

# References

*Anonymous* (2011), [Film] Dir. Roland Emmerich, USA: Columbia Pictures.

*Bill* (2015), [Film] Dir. Richard Bracewell, UK: Vertigo Films.

*Doctor Who* (2007), [TV series] 'The Shakespeare Code', BBC One, 7 April.

Kirwan, P. (2014), '"You have no voice!": Constructing Reputation Through Contemporaries in the Shakespeare Biopic', *Shakespeare Bulletin*, 32 (1): 11–26.

Lanier, D. (2002), *Shakespeare and Modern Popular Culture*, Oxford: Oxford University Press.

Lanier, D. (2013), '"There Won't be Puppets, Will There?": "Heroic" Authorship and the Cultural Politics of *Anonymous*', in P. Edmondson and S. Wells (eds), *Shakespeare Beyond Doubt: Evidence, Argument, Controversy*, 215–24, Cambridge: Cambridge University Press.

Orthia, L. A. (2010), '"Sociopathetic Abscess" or "Yawning Chasm"? The Absent Postcolonial Transition in *Doctor Who*', *The Journal of Commonwealth Literature*, 45 (2): 207–25.

Purcell, S. (2009), *Popular Shakespeare*, Basingstoke: Palgrave.

Semple, E. (2023), '"A Darker Story": Two Shakespeares, Art, and History in Emmerich's *Anonymous*', *Borrowers and Lenders: The Journal of Shakespeare and Appropriation*, 15 (1).

*Shakespeare in Love* (1998), [Film] Dir. John Madden, USA: Miramax.

Wardle, J. (2018), 'Time Travel and the Return of the Author: *Shakespeare in Love*, "The Shakespeare Code", and *Bill*', *Borrowers and Lenders: The Journal of Shakespeare and Appropriation*, 12 (1). Available online: https://borrowers-ojs-azsu.tdl.org/borrowers/issue/view/23.

# 13

# Reverse engineering Shakespeare with biofiction: TNT's *Will* as repertory studies criticism

## *Aaron Proudfoot*

In this chapter, I argue that *Will* – TNT's 2017 Shakespeare origin story series – functions as a piece of early modern repertory studies criticism by using an adaptive strategy I term 'reverse appropriation'. Literary biofictions generally draw from an artist's work to create an image, with varying degrees of fictionalization depending on the historical evidence available, of that artist's biography and their artistic process. As a show situated in Shakespeare's 'lost years', *Will* is an ideal text to examine the functionality of the 'reverse appropriation' strategy because the lack of historical evidence associated with the playwright's earliest days in London creates space for productive speculation on the biographical and professional gaps in the story. As I will argue, the subject matter, driving inquiry and the speculative approach of *Will* are all comparable to the scholarship of early modern repertory studies critics and should be considered alongside their scholarly conversations as speculative thought experiments that consider and play out potential answers to some of the unsolvable questions we have about Shakespeare's life and the workings of early modern theatre companies.

Put simply, reverse appropriation is the retrospective integration of material from an author's texts, typically recognizable as that author's work, into said author's biography. This strategy enables audiences and scholars to deliberate on the author and, more broadly, the relationship between life and art, and the material and professional contexts of the artistic process. *Will*'s use of reverse appropriation affords it the opportunity to explore imagined biographic spaces with productive possibilities because it consciously embraces speculation as a tool for understanding the unknowable. Instead of going for cheap jokes and encouraging a game of 'spot the reference' for seasoned Shakespeare initiates, *Will* embraces the ambiguities of the lost years and uses reverse appropriation to explore what life *might* have been like for Shakespeare when he first arrived in London and worked his way into a successful position within the theatre scene. In the rest of this chapter, I will argue that *Will*'s focus on how the theatre scene, its business implications and the personal and professional relationships within it, would have structured Shakespeare's early days in London allows the series to function as a piece of Shakespearean repertory studies scholarship. This is a particularly interesting approach to Shakespearean biofiction because it invites consideration of far more than the individual genius and character of Shakespeare himself. Repertory studies, which I will define and discuss in detail, is most simply summarized by Tom Rutter as 'an approach to the study of drama that takes the acting company – rather than, say, the individual dramatist or play' as its subject (2008: 336). Applying such a perspective to a piece of biofiction, then, works to destabilize the oft-depicted individuality of Shakespeare's authorial genius and affords the opportunity to feature other important figures, material contexts, professional challenges and collaborative resources as key components of the playwright's emergence on the stage of literary history.

There is an inherent contradiction within the biofiction genre because, as Jennifer Holl observes, 'Shakespeare – in *Will* or [other cultural artifacts] – is not a body of work, but a body' (2021: 125). Discussing the connection between the 'fleshy focus' of cultural artefacts that tend to hyperbolize Shakespeare's attractiveness and 'a preoccupation with celebrity', Holl argues that 'bodies are regularly scrutinized as texts that not only provide greater insight into the private lives concealed behind public faces, but are also inscribed with cultural meaning' (2021: 125). While there is a tension between Holl's claim that *Will* desires to know Shakespeare's body, not his texts, and her other claim that bodies are themselves scrutinized *as* texts, I contend that this is a productive tension rendered unavoidable by the uncertainty around Shakespeare's 'lost years'. *Will*'s setting in this time period of Shakespeare's biography affords it the opportunity to speculate about his private and professional life in ways that can be productive in learning more about what I find to be the most important part of Holl's claim – the 'cultural meaning' that we can imagine from an embodied experience of early modern theatre in Shakespeare's early London days.

Holl argues that it should be expected that repeated attempts to unveil Shakespeare's body from his body of work choose to make him more attractive than he probably was because we collectively want a Shakespeare that looks like what we imagine – which, of course, is an image that reflects the glamour and genius of the literature we know him through. Many early responses to *Will* criticized the show for its anachronisms in style, sound and image. However, *Will*'s punk rock mis-en-scène, with all of its corresponding excesses, is an intentional over-glorification of the sexiness of, not just Shakespeare's body (as Holl argues), but of the theatre scene itself and, in the spirit of repertory studies, the way budding celebrities like Shakespeare and Richard Burbage were able to emerge from such a complex and collaborative professional ecosystem.

Elsewhere in this volume, Michael Friedman builds on Peter Coogan's generic classification of the superhero origin story in a reading of *Will* that exemplifies this glamourization of the theatre industry *around* Shakespeare. While Friedman's focus is the actor Richard Burbage, I am more concerned with how *Will* draws on elements of the superhero origin story when it comes to Shakespeare himself. Instead of showing Shakespeare simply as an individual genius who emerges on the London stage in the early 1590s, it is specifically through his connections to others around him, including Burbage, and his attempts to find his way into the theatre *industry* that his origin story plays itself out. Joseph Roach argues in 'Celebrity Culture and the Problem of Biography' that 'stage history – which documents the ongoing collaboration by Shakespeare with celebrated actors and producers and expands the idea of what constitutes his "life" – is a more illuminating part of the playwright's proper biography than any of the extant [. . .] documents or portraits' (2014: 470–1). As Friedman argues in this volume, *Will* helps the budding celebrity of Richard Burbage along his superhero origin story journey by teaching him to tap into his humanity while acting. However, I think we can take this analysis a step further by observing the ways Burbage simultaneously helps Will with his own superhero origin story by teaching him how to be a celebrity; a skill that Will also hones with Marlowe and others throughout the series. With Roach's emphasis on the importance of stage history in any biographical speculation about Shakespeare in mind, we might even see the main 'superhero origin story' of *Will* as that of the Elizabethan theatre industry itself rather than of one or two individuals within it. Either way, the importance of Shakespeare's development as a celebrity within this biofictional tale makes it impossible for us to separate his individual authorial genius from his awareness of and reliance on the acting company around him, the positive reception from fickle audiences, and other components of the theatre industry of his time.

It is largely through its reverse appropriation of Shakespearean texts and historical records that *Will* demonstrates the speculative affordances of the biofiction genre and functions as a piece of repertory studies scholarship. *Will* is deeply invested in many of the major questions and interests of repertory studies and demonstrates an understanding of the relevant aspects of early modern theatre despite the liberties it takes in modernizing and thematizing it for TNT's audience. *Will* pushes the boundaries of and, I contend, enriches, repertory studies conversations by playing out possible answers to questions that are ultimately unanswerable through more traditional inquiry. As a medium, serial television is well-suited for this task. With multiple episodic plots and a longer running time than a film, *Will* can pose different questions about Shakespeare's experiences in the Elizabethan theatre industry and dwell on each one, playing out the potential answers and ramifications without rushing them or forcing a multitude of major questions and topics into one two-hour movie plot. While some of its speculative storylines – like Will's Catholicism, the existence of Alice Burbage and her affair with Will, and the exact nature of Will's relationship with historical figures like Aemilia Lanyer and Christopher Marlowe – may not have definitive historical sources, they allow us to think through possibilities and consider contexts and motivations that we might not otherwise have considered as scholars.

*Will* engages a repertory studies inquiry by focusing on collaborative composition and early modern company commerce, which, along with an emphasis on other authorial agents (actors, costume designers, patrons, etc.), works to destabilize the individuality of Shakespeare's author function. We should here be reminded of Tom Rutter's definition, from his detailed survey of the field, of repertory studies as 'an approach to the study of drama that takes the acting company – rather than, say, the individual dramatist or play – as the subject of its enquiry' (2008: 336). In this enquiry, which Rutter admits is often 'largely based on conjecture', '[t]he playwright is considered alongside other contributors to a company's dramatic output, such as actors, sharers, playhouse owners (and the buildings themselves), audiences and patrons, whereas the play itself is understood both as the company's basic commodity and as one of many plays that together constituted its repertory' (2008: 336). For Rutter, deindividualizing the 'author function' of early modern playwrights is the 'underlying methodological assumption' of repertory studies because 'the plays presented on early modern stages were shaped not just by the genius of individual dramatists, but by patterns of company commerce' (2008: 337). In the spirit of the field Rutter describes and without suggesting that Shakespeare was insignificant in his genius, *Will* proposes that while the 'author function' signified by 'Shakespeare' *includes* the celebrated Bard, it also includes actors like Richard Burbage and Will Kempe, theatre-owner James Burbage, the Theatre itself, the playhouse audiences, the rival company at the Rose, and various patrons, scribes, costumers and company apprentices, amongst others.

*Will* satisfies nearly every part of the definition of repertory studies provided by Rutter, acting almost as a dramatic narrativization of the entire field. The season pays sustained attention to the importance of acquiring and maintaining a patron's favour (episodes 1–3), the fragile nature of the company's reputation and tangible assets (episode 6), their theatre's situation within the daily life and culture of London (episodes 1–10), and the role of 'the play' as 'the company's basic commodity' (episode 2). In Burbage's pitch for money to build 'the Blackfriars theatre', *Will* even foreshadows the 'exclusive clientele', extended hours and improved lighting of the indoor theatres which grew increasingly popular in the years after the timeline of the series. Throughout the season, Will's ability to act and grow as a playwright, as well as his ability to live as a citizen of London, is mediated by the material conditions of his specific company and restrained by the physical space of the Theatre. The relatively small size of his claim to the company's profits and the necessity to navigate the already-established presence of the company's other contributors are driving forces not only in the show's plot but in the development of Will's human (as opposed to authorial) character.

Some of the show's most productive repertory studies arguments are made through its depictions of co-writing and language sharing. When he joins the acting company, Will is shocked and unsettled by the level of collaboration that takes place in the composition and production of 'his' plays. Struggling to write with an injured hand, Will is assisted by Alice Burbage, who offers to scribe for him saying, 'I am yours, dictate.' This early scene demonstrates the everyday practice of sharing the responsibility of writing for the theatre, albeit in its simplest, most literal form. Later in the scene, company owner James Burbage impacts what is written by demanding that 'we need [the script] now!' in order to rehearse before performing on their very tight schedule. Baxter (the company's other playwright) argues for revision, deploring Will's use of the word 'bedazzle' because 'you can't just *make up* words!' before star actor Richard Burbage silences Baxter and affirms Will's script, saying, 'I like "bedazzle".' Just as a repertory studies perspective encourages us to imagine, *Will* portrays the collaborative authorial work of the acting company not simply as a seamless process of splitting the work, but as an organic process based in dialogue, disagreement, emotional reactions and compromise.

Another backstage conversation summarizes the organic, collaborative process of language development within the company. A famous line from *As You Like It* is reverse appropriated when Richard walks up to Will and reflects on an encounter he just had with a young woman, saying that 'love is madness'. As he often does when other characters spontaneously spew recognizable lines, Will takes out his notebook and writes down the phrase for later use. Richard then implores Will to 'write a poem for me to bedazzle her with'. Using a word established five episodes earlier as Will's neologism, Richard's conversational deployment of 'bedazzle' symbolizes the applicability of the linguistic tools that the playwright gives the company. The cyclical and collaborative nature of the company's language is underscored by the fact that this comes immediately after the attribution to Richard of a line that is later, diegetically speaking, written by Shakespeare into a play to be performed by Richard. This brief interaction suggests that the linguistic development that we typically attribute to Shakespeare was likely actually an organic cycle that was collaboratively accomplished despite being penned into history by an individual.

*Will*'s speculative approach to the inquiries of repertory studies is not all too different from how scholars of the field scaffold what they do know about history with conjecture in order to paint a picture of what might have been. One such scholar is Roslyn Knutson, who in 'Marlowe, Company

Ownership, and the Role of *Edward II*', crafts a fascinating narrative about how Marlowe, Edward Alleyn and a series of happenstances might have been responsible for Shakespeare writing Alleyn-like lead roles for Richard Burbage. In a clever sequence of conjectures, Knutson says:

> I *suggest* that he still had Alleyn in mind when he [Marlowe] wrote *Edward II*, even though Pembroke's Men ended up with the play. In that company, Richard Burbage, not Edward Alleyn, *would have* debuted the part of Edward. Building on this *conjecture*, I *suggest* further that this nexus of Pembroke's Men, *Edward II*, and Richard Burbage had an influence on William Shakespeare [. . .] Seeing Burbage in the part of Edward II, Shakespeare *might well have* gained assurance that the up-and-coming competitor to Alleyn could handle a part on the scale of Richard III. (2005: 37, my emphasis)

Knutson's conjectures illustrate how an expert's informed speculation can enrich our understanding of Elizabethan theatre. In a similar vein, I argue, *Will* uses historical evidence, scholarly inference, and creative licence to reverse engineer the conditions of dramatic composition and production in the 1590s, producing a novel Shakespeare biofiction.

In the spirit of repertory studies scholarship like Knutson's, *Will* feels at times like a show as much about the company of actors and other contributors who worked at the Theatre in 1589 as it is about Shakespeare the individual. While most of the show's plot-driving adaptive work is performed through the allusions to, and reverse appropriations of, plays such as *Hamlet* and the Henriad, it also stages several adaptations per se of plays in the show's diegesis. *Will*'s staging of Shakespeare's early plays offers answers to some of the big questions posed by biographers and literary scholars about the lives of early modern writers, competition and collaboration between playing companies, and the development of their repertories. The answers proposed by the diegetic production of these plays can again be compared to the work of repertory studies experts. In a study of the repertory of Pembroke's Men, for example, Knutson argues that the titles of their 'history plays [. . .] deliberately advertised themselves as competitors to specific plays' belonging to other playing companies, creating audience expectation and interest (2001: 132). This marketing ploy is used by James Burbage in Episode 1 of *Will* when, after a bad performance, an angry audience moves him to announce the company's next play. Even though it seems like Marlowe will not deliver on the play he's promised the company, Burbage panics and makes up a title – '*Tamburlaine, The Ghost*!' – that sounds like a spin-off of the popular *Tamburlaine* series that Marlowe had been selling to the rival theatre. The play the company ends up performing turns out to be Shakespeare's *Edward III*, but, due to market pressure, the company continues to advertise and perform it under Marlowe's name and the hastily invented *Tamburlaine* title.

In Episode 6, 'Something Wicked this Way Comes', *Will* takes a particularly creative approach to the imitative and marketable titling of the same *Henry VI* plays that Knutson discusses. When Richard and Alice Burbage ask Will about his progress on 'the sequel' to his recent *Henry VI*, he replies, 'I've got a title – *Henry the Sixth Part 2, Return of the Roses*.' Later in the episode, Alice gives him the idea to write a prequel rather than a sequel and proposes the title, '*Henry the Sixth Part 1, The Rise of the Dauphin Menace*.' This is clearly not the straightforward way that Knutson works through the titling of these specific serial plays in the context of a popular rival repertory. *Will*'s double homage to *Star Wars*, however, accomplishes a similar outcome to Knutson's speculations and it does so in a way that is accessible to its own audience.

In order to depict Will's innovativeness in producing a prequel after the original, the show maps the process onto a modern film series that achieved great success by producing prequels to its own original story. *Will* creates an ingenious set of parallels by evoking *Star Wars: Return of the Jedi* (a sequel of the original) when its hero considers a sequel to *Henry VI*, and then evoking *Star Wars: Episode 1 – The Phantom Menace* (the first prequel in the series) as Will decides to write the prequel instead. Like Knutson, *Will* uses a repertory studies approach to demonstrate that the titles of the *Henry VI* plays were crafted in a way that would 'deliberately advertis[e]' themselves in the context of a well-known contemporary repertory. Punning on the titles of a repertory familiar to its own contemporary audience, *Will* attempts to recreate the recognition that would have been evoked by the plays' actual titles in the minds of Shakespeare's contemporaries. Viewers who hear 'The Return of the Roses' and 'The Dauphin Menace' won't necessarily think of the repertory of Lord Strange's Men, but they *will* get the feeling that Shakespeare is ripping something off.

This choice harnesses modern cultural knowledge to encourage a repertory studies perspective on the composition of early modern professional drama, but it also goes a step further. By drawing the *Star Wars* parallel, *Will* invites its audience to turn the repertory studies perspective deployed by the show onto its own contemporary moment. Even in its early modern English setting, the professional choices made by *Will*'s characters point to similar choices made by modern producers of popular culture. Recognizing the fact that collaborative composition and the influence of rival repertories have as much an impact on the production and marketing of popular culture now as they did in the sixteenth century, *Will* opens a temporally reflexive inquiry through which the perspectives of repertory studies become more widely applicable.

This temporally reflexive inquiry can be seen not only in the show's nods to popular modern repertories, like *Star Wars*, but in its awareness of its own position as a series originally contracted for only one season and clearly in competition for a long-term place in its network's repertory with *Claws* (2017–22), another TNT drama whose first season aired weekly alongside

*Will* and which was eventually chosen by the network for continuation while *Will* was cancelled. Even though *Will* failed in comparison to its internal competition at TNT, it is notable in a repertory studies sense that much of what *Will*'s creators did to set it apart from the network's other shows seems like an attempt to style it as comparable to HBO's *Game of Thrones* (2011–19). Having been at the peak of its popularity while *Will* was being produced and released, *Game of Thrones* is arguably the most successful piece of HBO's repertory – a repertory widely considered to be the most successful in modern television history. With that said, *Will*'s attempts to style itself as comparable are not altogether unlike the competitive titling highlighted in Knutson's work or deployed by Shakespeare and his company within the series. While restrictions of space prevent a detailed discussion of the specific connections between *Will* and *Game of Thrones* (from imitative cinematography to over-the-top orgies and unnecessarily extensive torture scenes), it's worth noting that for a show about early modern theatre repertories and commercial competition, *Will*'s own attempt at commercial success was at least partially intertwined with its desire to recreate what has worked for the most successful modern media repertories of its own time – a lesson the show seems to have learned from its eponymous hero, even if the execution wasn't quite as strong.

The fact that such an attempt ultimately failed to secure a place in TNT's repertory also raises questions about *Will* itself, the network that aired its one season, the audiences of that network compared to others, and the decision to apply *Game of Thrones*-like creative decisions to Shakespearean and biofictional subject matter. The decision to imitate or invoke *Game of Thrones* is certainly not an uncommon one these days, most notably, when it comes to Shakespeare, in the case of the battle cinematography in *The King* (Michôd, 2019). *Will*'s choices, however, are particularly relevant because they raise questions about the place of not only Shakespeare but of literary biofiction in modern media repertories. Throughout its exploration into the lost years of Shakespeare's biography, *Will* is a self-reflexive piece of Shakespearean biofiction that is acutely aware of its own form, genre and overall precarity. Through its reverse appropriation of Shakespeare's texts and historical records, it speculates productively on the professional and material contexts of the theatre industry its protagonist worked his way into and should be considered in repertory studies conversations that focus on Elizabethan and Jacobean theatre.

# References

*Game of Thrones* (2011–2019), [TV series] HBO.
Holl, J. (2021), 'A Shakespeare that Looks Like Shakespeare', in *Shakespeare and Celebrity Cultures*, London: Routledge.

*The King* (2019), [Film] Dir. David Michôd, USA: Netflix.

Knutson, R. L. (2001), 'Pembroke's Men in 1592–3, their Repertory and Touring Schedule', *Early Theatre: A Journal Associated with the Records of Early English Drama*, 4: 129–38.

Knutson, R. L. (2005), 'Marlowe, Company Ownership, and the Role of Edward II', *Medieval and Renaissance Drama in England: An Annual Gathering of Research, Criticism and Reviews*, 18: 37–46.

Roach, J. (2014), 'Celebrity Culture and the Problem of Biography', *Shakespeare Quarterly*, 65 (4): 470–81.

Rutter, T. (2008), 'Repertory Studies: A Survey', *Shakespeare*, 4: 336–50.

*Will* (2017), [TV series] TNT, 10 July–4 September.

# 14

## Enter Burbage

## The origin story of an acting superhero in Craig Pearce's *Will*

### *Michael D. Friedman*

When actor Richard Burbage died in 1619 after a thirty-five-year career, public lamentation exceeded that offered for Queen Anne, whose demise befell two weeks previously. Burbage's passing provoked numerous elegies and epitaphs, the briefest of which was the pithy phrase 'Exit Burbage' (Nungezer 1929: 73). Such tributes detail Burbage's mature life as a player, but we know comparatively little about his birth, his apprenticeship in the theatre, or the early development of his talent. Shakespearean biofiction on screen has therefore tended to portray Burbage as if he sprang fully grown into Elizabethan theatre. In two television series: *Will Shakespeare* (1978) and *Upstart Crow* (2016–18), and in the film *Shakespeare in Love* (1998), Burbage is depicted as a middle-aged man, already his company's leading actor. Craig Pearce's *Will* (2017) diverges from these earlier portrayals by dramatizing an obscure portion of Burbage's biography: the events that perfected him in his craft. Concurrently, Pearce adapts conventions from the comic book superhero genre, particularly the feature of the origin story, which tells the tale of the protagonist's acquisition of superpowers. Although *Will* was advertised as 'the young and sexy treatment that Shakespeare's origin story has been waiting for!' (Agard 2017), the series more closely adheres to the elements of the superhero origin story in its treatment of the entrance of the great actor Richard Burbage.

Peter Coogan defines a superhero as a 'heroic character with a selfless, pro-social mission; with superpowers – extraordinary abilities, advanced technology, or highly developed physical, mental, or mystical skills; who has a superhero identity embodied in a codename and iconic costume, which typically express his biography, character, powers, or origin' (2006: 30). In a sense, the entire first season of *Will* dramatizes the origin story of Richard Burbage in that we observe him acquiring the core elements of mission, powers and identity as he evolves from a selfish, immature actor into a costumed version of King Richard III, in whose person Burbage defeats Richard Topcliffe, Queen Elizabeth's real-life Jesuit hunter and torturer, who functions as the supervillain opposing the superhero. Coogan identifies another aspect of the superhero genre: the use of 'resonant tropes', which he describes as 'familiar and repeated moments, iconic images and actions, figures of speech, patterns of characterization – that have resonance; that is they embody or symbolize some aspect of the character, and have gained this resonance through repeated use by storytellers' (2006: 6–7). Pearce selects three resonant tropes from Burbage's life: the Manningham anecdote, Hamlet's advice to the players, and Burbage's rivalry with Edward Alleyn, which Pearce adapts to set up the traumatic event (the plague death of Richard's best friend) that transforms Burbage into the greatest actor of the Renaissance stage.

The screenplay for the Pilot episode of *Will* introduces young Richard as 'arrogant, impossibly handsome and hugely talented, (but prone to over-act)' (Pearce n.d.: 11). At the outset, Richard does not resemble a superhero because his mission is self-centred (he exploits his profession and handsomeness to attract women) and his acting powers are not yet well-developed, so he cannot subsume his own persona within the alternative identity of the characters he embodies. Pearce demonstrates Richard's egotistical libidinousness through a revision of the famous anecdote recorded in the diary of John Manningham:

> Upon a tyme when Burbidge played Rich[ard] 3. there was a Citizen grewe soe farr in liking with him, that before shee went from the play shee appointed him to come that night unto hir by the name of Ri[chard] the 3. Shakespeare, overhearing their conclusion, went before, was intertained, and at his game ere Burbidge came. Then message being brought that Richard the 3$^d$. was at the dore, Shakespeare caused returne to be made that William the Conquerour was before Rich[ard] the 3. (Sorlien 1976: 75)

Pearce's version of this story begins in Episode 2, with Richard on stage performing in a production of *Edward III*. He flirts shamelessly and arranges an assignation with a woman in the audience, Lady Cressida Deveraux, to the detriment of his portrayal of his character. After the show, Cressida invites Richard to the Deveraux home, where the Lady expects Richard to make love to her. Richard, arrogantly believing that she is mesmerized by his acting talent, tries to recite lines from the play as he 'performs', but Cressida insists, 'Don't speak. Unbutton.'[1] In the Manningham anecdote, the female citizen is enamoured with Burbage in his embodiment of Richard III, but in Pearce's retelling, the Lady has no interest in Richard's character; she is lustfully drawn only to his good looks. Shakespeare does not figure directly in this encounter, but at the end of the episode, Richard's sister Alice refers to Shakespeare as 'William the Conqueror'. While this resonant trope usually establishes a sexual competitiveness between Burbage and Shakespeare, in *Will*, Pearce uses it to characterize Richard initially as a selfish philanderer who pursues his mission to seduce women at the expense of the quality of his company's stage performances.

To upgrade these productions, Pearce's Shakespeare attempts to enhance Richard's acting expertise with instructions that introduce a second resonant trope, Hamlet's advice to the players, often interpreted as praise for the real-life Burbage's naturalistic acting style in comparison to the artificial histrionics of his main competitor: 'Alleyn was most remarked on for his characteristic "stalking and roaring" [. . .] His peer, Burbage [. . .] who spoke Hamlet's words to the Players about unnatural actors strutting and bellowing, was himself never spoken of except as a master of "lively" or life-like acting' (Gurr 1992: 113).[2] Pearce transforms Hamlet's remarks from a critique of Alleyn's ranting style in comparison to Burbage's modest personation to a criticism of Richard's own unnatural overacting, which Shakespeare hopes to develop into a more realistic mode of representation.

In the Pilot screenplay, Richard's first appearance on the stage is accompanied by the following stage direction: 'Richard Burbage is bellowing out a speech. He is ridiculously loud, and his overly emphatic hand gestures make the speech look forced and artificial' (Pearce n.d.: 29). Richard's 'bellowing' and 'overly emphatic hand gestures' violate Hamlet's advice neither to 'o'erstep [. . .] the modesty of nature' nor to 'saw the air too much with your hand' (3.2.19, 4-5). Alice Burbage underlines her brother's transgression by whispering to Will, 'When he gets excited he saws the air like he's chopping wood – I call him "the carpenter"' (Pearce n.d.30). Later in the episode, Will tries to help Richard to improve his technique:

> WILL Well, ah, when actors, *act* they . . . Hold up a mirror to, *nature* – as it were . . .
> RICHARD BURBAGE A mirror up to nature . . . ?
> WILL So that audiences can recognize themselves on stage. (Pearce n.d.: 40)

Paraphrasing Hamlet's advice, which Richard ironically revises into an accurate allusion, Shakespeare initiates a collaboration between the two players that will eventually produce some of mankind's best theatre. As Richard exclaims, 'You will write the greatest parts this world has ever seen, and I will illuminate them by holding the mirror up to . . . what was it? . . . Nature! Together we will achieve greatness' (Pearce n.d.: 41). This prediction foreshadows a flash of acting brilliance that Richard evinces at the end of the episode, when Richard 'thunders' the first line of his most crucial speech, but then abruptly halts:

> As if suddenly remembering, he turns toward Will and holds his hand before his face like a looking glass. Richard and Will's eyes connect. A smile. The enigmatic gesture creates a strangely powerful moment. The audience are rapt as Richard turns back to them and continues more softly, connecting deeply with the emotion. (Pearce n.d.: 58)

Richard's fortuitous recollection of what will become Hamlet's advice manifests his latent acting talent. However, his lingering inability to retain the memory of what he is supposed to hold the mirror up to, which becomes a running joke, alerts us to the fact that he has not yet achieved the naturalistic acting 'greatness' for which he strives.

Greatness serves as *Will*'s equivalent for the superpowers of the superhero. In the same way that the superhero possesses some exceptional ability that sets him or her apart from ordinary human beings, a 'great' Renaissance actor has talents that raise him above the level of a run-of-the-mill thespian. Pearce sets the bar for greatness by incorporating a third resonant trope: several references to 'Burbage's principal rival, Edward Alleyn' (Roach 1985: 41). The Pilot screenplay includes the following exchange:

> RICHARD BURBAGE My acting tis far greater than All[e]yn's. Speak truth, tis great, tis not?
> WILL [diplomatic] Great? Yes . . . Perhaps even a little . . . too great. (Pearce n.d.: 39-40)

In Episode 1, Richard arrogantly announces that he is a greater actor than Alleyn, but he seeks confirmation from Will, who diplomatically attempts to stroke Richard's ego while at the same time moderating his overacting, which makes him 'too great'. The rest of the viewing public does not share Richard's high opinion of his own capacity, as is displayed when Richard tries to enter the VIP section of a party at Sir Francis Bacon's house:

> RICHARD Who says I'm not on the list? Do you know who I am . . . ? I'm the greatest actor in London.
> BOUNCER #1 Thou art no Edward Alleyn.
> RICHARD Nay! I'm Richard bloody Burbage!
> BOUNCER #2 I love Ned Alleyn.

Like *Shakespeare in Love*, Pearce's *Will* conceives of the early modern theatre world as an industry no less obsessed with fame and celebrity than modern Hollywood. Although Richard considers himself 'the greatest actor in London', the bouncers clarify that Ned Alleyn currently holds that title and Richard is merely a common player. Not until he endures a life-changing event that grants him his 'superpower' does Richard become the great actor whose roles made theatrical history.

The core of a superhero's origin story is the single event that transforms the protagonist from a commonplace individual to an extraordinary figure, like the moment when Peter Parker is bitten by a radioactive spider and becomes Spider-Man. Coogan argues that the superhero origin story is 'a metaphor for adolescence' in that 'origin stories tell of selfish boys made into selfless men' (2006: 15, 24). Peter Parker, for example, initially uses his spider strength for personal gain, but this choice leads indirectly to the death of his beloved Uncle Ben, which shows 'the dangers of selfishly withdrawing from the group and refusing to use one's abilities to help others' (Coogan 2006: 25). As a result, Peter altruistically resolves to serve society by fighting crime. The core event of the superhero origin story also usually involves 'trauma and recovery from trauma' (Gavaler 2015: 250). Therefore, as Sarai Mannolini-Winwood suggests, 'origin stories can inspire us or provide models for coping with adversity, or finding meaning from loss and trauma, or perhaps even discovering hidden strengths that can be used for good' (2018).

Richard Burbage spends much of *Will* as a self-centred, overgrown adolescent. As his father James, expecting to be arrested for debt, tells his son in Episode 7, 'I've never asked much of you, Richard. Your heart's in the right place. But you've been raised spoilt, vain, selfish. But in my absence, you have got to grow up.' The traumatic event that impresses itself upon Richard's body is the death of his best friend and fellow actor, the fictional character Autolycus Brewit. Here, Pearce adapts a movie and comic book trope known as 'fridging', whereby a character close to the protagonist (usually female) is killed off in order to cause emotional distress that propels the hero forward ('Stuffed' n.d.). The demise of Autolycus in Episode 8 provides the traumatic loss that will transform Richard into a great actor. Will explains to Richard that he is writing the play *Richard III* in order to attack Richard Topcliffe, Elizabeth's torturer, but Burbage resists playing the title role:

> WILL The first night we met, we said there was greatness in our stars. Do you still believe that? I'm writing this for you. This is where we start.
> RICHARD I am but a player, Will, not a man of politics or religion.
> WILL Do you believe in anything?
> RICHARD Of course! Women! Beer! Fame! Money! Did I mention women?

At this point, Pearce stresses that Richard lacks all three defining elements of a superhero: his life *mission* is not altruistic but selfishly sensual; he has not achieved the *power* of greatness as an actor, and he is unwilling to adopt the alternative *identity* with which he will be famously associated. However, when Autolycus contracts the plague, Richard accompanies his friend into the boarded-up plague house, answering Will's objections with the reply, 'This is what I believe in.' When Richard emerges from the house at the beginning of Episode 9, the harrowing experience of watching his friend and others die has impressed itself upon Richard's body, particularly his eyes, which are sunken and dark. He walks towards a bonfire and removes all of his clothes, which he throws into the flames. Standing naked in the square, he is, in a sense, reborn; altered by this traumatic event, which will eventually grant him the mission, powers and identity of a superhero.

Richard's mission ultimately becomes the protection of his family's theatre company against the threat posed by the Puritan Topcliffe, who wants to see all of London's stages closed down. Like many superheroes, Richard is at first reluctant to use his newfound powers. He must be pressured by Will to assume the role through which his greatness will defeat their adversary:

WILL I've finished *Richard III*.

RICHARD I'm not doing the play. I can't.

WILL Richard, it's monumental. You'll be hailed as the greatest . . .

RICHARD I said I'm not doing it.

WILL Hunsdon is going to recommend to the Queen that Topcliffe replace Walsingham as England's spymaster.

RICHARD What?

WILL He will wield total power. We must bring him down. It's our duty.

Despite Will's urging, Richard is not yet ready to assume the costumed identity of Richard III, by which means he will fulfil his unselfish duty to defend the theatre against the menace posed by Topcliffe, whom Pearce models after the conventions of the supervillain.

In a typical superhero tale, the protagonist 'represents the virtues and values of a society' while the supervillain 'represents an inversion of those values'; moreover, the supervillain 'has the ability to enact that inversion, to bring the normal activities of a society to a halt and force a hero to arise to defend those virtues' (Coogan 2006: 61). In *Will*, Topcliffe represents the antitheatrical prejudice of radical Protestantism, and if he is appointed spymaster, he will destroy Elizabethan theatrical society. Unlike the selfless superhero, the supervillain is motivated by selfishness, commonly an ego-driven ideological mission 'to save society from itself'. This maniacal 'singleness of purpose' prevents the supervillain from perceiving 'the inhumanity of what he does' or the fact that his actions primarily benefit himself (Coogan 2006: 82). Similarly, Topcliffe's Puritan crusade against the theatre putatively aims to save the souls of the reprobate players and their audiences, but Topcliffe stands to gain the most in terms of worldly power from his inhumane persecution of Burbage and his company.

Coogan's taxonomy of supervillains delineates five types, the first of which is 'the monster'. This version generally appears in beast form, but when 'a monster has a human form, it is monstrous morally – it has no moral sense of right or wrong, or a perverted one'; it 'lacks human compassion' (2006: 61–2). Topcliffe graphically demonstrates his perverse morality and inhuman lack of fellow feeling throughout the series by torturing to death various characters, including Baxter, Will's predecessor as the company's playwright. Topcliffe's devotion to the Protestant cause justifies, in his own mind, the violence of his endeavours, while simultaneously blinding him to the source of his god complex, which arises from the trauma of his own origin story. Coogan explains that the grandiose self-image of the supervillain

> arises from a sense of victimhood, originating in a wound that the supervillain never recovers from. He creates a superiority complex that most often emerges as a defense mechanism to make up for feelings of inferiority and inadequacy that arose from maltreatment received when he was younger (2006: 83–4)

Pearce gives both Burbage and Topcliffe a backstory that involves childhood maltreatment, but while Burbage grows beyond his wound, Topcliffe relishes his eternally. As Will and Alice discuss her brother's fitness to play Richard III, who represents Topcliffe, she reveals,

> ALICE You wouldn't believe it, but Richard was a sore, ugly little boy ... with a stutter. He was bullied horribly. But when Father put him on stage for the first time as a page ... In that moment, he suddenly grew taller and handsome. He could feel that the audience liked him ...
> WILL The audience can't like him. It's Topcliffe.
> ALICE No, but they can understand him. If you really want to terrify the audience, make us see ourselves in him.
> WILL Make the monster human. That's it. I have to show how a boy named Richard became Topcliffe.

Whereas Richard Burbage leaves behind the bullying he received as a boy and finds his place on the stage, Richard Topcliffe holds on to the victimhood that shaped him into a supervillain. To humanize this monster in the form of Richard III, Will must learn 'how a boy named Richard became Topcliffe'. Later in Episode 9, Topcliffe tells Will his origin story:

TOPCLIFFE I was packed off to a brutal school where the other boys had wealth and privilege. They scorned me. I found solace on the rooftop of my dormitory. I would pray in all weathers, beseeching God for salvation. One of the cruellest of the boys discovered me there. Mocked me, kicking me again and again, until he lost his footing. Fell off the roof and cracked his head. He was still breathing, so I stepped upon his neck.

WILL To be merciful?

TOPCLIFFE To be strong. It was a sign from God. For the first time, I felt absolute.

WILL And his death did not trouble your conscience?

TOPCLIFFE Conscience? 'Conscience' is a word only cowards use.

As a defence mechanism to compensate for the inferiority that he felt in relation to the wealthy boys who tormented him, Topcliffe, like a supervillain, develops a superiority complex, a conviction of divine sanction that frees him from any duty to show compassion to other humans.

To vanquish Topcliffe, Richard Burbage must draw upon the superpower granted to him by the trauma of his origin story, which Pearce envisions as method acting. In 1660, Richard Flecknoe wrote of the real-life Burbage that 'he was a delightful Proteus, so wholly transforming himself into his part and putting off himself with his clothes, as he never [. . .] assumed himself again until the play was done' (Richmond 1989: 35). Hugh Richmond observes that in this fashion, 'Burbage seemingly anticipates the total self-involvement in a role solicited by modern Method Acting' (1989: 34). Pearce's Burbage also learns how to employ the Stanislavskian technique of drawing upon personal experiences of emotions in order to create a believable portrayal. Although James Burbage has agreed to portray Richard III in Will's play, he cannot embody the character, so Will continues to pressure a reluctant Richard to assay the part:

RICHARD I've just lost my best friend, and now you want me to tell my father he's an old fool who can't act.

WILL I want you to stop cloaking your greatness in fear and self-pity. That's not why you lived and Autolycus died.

Richard continues to experience the traumatic loss at the core of his origin story, but Will urges him to bring out his greatness by using this pain as a method actor would: to enhance his portrayal of the character. 'Pour your nightmare into this part', Will tells him. Out of respect for his parent, Richard attempts to advise James how to perform the role: 'Father, if I may. Perhaps if you think of Richard's deformities more as a shoulder that rises as a shield against mockery, the arm twisted from being jeered at, hand withered like his unloved heart.' Richard clearly recalls the mockery and jeering that he received when he was a 'sore, ugly little boy [. . .] with a stutter', and therefore he possesses the emotional memories that a method actor could draw upon to offer a great performance of this role. Eventually, Richard convinces his father to relinquish the part to him, and Richard dons the costume and identity of his alter ego, Richard III, complete with the dark sunken eyes that recall his emergence from the plague house where the trauma of his origin story occurred. Using the powerful techniques of method acting, Richard Burbage as Richard of Gloucester reveals the true nature of the monstrous supervillain Topcliffe, prevents his appointment as spymaster and rescues the world of Elizabethan theatre.

Ronan Hatfull recognizes the economic incentive for screen artists re-imagining the life of Shakespeare and his company to employ superhero conventions in their works, which are 'designed to capitalise on the tropes of commercially successful cinema in order to transfer their popularity to Shakespeare and attract the audiences of those film franchises' (2020: 169). Yet creators like Pearce borrow from the superhero genre not only for commercial purposes but also to dramatize the little-known biography of figures like Burbage in a manner accessible to young viewers. By specifying the mission, powers and identity of their protagonists, such creators mirror back to us a vision of our own fantasies and aspirations. If *Will*'s portrayal of Richard Burbage is any indication, then we strongly wish to believe that the acting style on the Elizabethan stage evolved from an overblown rhetorical approach to a more naturalistic personation epitomized by Burbage's Protean transformation into his characters, aided by a dependence upon emotional memories that anticipates the techniques of modern method acting. We also want to believe, presumably, that theatre *matters*, in a political sense, and that the unselfish heroism of our contemporary players can overcome adversity and save us from villains cloaked in self-righteous piety.

## Notes

1 Quotations from *Will* (other than the Pilot episode) are my own transcriptions of the dialogue based on the episodes temporarily posted online at the TNT site.
2 Gurr quotes Everard Guilpin's *Skialetheia* (1598: B2$^v$).

## References

Agard, C. (2017), 'TNT's Young Shakespeare Drama *Will* Gets a Fresh Teaser', *Entertainment Weekly*, 30 January. Available online: http://ew.com/tv/2017/01/30/tnt-young-shakespeare-will-teaser-trailer (accessed 5 February 2022).
Coogan, P. (2006), *Superhero: The Secret Origin of a Genre*, Austin: MonkeyBrain Books.

Gavaler, C. (2015), *On the Origin of Superheroes: From the Big Bang to Action Comics No. 1*, Iowa City: University of Iowa Press.

Gurr, A. (1992), *The Shakespearean Stage 1574–1642*, 3rd ed., Cambridge: Cambridge University Press.

Hatfull, R. (2020), '*Bill* Begins: The Rise of the Contemporary Shakespeare "Origin Story"', in M. Gerzic and A. Norrie (eds), *Playfulness in Shakespearean Adaptations*, 160–77, New York: Routledge.

Mannolini-Winwood, S. (2018), 'The Superhero Origin . . . Again?', *The Artifice*, 26 January. Available online: http://the-artifice.com/superhero-origin (accessed 6 February 2022).

Nungezer, E. (1929), *A Dictionary of Actors and of Other Persons Associated with the Public Representation of Plays in England Before 1642*, New Haven: Oxford University Press.

Pearce, C. (n.d.), *Will: Pilot First Revision*, Screenplay. Available online: http://www.zen134237.zen.co.uk/Will_1x01_-_Pilot.pdf (accessed 19 September 2017).

Richmond, H. (1989), *King Richard III, Shakespeare in Performance*, Manchester: Manchester University Press.

Roach, J. (1985), *The Player's Passion: Studies in the Science of Acting*, Ann Arbor: University of Michigan Press.

Sorlien, R., ed. (1976), *The Diary of John Manningham of the Middle Temple 1602–03*, Hanover, NH: University Press of New England.

'Stuffed into the Fridge' (n.d.), *TV Tropes*. Available online: https://tvtropes.org/pmwiki/ pmwiki.php/Main/StuffedIntoTheFridge (accessed 30 April 2022).

*Will* (2017), [TV series] TNT, 10 July–4 September.

# 15

## '#Sharlowe'

## Connecting Shakespeare and Marlowe in *Only Lovers Left Alive*, *Upstart Crow* and *Will*

### *Ronan Hatfull*

In the casting call for supporting players in Shakespeare's life on screen, Christopher Marlowe is frequently at the front of the queue. Marlowe's life has been subject to intense scrutiny, encompassing his reputed criminal activities, atheism, homosexuality, occult status and work as a government spy. However, his violent and untimely murder in a Deptford tavern brawl on 30 May 1593 – aged just twenty-nine – has spawned even greater speculation and intrigue. It partly fed into one theory of the Shakespeare authorship conspiracy, which suggests that Marlowe 'faked his own death, fled to northern Italy, and wrote the works attributed to Shakespeare' (Barber 2010: 167). The reasons for and exact nature of his death – whether due to a disagreement over a bill or a government assassination – have also contributed to Marlowe's mythology. Biofiction has often reimagined Marlowe as Shakespeare's superior in age or class, transforming him into a mentor, companion or rival. In this chapter, I explore how screenwriters and directors have used Marlowe as a means by which either to confer cultural authority on Shakespeare and preserve his place atop the literary perch of his period, or to question this rarefied position and set their Marlowe in opposition to Shakespeare.

My principal focus is on Marlowe, and I begin with a previously unexplored, ephemeral portrayal of his on-screen dynamic with Shakespeare in the fantasy comedy-drama film *Only Lovers Left Alive* (2013), which portrays Marlowe as a jaded vampire who has kept secret the truth that he wrote the long-dead Shakespeare's plays and laments his rival's fame for this illegitimate authorship. I then consider two sustained representations of their relationship: the BBC sitcom series *Upstart Crow* (2016–20), which accentuates Marlowe's university background by depicting him as Shakespeare's entitled, upper-class companion, and the TNT drama series *Will* (2017), which casts Marlowe as a secret agent and explores homoerotic tension between him and Shakespeare. These representations have been chosen for their contrasting interpretations of Shakespeare and Marlowe's hypothetical connection, as well as the varying scale on which this relationship is able to be presented, from two-hour feature film to fifty-minute drama to half-hour sitcom.

As Shakespeare's life is remade on-screen, so Marlowe – as one of his most notorious contemporaries – has been utilized in myriad ways to hold the mirror up to Shakespeare to create a rival or collaborator. Artists imagine the playwrights' relationship to explore their own attitudes and anxieties about appropriation and legacy, while also celebrating collaboration and rivalry as key aspects of their own creative endeavours. Are these Marlowes fundamentally reverse-engineered by their creators, who begin by asking 'what kind of Shakespeare do we need' and then tailor him to fit their desired Shakespeare? To what extent does Marlowe play a supporting role in the story of Shakespeare's life?

*Only Lovers Left Alive* follows vampires Adam (Tom Hiddleston) and Eve (Tilda Swinton), and their attempts to rekindle a centuries-old relationship. Marlowe (John Hurt) is a minor character though he bookends *Only Lovers Left Alive*; at the beginning, he supplies Eve with blood and at the end he appears on his deathbed being comforted by both lovers. Although writer-director Jim Jarmusch never explains why Marlowe chose to keep his secret, the playwright's presence in a film which meditates on both the curse and mundanity of eternal life is significant. Without a physical manifestation of Shakespeare in *Only Lovers Left Alive*, Marlowe is defined by that very absence. This liberates him from his supporting role and, through the vampiric metaphor, offers a glimpse of how dead writers are sustained by the continuing utterance of their words.

While it takes the traditions of both Marlowe and vampires seriously, *Only Lovers Left Alive* retains a sense of humour, with several conspicuous literary references which, through their lack of subtlety, provoke amusement. For example, when Adam makes a pre-arranged visit to a doctor in a local blood bank, he wears a medical coat labelled 'Dr. Faust', in a nod to the title character of Marlowe's play *Doctor Faustus*. Jarmusch also peppers the film with allusions and direct references to Shakespeare's work, such as Eve reading Sonnet 116 to herself on an overnight flight to America and afterwards intoning 'Marlowe', in reflection of its true author, while Marlowe reflects on Adam's beauty, telling Eve that 'I wish I'd met him before I wrote *Hamlet*.' This connection finds its logical conclusion when Marlowe quotes Hamlet's 'what a piece of work is a man' as he dies, and Adam responds with another part of the same speech: 'what is this quintessence of dust?'

In their first shared scene, Eve longs for Marlowe to let 'the cat out of the bag' and reveal to the world that he was responsible for Shakespeare's work. In the deathbed scene, Shakespeare's image is shown on the wall of Marlowe's room, in the form of a Droeshout portrait poster with a dart sticking out, suggesting that Marlowe has been using the image of his enemy as target practice. Jarmusch thereby inverts the image of a fan plastering their walls with images of their heroes to suggest that Marlowe resents Shakespeare's fame and has been haunted by the playwright's very image right up to the end of his life. The playwright dismisses Shakespeare as an 'illiterate zombie philistine', referencing the word 'zombie', which the vampires attribute to humans throughout the film in a derogatory fashion, suggesting, that in comparison to themselves, humans are mindless lower life forms, incapable of appreciating art or existence. Finally, Marlowe reflects that 'humility will get you nowhere. There's the proof of that' and gestures to the poster, further underscoring his sense of regret. Jarmusch thus pays little attention to sexuality or class in comparison to *Upstart Crow* and *Will*, choosing instead to depict the two playwrights as ontologically in direct opposition to each other, even beyond the grave – zombie versus vampire. Instead, by creating the fiction of Marlowe remaining alive to represent how his image in popular culture is, conversely, sustained by his untimely death, Jarmusch reflects on the continued fascination with the playwright's mystique, the nature of his death and his connection to Shakespeare. Consequently, there is a reversal of Marlowe and Shakespeare's cultural roles as the renegade figure who died young in suspicious circumstances, and the prolific playwright who became England's most celebrated poet and passed away in middle age at his family home. Presented thus, Marlowe suffers the ignominy of witnessing Shakespeare's global success, while Shakespeare lies long dead.

By casting Marlowe as a vampire who faked his own death, *Only Lovers Left Alive* not only parodies the speculation about the true nature of the playwright's death, but implicitly comments on the nature of adaptation and influence itself. Taking Thomas Leitch's 'theory of vampiric adaptation', Adam Hansen and Kevin J. Wetmore Jr. propose 'the idea of Shakespeare as a vampire, feeding on texts and also being fed upon and breeding a new generation of vampires. Shakespeare's textual life is prolonged by those he feeds and feeds upon though the process of adaptation' (2015: 15). Through this lens, Jarmusch is decidedly vampiric in the way he seizes upon Shakespeare as a resource and is sustained by the playwright's work, and, in turn, figuratively extends Shakespeare's life through adaptation. In exploring the afterlife of Shakespeare's relationship with his most notorious contemporary, and by doing so through the prism of vampirism, Jarmusch questions the fetishization of Shakespeare and satirizes the idea that the playwright's contemporaries, such as Marlowe, are only sustained in the imagination of mainstream audiences by the ghostly presence of the Bard.

In *Upstart Crow*, series creator Ben Elton takes a more explicitly comic approach to the playwrights' relationship while also probing questions of cultural legacy and influence. His Marlowe (Tim Downie) appears to the audience as an upper-class twit who can be both buffoonish and streetwise. Shakespeare (David Mitchell) views his contemporary as the aspirational epitome of cool, despite Marlowe spending much of his time either demeaning Shakespeare, womanizing or engaging in espionage. The 'Mitchell-Shakespeare' (Blackwell 2021: 128) is, conversely, a middle-aged commuter, supporting his family in Stratford-upon-Avon and gradually building his authorial reputation in London. In contrast to Jarmusch, Elton's Marlowe functions in service to his Shakespeare and the bombastic extremes of Downie's comic performance in the role is designed to throw into sharp relief Mitchell's comparatively conservative approach to Shakespeare.[1] Their relationship, as this section of my chapter will illustrate, is built on mutual manipulation and exploitation.

Elton presents his version of Shakespeare as a man whose talent is without question, but who is pulled in several different directions by external social and personal pressures, chiefly imposed by three men in his life: his friend, Marlowe (Tim Downie), his nemesis, Robert Greene (Mark Heap) and his father, John Shakespeare (Harry Enfield). These men exert their superiority through snobbery (Marlowe), authority (Greene) and disapproval (John). These adversarial factors root *Upstart Crow* in the tradition of the British sitcom, which, with consummate self-awareness, it simultaneously embraces and mocks. Within this tradition, *Upstart Crow*'s most recognizable connection is to *Blackadder* (1983–9), the British sitcom co-written by Elton and Richard Curtis. Shakespeare's insecurity about Marlowe, who he confesses is 'cool, confident, everything I'm not', (60) is a direct extension of the embattled Edmund Blackadder's attitude to the flamboyant Lord Flashheart in *Blackadder II*. Like Marlowe, who frequently describes himself as a 'roister', Flashheart boasts of his sexual prowess and enjoys openly mocking his comparably conservative friend. For instance, Blackadder appoints him as best man at his wedding, due to Flashheart's reputation as 'the best sword, the best shot, the best sailor and the best kisser in the kingdom', only for his friend to seduce and steal his bride.

In *Blackadder Goes Forth*, set during the First World War, Flashheart reappears as a devil-may-care RAF commander who refers derogatorily to Blackadder as 'Slackbladder'. This mirrors the depiction of Marlowe as an attractive, dangerous radical in *Upstart Crow*, a portrayal influenced, no doubt, by the antireligious themes in his plays, as well as his espionage activities and reported death by brawl. Elton thus uses Marlowe, as he did Flashheart, to emphasize the protagonist's sense of inferiority when brought into contact with a dominant, virile free spirit. In urging her husband to 'own' his comparatively dull lifestyle, Shakespeare's wife Anne (Liza Tarbuck) notes – with prophetic irony – that 'Kit Marlowe will probably die in some bleedin' tavern fight somewhere, whereas you will die in your own bed with me, your loving wife' (Elton 2018, 60).[2] This further diminishes Shakespeare's character to that of a typical everyman figure governed by domesticity, far removed from the adventures and extreme passions, as portrayed by many of his dramatic characters and represented in *Upstart Crow* by Marlowe's love affairs and journeys as a spy to exotic locations.

In Series 2, Episode 3, Elton creates the authorial conceit that Shakespeare vicariously uses Marlowe's experiences as direct inspiration for his comedies. Marlowe vows to leave behind his promiscuous days when he falls in love with Kate (Gemma Whelan), the landlady's daughter, before being forced to travel to Verona on a government mission, where he quickly forgets her after meeting Silvia (Margaret Clunie), a glamorous Italian Contessa. Drawing on the abiding fantasy that Shakespeare travelled overseas (Franssen 2016: 195), Mitchell's Shakespeare follows his friend to Verona with Kate and his servant Bottom (Rob Rouse). Shakespeare has her dress as a boy to ascertain Marlowe's true feelings and, thereby, achieve the dual purpose of keeping Kate close to Marlowe and gain inspiration for his new comedy. Shakespeare is depicted taking notes as the scene progresses, metatheatrically following the same pattern as many of his cross-dressing comedies in their final acts, where a woman disguised as a man reveals her true identity and a marriage ensues. Here, Shakespeare sends Kate to speak to Marlowe, who does not recognize her, and tells her to woo Silvia for him. Kate does so, only for Silvia immediately to see through the disguise and admit that she has instead fallen for Marlowe's rival and government colleague, Valentine (Jack Fox). All looks to be going according to plan, when Valentine enters and proposes to her, whereupon Marlowe, realizing his error, emerges to tell Kate that he's 'been a fool', to which the hidden Shakespeare and Bottom react:

> WILL: Boom! Textbook stuff! I predict a double marriage.
> BOTTOM: Or not (Elton, 271).

Following Valentine's lead, Marlowe asks for Kate's hand in marriage, to which she replies positively, leading Shakespeare to exclaim in triumph to Bottom 'What did I tell you?' (Elton, 271). However, Kate breaks the rules of Shakespearean comedy. Instead of giving Marlowe her hand in marriage, the scene concludes with Kate repeatedly punching him. This climax makes Marlowe the butt of a slapstick comedy joke and further strips him of any romantic mystique, underlining still further his role as the upper-class sitcom twit in contrast to Shakespeare's middle-class sitcom everyman. The scene ends with Shakespeare's apprehensive expression and Bottom, who had already expressed his concern at his master manipulating Kate's feelings for literary gain, shown to be quietly satisfied that he was proven correct. Elton thus depicts Shakespeare as not only recording his first-hand experiences for inspiration, but rewriting them to be more palatable, when he tells his friends that he 'shall use it all. The only tiny change is that in my play, I'll have both couples marry at the end, instead of only one while the other lover gets punched unconscious' (Elton, 272). In contrast to *Shakespeare in Love* (1998) and *Bill* (2015) which depicts Shakespeare as being inspired by Marlowe's creative genius, Elton's Shakespeare engages in acts of manipulation, feeding off Marlowe's romantic adventures as a source of artistic invention for commercial profit.

However, Shakespeare himself is also subject to manipulation, as seen in Series 1, Episode 6, which parodies *The Merchant of Venice* by having Greene trick Shakespeare into borrowing money from him and, when the investment fails, seeking his 'pound of flesh' (Elton, 174). Greene's Machiavellian schemes commence with his use and understanding of Latin, a language which Elton constructs as being unfamiliar to the non-university educated Shakespeare. When Marlowe and Greene share a private joke at Shakespeare's expense, Marlowe patronizingly remarks: 'Sorry, Will. You wouldn't get it. Latin joke. Need to have gone to Cambridge' (Elton, 152). Despite historical evidence that Shakespeare's attendance at grammar school would have meant that he studied Latin, by constructing the playwright's grasp of the language as rudimentary, at best, particularly in relation to that of Marlowe and Greene, Elton further emphasizes the class boundaries and limitations which Shakespeare faces in *Upstart Crow*. The series thus constructs Shakespeare's identity as a recognizable, middle-class sitcom character through the representation of contemporary playwrights as inherently 'other' and opposed to Shakespeare's ambitions and background.

In the first episode of *Will*, James Burbage (Colm Meaney), actor, owner and builder of the Theatre, turns to Marlowe (Jamie Campbell Bower), 'in his now-conventional role as sexy gay spy', (O'Brien 2018: 530) hoping the playwright's lauded work will revive the fortunes of his theatre. Facing an audience revolt against the substandard work delivered by the 'fictional hack playwright John Baxter' (O'Brien 2018: 530), Burbage is told by one of his subordinates that 'he's here'. This ominous pronouncement, combined with a distant drum roll and an immediate hush from Burbage's gathered company, implicitly informs the viewer that they are about to meet a character of significance. Burbage subsequently hurries upstairs and is met by the lithe figure of a dissolute but attractive, tattooed, long-haired, leather-clad man lounging in the shadows. The casting of Bower indicates *Will*'s intended teen demographic, given the actor's previous appearances in film adaptations of young adult novels, such as *Harry Potter and the Deathly Hallows: Part 1* (2010), *The Twilight Saga* (2008–12) and *The Mortal Instruments: City of Bones* (2013), and his subsequent following amongst fans of the young adult genre.

In his reply to Burbage's immediate question of where the finished play is, Marlowe quips that he has 'been far too busy on her majesty's secret service', a line which refers to the 1969 James Bond film *On Her*

*Majesty's Secret Service*. Craig Pearce, who created *Will* and wrote this episode, intends this reference to draw the audience's attention to his construction of Marlowe as a glamorous intelligence agent in the mould of an Elizabethan 007. Although, as David Riggs suggests, 'over the course of his brief lifetime, the evidence for Marlowe's involvement with espionage and crime is too substantial to be explained away' (2004: 4–5), *Will*'s Marlowe is unquestionably a hyperbolic representation of this aspect of the playwright's cultural mythology. In keeping with such anachronistic references, *Will* was marketed for various contemporary audiences through contrasting promotional trailers. One used a cinematic score and featured dramatic, slow-motion previews of the series, while another paired a fast-paced, Day-Glo aesthetic with a modern soundtrack that blended electronic music and rap vocals, promising an irreverent, youth-orientated take on Shakespeare's biography.

The first of these trailers capitalizes on the success of prestige drama series such as *Game of Thrones* (2011–19) and *The Tudors* (2007–10), while the second aims to recruit a twenty-first-century teen audience through its combination of popular music and bold colour scheme. Despite such aspirations, the series is in fact built on the late 1990s foundations of its creator/head writer Pearce and executive producer/director Shekhar Kapur's previous successes, as made plain in the teen-focused trailer. *Will* combines the incongruity and irreverent postmodernity of *Romeo + Juliet* (1996), which Pearce co-wrote with director Baz Luhrmann, with the themes of political division, uncompromising visuals and lavish period sensibilities of Kapur's *Elizabeth* (1998). This is captured by the contrasting scenes of playful wonder as Shakespeare walks the streets of London, or during performances of his work, with intensely violent scenes of abuse and torture. The lighting of these scenes is strikingly different, with exterior scenes at the theatre presented in a garishly bright colour palette, whereas some interior scenes, such as those of Catholic persecution, are more sombre.

These stark contrasts not only serve as a metaphor for theatre's role as an escape from the harsh realities of the period but also as the symbolic division between Shakespeare and Marlowe, particularly since the series suggests Shakespeare as a closet Catholic and Marlowe as a secret government operative. Magpie-like, Campbell Bower offers an interpretation of Marlowe that channels his various reputations as an atheist, secret agent and homosexual, and Lisa S. Starks commends *Will* for 'presenting a range of sexualities in the theatre world, as well as developing and championing a queer Marlowe' (2019: 224). Laurie Davidson's Shakespeare is, conversely, conventional in his sexual orientation, as shown by his heterosexual attraction to Burbage's fictional daughter Alice (Olivia DeJonge). There is no sexual fluidity visible in his character, which is presented as fluctuating between commitment to his Catholic faith and the temptations of theatre. Although *Will* was cancelled after its first season due to poor viewing ratings, thereby denying Pearce the opportunity to explore Marlowe's death and Shakespeare's potential reaction to it, the two playwrights do engage in some token homoerotic exchanges and share one kiss.

This has given birth to the portmanteau #Sharlowe in several fanvids uploaded to YouTube, compiling the shared moments between the two men set to a pop soundtrack. In the fashion of slash fiction, a subgenre of fan fiction which involves romantic or sexual relationships between characters of the same gender, the creators of these pastiches imagine what the future might hold for 'Sharlowe', had *Will* been renewed for a second season (Starks 2019: 226–8). Indeed, the linguistic conflation of the playwrights' names suggests the viewers' impulse to add Shakespeare and Marlowe to the canon of modern celebrity super couples such as 'Brangelina' or 'Kimye'. Furthermore, the practices both of vidding amongst *Will*'s fan base, and the creation of musical pastiches, sets Shakespeare and Marlowe's most erotically charged moments on-screen to contemporary pop songs including Lady Gaga's 'Bad Romance' (2009) and Cascada's 'Dangerous' (2009), each of which contains lyrics which focus on complex relationships and forbidden love. In creating these mash-up videos, fans knowingly reflect the Lurhmannian musical choices made throughout the series, which include Will arriving in London to the anachronistic sound of 'London Calling' (1979) by The Clash.

Despite the closeness fostered by these constructs, *Will* itself focuses on the two characters as inherently separate figures with fundamentally different destinies. Douglas Lanier states that 'Marlowe is often portrayed as homoerotic, promiscuous, hedonistic and recklessly drawn to political and religious intrigue, doomed by his passions – everything the mythic Shakespeare is not' (2007: 103). Although *Will* explores Shakespeare's sexual fluidity in greater detail than predecessors such as *Shakespeare in Love*, his strongest romantic passions in the series revolve around a young blonde woman, thus echoing the similarly fictionalized character of Viola (Gwyneth Paltrow) in John Madden's film. Shakespeare's romantic focus locks Marlowe into the role of an isolated, lawless celebrity. In contrast to other portrayals of his life on screen, Marlowe does function independently from Shakespeare in *Will*. However, these moments are still treated most often as subplots, which serve to further the central Shakespeare-related narrative. Pearce turns Marlowe into a troublemaking overreacher in the manner of the playwright's own tragic heroes, Faustus and Tamburlaine, framed against Shakespeare's path to security and success. Elton imagines Marlowe's Italian flirtations in *Upstart Crow* as having contributed to the accomplishments of Shakespeare; more upstart magpie than crow in this series. *Only Lovers Left Alive* presents an exception to this concept, retaining Shakespeare's ghostly stranglehold over Marlowe's cultural legacy, but erasing him from the narrative as a physical presence. Jarmusch thus allows Marlowe more agency, rather than casting him as merely a reactive player in service to Shakespeare's story.

The #Sharlowe binary varies in levels of extremity, from *Only Lovers Left Alive*'s radical zombie/vampire formulation, to the variations on a shared theme in *Upstart Crow* and *Will* of Shakespeare as a dreaming everyman and Marlowe as a roguish spy. Beyond the examples discussed in this chapter, *Anonymous* (2011) offers another version of Marlowe engaged in espionage and as an upper-class superior to an everyman Shakespeare, while *Bill* 'casts Shakespeare as a young, naïve writer of "bum jokes, people hit with sticks, comedy," in stark contrast to the elder and more experienced Marlowe, who says he writes "dramas, tragedies, tales of betrayal and revenge, frailties of the human condition"' (Hatfull 2020: 171–2). Alongside the ongoing fascination with Marlowe's untimely death and its potential for tragic interpretation, this binary is rooted in a desire to draw generic differences between Shakespeare as comic and Marlowe as tragic, which reflects twenty-first-century society's need for the compartmentalization of genre and a predilection for watching creative artists compete, as on reality television. Moreover, Shakespeare's cultural ubiquity is such that, for both artistic and commercial reasons, the Marlowe that is remade by creators of Shakespearean biofiction on screen will almost inevitably be made in the image opposite to the creator's own, such is the desire of these artists to align their own reputation, ideals and legacy with Shakespeare.

# References

Barber, R. (2010), 'Exploring Biographical Fictions: The Role of Imagination in Writing and Reading Narrative', *Rethinking History*, 14 (2): 165–87.

*Blackadder II* (1986), [TV programme] BBC One, 9 January–20 February.

*Blackadder Goes Forth* (1989), [TV programme] BBC One, 28 September–2 November.

Blackwell, A. (2021), 'Sympathise with the Losers: Performing Intellectual Loserdom in Shakespearean Biopic', in V. M. Fazel and L. Geddes (eds), *Variable Objects: Shakespeare and Speculative Appropriation*, 127–50, Edinburgh: Edinburgh University Press.

Elton, B. (2018), *Upstart Crow: The Scripts*, London: Bantam Press.

Franssen, P. (2016), *Shakespeare's Literary Lives: The Author as Character in Fiction and Film*, Cambridge: Cambridge University Press.

Hansen, A. and K. J. Wetmore, Jr. (2015), 'Introduction', in A. Hansen and K. J. Wetmore, Jr. (eds), *Shakespearean Echoes*, 1–20, Basingstoke: Palgrave.

Hatfull, R. (2020), 'Bill Begins: The Rise of the Contemporary Shakespeare "Origin Story"', in M. Gerzic and A. Norrie (eds), *Playfulness in Shakespearean Adaptations*, 160–77. London: Routledge.

Lanier, D. (2007), 'Shakespeare™: Myth and Biographical Fiction', in R. Shaughnessy (ed), *The Cambridge Companion to Shakespeare and Popular Culture*, 93–113, Cambridge: Cambridge University Press.

O'Brien, R. (2018), '*Will* Produced by Monumental Television for TNT (review)', *Shakespeare Bulletin*, 36 (3). Available online: https://doi.org/10.1353/shb.2018.0049 (accessed 20 December 2020).

*Only Lovers Left Alive* (2013), [Film] Dir. Jim Jarmusch, UK: Soda Pictures.

Riggs, D. (2004), *The World of Christopher Marlowe*, London: Faber and Faber.

Starks, L. (2019), 'Queering Will and Kit: Slash and the Shakespeare Biopic', in K. Graham and A. Kolentsis (eds), *Shakespeare on Stage and Off*, 212–29, Montreal: McGill-Queen's University Press.
*Will* (2017), [TV series] TNT, 10 July–4 September.

# PART FOUR

# Afterlives

# 16

## More 'Shakespeare' than Shakespeare

## The notion of 'Uber-Shakespeare' in *The Lego Movie*

### *Benjamin Broadribb*

In the final moments of the *Looney Tunes* cartoon short 'A Witch's Tangled Hare' (dir. Levitow 1959), Bugs Bunny runs past a man sitting on a rock tearing up pieces of paper and sobbing. 'Oh blimey', he says, as Bugs screeches to a halt, 'I'll never be a writer, never!'. 'Oh yes you will', Bugs tells him, 'because *you're* William Shakespeare!'. 'But I'm *not* William Shakespeare', comes the reply, 'I'm Sam Crubish.' Bugs's assumption that Crubish is Shakespeare is forgivable – the writer looks like Shakespeare, after all. The audience is also led to believe the character is Shakespeare through his sporadic appearances throughout the short, which features numerous Shakespearean references, many of which Crubish is seen using as inspiration for his writing. While the reveal at the end of the short confirms that Crubish *is not* Shakespeare, for the majority of the episode Crubish *is* Shakespeare from the perspective of the audience (and Bugs). Moreover, even when he is revealed *not to be* Shakespeare, Crubish paradoxically continues *to be* Shakespeare, existing as he does only through the Shakespearean signifiers which have been used in his character design.

Sam Crubish offers a biofictional example of the contemporary phenomenon in popular culture, identified by Christy Desmet, Natalie Loper and Jim Casey, 'that something – a play, a film, an object, a story – may [...] at once "be" and "not be" Shakespeare', encapsulating 'the liminality of the category "Shakespeare" itself, with works and performances and ideas constantly phasing in and out of the Shakespeare-plane – now Shakespeare, now "not Shakespeare," now "really Shakespeare" once again' (2017: 2, 5). But, if Crubish exists only as a collection of Shakespearean signifiers, then the next question is what these Shakespearean signifiers are, and what they say about conceptions of Shakespeare in popular culture. Put more simply, if Crubish 'looks like Shakespeare' as I have suggested earlier, what does Shakespeare 'look like'? Mya Gosling, the author of the webcomic *Good Tickle Brain*, provides some initial answers to these questions in an instalment of the comic titled 'Stick Figure Iconography: Shakespeare' (2019). The features Gosling identifies in the comic as the '[m]ost important piece[s] of Shakespeare iconography' are a '[r]eceding hairline paired with wispy mustache and pointy beard' (2019). This defining cranial and facial hair combination is a key part of Crubish's appearance in 'A Witch's Tangled Hare', and can be seen throughout visual representations of Shakespeare as a character in modern popular culture, with many examples to be found elsewhere in this volume.

These and other features identified by Gosling can be traced back to the two surviving portraits of Shakespeare that were made in living memory of the playwright's lifetime: the funerary monument located in Holy Trinity Church in Stratford-upon-Avon; and Martin Droeshout's engraving of Shakespeare, which appears on the title page of the First Folio. Together, these depictions irrefutably suggest that Shakespeare had this appearance towards the end of his life. Moreover, the likeness of Shakespeare immortalized by both the Holy Trinity monument and the Droeshout portrait has become instantly recognizable around the world as *the* image of Shakespeare. As Erin C. Blake argues, the monument and portrait now embody 'the idea of Shakespeare, which itself has come to represent such things as the theatre, Englishness, culture and scholarship' even more than they depict the playwright himself (2011: 421). Together, they stand as two of the earliest examples of something being and not being Shakespeare simultaneously: they are both inanimate objects offering subjective representations of the playwright; and at the same time, both offer visual metonyms for Shakespeare, the image they put across now inextricable from the popular consciousness of what 'Shakespeare' – both the historical man and, by extension, his cultural cachet – looks like.

The Droeshout portrait in particular has played a central role in establishing the archetypal image of Shakespeare. Douglas Lanier has described the portrait as 'the most famous image of an author ever produced', noting how it 'inaugurates the myth of Shakespeare the self-made author' through its establishment of Shakespeare as a literary genius:

> His eyes engage the viewer directly, but the gaze is neither challenging nor penetrating. Rather, the expression, poised between seriousness and an

ever-so-slight smile, is one of self-containment, conveying intelligence but betraying nothing of what Shakespeare is thinking [. . .] Whether or not Droeshout captured Shakespeare's likeness accurately, what he conveys is Shakespeare's compelling, mature, self-possessed but finally enigmatic intellect. (2002: 110)

The Droeshout portrait is therefore foundational to Shakespearean biofiction, setting in motion not only the iconic physical features which make a character recognizable as Shakespeare, but also many of the characteristics which fictionalized Shakespeares either embody or subvert. The portrait has also endured at least in part through its ability to make Shakespeare into a symbol in multiple senses of the word. It not only encapsulates the qualities and values the playwright is considered to represent, but also enables his face to be turned into a metonymic logo, ultimately taking on 'the iconic status of a global trademark' for the Shakespeare brand (Shaughnessy 2011: 71).

Gosling's stick figure Shakespeare is just one example of this trademark status. Visit Shakespeare's hometown of Stratford-upon-Avon today, for example, and you will be inundated with images of Shakespeare which conform to the Droeshout archetype, from historic statues to novelty memorabilia. The Royal Shakespeare Company offers a typical example of this phenomenon through a toy duck sold in its gift shop ('RSC Shakespeare rubber duck'). Combining the iconography of the popular bath toy – a yellow plastic bird with a bright orange bill – with that of Shakespeare – receding hairline, thin moustache, pointy beard, prominent collar – the RSC's gift shop souvenir is the Droeshout portrait reimagined in rubber duck form. The duck also presents another example of the 'Shakespeare/ not Shakespeare' phenomenon which parallels Crubish in the *Looney Tunes* short. It simultaneously *is* Shakespeare through the signifiers used in its design, given further weight by its association with a prestigious professional Shakespearean theatre company; and *is not* Shakespeare most obviously through being a toy duck, but also through the inherent kitschness of the novelty item, which is in direct contrast to the perceived high culture status of Shakespeare within contemporary Western society.

Desmet, Loper and Casey's 'Shakespeare/not Shakespeare' phenomenon and the Droeshout archetype together offer the starting point for this chapter's analysis of Shakespeare's figurative biofictional presence in *The Lego Movie* (dirs. Lord and Miller 2014). I use 'figurative' intentionally to evoke multiple meanings of the word. Like all other characters who inhabit the Lego universe of the film, Shakespeare is literally depicted as a plastic Lego minifigure; but, through the way in which Lord and Miller use Shakespearean signifiers to create Lego Shakespeare, the character becomes representative of Shakespeare's emblematic afterlife in twenty-first-century culture. Moreover, Lego Shakespeare represents an example within popular culture of what I have termed 'uber-Shakespeare'. I have opted for the prefix 'uber-' over other possibilities, such as 'super-' or 'hyper-', for two main reasons. Firstly, to avoid the loaded nature of those prefixes, which regularly take on inherently positive or negative associations depending on the context in which they are used, whereas 'uber-' currently remains relatively neutral in this respect; and secondly, to connect with the contemporary popular culture starting point of my conceptualization of 'uber-Shakespeare' (this is also the reason for not including the umlaut over the letter 'u' as in the root German word 'über'). Since the closing decades of the twentieth century onwards, 'uber' has been used within pop culture contexts to indicate 'an outstanding, supreme, or pre-eminent example of its kind, or a person or thing markedly surpassing others of its class or type', and in adjectival forms which denote a quality 'to a great, extreme, or excessive degree' ('uber-, prefix' 2022). 'Uber-Shakespeare' notionally takes in both of these related senses: a representation of Shakespeare which is a distinct product of the liminality inherent to 'Shakespeare/not Shakespeare' which, through pushing the contradictory positions of both being and not being Shakespeare to extremes, becomes more 'Shakespeare' than Shakespeare. My phrasing here intentionally recalls 'More Human than Human', the slogan of the fictional Tyrell Corporation in *Blade Runner* (dir. Scott 1982), used to describe the bioengineered 'replicants' which are virtually indistinguishable from humans, but which have mental and physical capabilities beyond the limits of humanity.

*Blade Runner*'s replicants offer an opportune pop culture segue into the concept of 'Master Builders' within the universe of *The Lego Movie*, which is the starting point of deconstructing Shakespeare's presence within the film. Just as replicants have heightened human faculties, Master Builders are identified as having the innate ability to create anything from the world around them without the need to follow instructions. As well as playing a key role in the lore and narrative of *The Lego Movie*, Master Builders are also a significant way in which Lord and Miller postmodernistically smash together figures from history, fantasy and popular culture throughout their film. The eclectic mix is demonstrated when *The Lego Movie*'s protagonist Emmet Brickowski is taken by Master Builders Wyldstyle and Vitruvius to meet the council of Master Builders. In his opening address to the assembly, Vitruvius names (amongst others) English folk hero Robin Hood; Gandalf, the wizard from the *Lord of the Rings* franchise; a mermaid; the 2002 NBA All Stars; DC Comics superhero Wonder Woman; Michelangelo, the historical Renaissance artist; and Michelangelo, the character from the *Teenage Mutant Ninja Turtles* franchise. Although he is not named, Shakespeare is included amongst the Master Builders in the scene. It is the most prominent of his fleeting appearances in only a handful of scenes throughout the film, and it is also the only scene in which Shakespeare speaks. Richard Burt suggests that Shakespeare's 'strange inclusion as one of the main Master Builders and yet nearly complete exclusion from the dialogue makes him almost literally unspeakable and [...] unreadable [...] he is negated and he negates' (2016:

103). However, if the minifigure representing Shakespeare is recognizable as Shakespeare from such brief screen time and dialogue, then the character's readability is not just present, but potent. As Sarah Hatchuel and Nathalie Vienne-Guerrin suggest, '[t]he presence of the Shakespeare minifigure in *The LEGO Movie* may be less fleeting than profoundly eloquent and revelatory' (2018).

The scene in which Vitruvius namechecks numerous Master Builders encapsulates the minimalist aesthetic of representing figures from *The Lego Movie*'s multifarious sources as Lego minifigures. Lord and Miller quickly cut to each Master Builder as they are named, allowing the audience to read the signifiers of each minifigure to decipher who or what each represents. For example, when the audience sees a minifigure in a green outfit, wearing a pointed cap with a protruding feather and holding a bow and arrow, they recognize it as a stereotypical representation of Robin Hood. Correspondingly, while Shakespeare is not named and only seen fleetingly, the audience sees a minifigure with a receding hairline, wispy moustache and pointy beard, and they recognize him as Shakespeare. In a manner which parallels the RSC's novelty duck, *The Lego Movie*'s figurative Shakespeare can be considered to reimagine the Droeshout portrait in minimalist Lego minifigure form.

As well as being reduced to simple Lego versions of themselves, each Master Builder is liberated from their conventional historical or narrative setting. The council of Master Builders gathers in the fantastical realm Cloud Cuckoo Land, where there are 'no rules' and 'no consistency'. As a result, Lego Shakespeare is never depicted in a Lego version of either Stratford-upon-Avon or London. He is never seen writing anything and never quotes a Shakespeare play. He is not married to Lego Anne Hathaway, and he never mourns Lego Hamnet. This stripping away of the staples of biofictional representations of Shakespeare in one sense pushes Lego Shakespeare further towards being 'not Shakespeare', rendering the character as a postmodernistically depthless depiction which exists purely through pop culture referentiality. At the same time, however, Lego Shakespeare is liberated from the literary, historical and domestic baggage that comes with his human original, unfixed in time to become eternal in a further echo of the Droeshout portrait, which similarly renders Shakespeare timeless. As a result, Lego Shakespeare is brought closer to the near-mythical status Shakespeare now occupies in contemporary culture. Through his status as a Master Builder, Lego Shakespeare is inherently not ordinary but extraordinary – someone who sees and interacts with the world in a way most people cannot. By casting aside the signifiers of Shakespeare as an ordinary man and transforming him into a timeless Master Builder, Lord and Miller shift Lego Shakespeare further towards representing Shakespeare the contemporary cultural phenomenon. This simultaneous push towards both 'Shakespeare' and 'not Shakespeare' offers the foundations for Lego Shakespeare's uber-Shakespeare status.

While Lego Shakespeare conforms to the Droeshout archetype in most respects, the minifigure sports an Elizabethan ruff 'piece' around his neck rather than a characteristic pointed collar as in the portrait. Ella Hawkins notes that 'no ruff features in any early modern portrait or sculpture associated with Shakespeare', but suggests that 'the image of Shakespeare wearing a ruff has become so prevalent in modern culture that the playwright seemingly appears incomplete without one' (2021: 193). Hawkins cites as an example of this phenomenon the Shakespeare masks commissioned by the councils of Stratford-upon-Avon for the quatercentenary in 2016, which were based on the Droeshout portrait – however, artist Geoffrey Tristram considered the mask to be incomplete until he added a ruff to his design (2021: 193). In this sense, the inclusion of the ruff 'piece' in Lego Shakespeare's character design offers a visual example of what Jennifer Holl describes as the audience's 'desire to *see* a Shakespeare that *feels* appropriately Shakespearean' (2021: 126). Moreover, Hawkins asserts that 'the ruff is used widely in popular culture to imbue other figures with "Shakespearean" qualities', becoming a visual shorthand for traditional theatrical performance (2021: 194). On a practical level, Lego Shakespeare's ruff gives the audience an extra pop culture indicator of Shakespeare, ensuring the simplification of the recognizable Droeshout features do not obscure the figure's Shakespeareness. Younger viewers, for example, may more easily be able to recognize the ruff as a Shakespearean marker than the Droeshout archetype. However, it also identifies Lego Shakespeare as a heightened, parodic representation of the playwright. Thus, by layering an additional Shakespeare signifier on top of the character's already recognizably Shakespearean appearance, Lego Shakespeare becomes more 'Shakespeare' than Shakespeare.

Lego Shakespeare only speaks one word during *The Lego Movie*. After announcing Emmet as 'the Special', a figure prophesied at the beginning of the film to be the saviour of the Lego universe, Vitruvius tells the Master Builders that Emmet will give them 'an eloquent speech'. However, when his speech fails to impress and he admits that he is not yet a Master Builder, the assembly turns on Emmet – including Lego Shakespeare, who is briefly seen shouting 'Rubbish!' and throwing a pizza in protest. It is a moment so brief as to appear initially inconsequential and, to use Burt's term, 'unreadable'. On the surface, the choice to have Lego Shakespeare hurl a pizza at Emmet is a surreal piece of physical comedy which fits into the fantastical location of Cloud Cuckoo Land. It contributes to Lego Shakespeare's detachment from his historical source and other biofictional Shakespeares through its incongruity and anachronicity, pushing the character further towards 'not Shakespeare' as a result.

However, the character's hurling of food and loud heckling also plays into the popular belief that theatre audiences in the early modern period did precisely this, even though reports of it ever happening are both incredibly scarce and likely apocryphal. So ingrained is this belief in contemporary popular conceptions of early modern theatre-going that audiences attending early performances of Richard Olivier's 1997 production of *Henry V*, the inaugural production at Shakespeare's Globe Theatre on London's Bankside, brought bags of vegetables with them to throw at the stage. As Stephen Purcell suggests, 'spectators might have come to the theatre ready to enact, self-consciously or otherwise, the modes of participation they had learned from popular culture' (2017: 117). While Mark Rylance, artistic director of Shakespeare's Globe at the time, recalls that some actors 'were very, very angry and upset that their scenes were dominated by vegetables flying in on them', he also notes that Olivier described it as 'a completely authentic, legitimate response' (2017: 191–2). Together, Lego Shakespeare's anachronistic food of choice, and his apocryphal use of it as a projectile, shift the character further towards 'not Shakespeare'. And yet, much like the character's ruff, having Lego Shakespeare throw food and heckle Emmet's 'performance' aligns him with ideas of 'Shakespeare' in collective popular consciousness. As a result, Lego Shakespeare is also pushed beyond Shakespeare, contributing to his uber-Shakespeare pop culture status.

However, Lego Shakespeare's declaration of Emmet's speech and lack of Master Builder status as 'Rubbish!' also complicates the character's uber-Shakespeare status. Hatchuel and Vienne-Guerrin argue that the moment

> reduc[es] such a master builder as Shakespeare to the status of a reactionary, old-fashioned figure [. . .] Shakespeare's exclamation could mean 'You will not build beyond me.' The Shakespeare figure itself thus states and feeds its own mythical stature as a builder 'for all time,' never to be equalled. (2018)

In this moment, criticizing both Emmet's ordinariness and lack of eloquence, Lego Shakespeare embodies a particularly harmful aspect of Shakespeare's contemporary afterlife: the idea that those who do not care for Shakespeare are either not sophisticated or intellectual enough to appreciate his works. Punctuated by the Frisbee-style throwing of a pizza, the moment is played for laughs, but Lego Shakespeare's denouncement of Emmet as 'Rubbish!' is not challenged at this point – on the contrary, it encapsulates the wider mood of the Master Builders. In this moment, Lego Shakespeare upholds the idea that to be ordinary is not good enough, thereby perpetuating the idea that the historical Shakespeare was born an extraordinary individual and destined for greatness. Ironically, it is the elitist idea that a person from Shakespeare's relatively ordinary beginnings could not have possibly written the works attributed to him which primarily fuels contemporary anti-Stratfordian conspiracy theories.

Ultimately, however, the contempt for Emmet's ordinariness displayed by the Master Builders and embodied within Lego Shakespeare's denouncement of him as 'Rubbish!' is proven wrong. It is precisely Emmet's ordinary rather than exceptional nature that leads to him saving the day. As Hatchuel and Vienne-Guerrin observe, '[t]he LEGO world values both regular, generic construction workers who are keen on following the instructions precisely and the master builders who are inspired, inspiring, and cultivate freedom', demonstrated through the film's ultimate message of self-belief and individuality (2018). The shift away from Lego Shakespeare's elitist perspective is encapsulated in Wyldstyle's change of heart after she believes Emmet has sacrificed himself to save the Lego universe (he later returns, having achieved Master Builder status through his selfless act). In an inspirational speech before the final battle, Wyldstyle tells the citizens of the Lego universe that Emmet 'was just like all of you: a face in the crowd, following the same instructions as you [. . .] and I owe you an apology, because I used to look down on people like that. I used to think they were followers with no ideas or vision'.

Lego Shakespeare is seen twice during *The Lego Movie*'s finale: first fighting alongside the citizens, inspired by Wyldstyle's rousing speech, with two other Master Builders – Michelangelo (the artist, not the turtle) and Abraham Lincoln – and then celebrating as part of a large group of citizens and Master Builders once the battle has been won. While all of Lego Shakespeare's appearances in *The Lego Movie* are brief, these final two are by far the most fleeting, with the character appearing momentarily first as part of a much longer battle sequence and then, to use Wyldstyle's phrase, as 'a face in the crowd'. Lego Shakespeare shifts away from the elitist and reactionary brand of Shakespeare he previously embodied to instead present a more egalitarian and inclusive identity. The character moves back towards the Droeshout portrait's establishment of Shakespeare's 'self-made author' status – an identity all the inhabitants of the Lego universe, citizens and Master Builders, have now embraced.

So much for the Lego universe – but where do Lego Shakespeare and the notion of uber-Shakespeare fit into the wider concept of 'Shakespeare' in contemporary culture? The answer potentially comes from critical reactions to *The Lego Movie*. In his review, Joel Arnold argued that '*The Lego Movie* may be one giant advertisement, but all the way to its plastic-mat foundation, it's an earnest piece of work – a cash grab with a heart' (2014). His sentiments were echoed by Susan Wloszczyna, who admitted that the film 'might be a 100-minute commercial, but at least it's a highly entertaining and, most surprisingly, a thoughtful one' (2014). Responses such as these characterize the wider feeling that while *The Lego Movie* never hides its corporate goal of marketing Lego and making a profit for the company, its messages of individualism and creativity are presented with sincerity. Lego Shakespeare encapsulates how this extreme dichotomy is paralleled within the Shakespeare brand, presenting an example of how 'under the pressure of mass mediatization, contemporary Shakespeare may be undergoing something of a paradigm shift that raises foundational questions about how we, as Shakespearian professionals, conceptualize the "essential" or "authentic" Shakespeare and situate his cultural value' (Lanier 2011: 145).

Lego Shakespeare represents the increasingly symbiotic relationship between Shakespeare and popular culture, not only pushing at the extremes of what is and is not Shakespeare but blurring and distorting the boundaries between the two. 'Not Shakespeare' is absorbed into the contemporary Shakespeare brand, making it more 'Shakespeare' than Shakespeare has arguably ever been before. Moreover, Lego Shakespeare simultaneously embodies the massive cultural and commercial capital of Shakespeare, while sincerely capturing the 'self-made author' ethos and unrestricted access to creativity his work and legacy also embodies. In this way, the character also provides 'a human architecture to narrate our own experiences, desires, concerns, and fixations', as Holl suggests is the underlying aim of all fictionalized Shakespeares (2021: 127). In short, Lego Shakespeare reflects the perpetual tug-of-war between capitalism and individualism identifiable not just within the Shakespeare brand, but throughout twenty-first-century society as a whole.

# References

Arnold, J. (2014), '"Lego Movie": A Goofy Toy Story That Genuinely Clicks', *NPR*, 6 February. Available online: https://www.npr.org/2014/02/06/271422040/lego-movie-a-goofy-toy-story-that-genuinely-clicks (accessed 10 July 2022).

Blake, E. C. (2011), 'Shakespeare, Portraiture, Painting and Prints', in M. Thornton Burnett, A. Streete, and R. Wray (eds), *The Edinburgh Companion to Shakespeare and the Arts*, 409–34, Edinburgh: Edinburgh University Press.

Burt, R. (2016), 'What Is Called Thinking with ShaXXXspeares and Walter Benjamin?: Managing De/Kon/struction, Toying with Letters in *The Lego Movie*', *Journal for Early Modern Cultural Studies*, 16 (3): 94–115.

Desmet, C., N. Loper, and J. Casey (2017), 'Introduction', in C. Desmet, N. Loper, and J. Casey (eds), *Shakespeare / Not Shakespeare*, 1–23, Cham, Switzerland: Palgrave Macmillan.

Gosling, M. (2019), 'Stick Figure Iconography: Shakespeare', *Good Tickle Brain*, 23 April. Available online: https://goodticklebrain.com/home/2019/4/23/stick-figure-iconography-shakespeare (accessed 10 July 2022).

Hatchuel, S. and N. Vienne-Guerrin (2018), '"To Build or Not to Build": LEGO® Shakespeare™ and the Question of Creativity', *Borrowers and Lenders: The Journal of Shakespeare and Appropriation*, 11 (2). Available online: https://borrowers-ojs-azsu.tdl.org/borrowers/article/view/253/503 (accessed 10 July 2022).

Hawkins, E. (2021), 'The "Shakespearean" Ruff', *Shakespeare Bulletin*, 39 (2): 191–213.

Holl, J. (2021), *Shakespeare and Celebrity Cultures*, London: Routledge.

Lanier, D. (2002), *Shakespeare and Modern Popular Culture*, Oxford: Oxford University Press.

Lanier, D. (2011), 'Post-Textual Shakespeare', *Shakespeare Survey*, 64: 145–62.

*The Lego Movie* (2014), [Film] Dirs. Phil Lord and Christopher Miller, USA: Warner Bros.

*Looney Tunes* (1959), [TV programme] 'A Witch's Tangled Hare', Dir. Abe Levitow, Warner Bros. Cartoons, 31 October. Available online: https://www.b98.tv/video/a-witchs-tangled-hare/ (accessed 9 July 2022).

Purcell, S. (2017), *Shakespeare in the Theatre: Mark Rylance at the Globe*, London: Bloomsbury Arden Shakespeare.

'RSC Shakespeare Rubber Duck'. Available online: https://shop.rsc.org.uk/products/shakespeare-rubber-duck (accessed 10 July 2022).

Shaughnessy, R. (2011), *The Routledge Guide to William Shakespeare*, London: Routledge.

'uber-, prefix' (2022), *OED Online*, Oxford University Press. Available online: www.oed.com/view/Entry/36144911 (accessed 10 July 2022).

Wloszczyna, S. (2014), 'The Lego Movie', *RogerEbert.com*, 7 February. Available online: https://www.rogerebert.com/reviews/the-lego-movie-2014 (accessed 10 July 2022).

# Afterword

# Global Shakespearean biofictions

## *Ramona Wray*

In this afterword, I want to take up the challenge of biofiction as a way of celebrating Edel Semple and Ronan Hatfull's *Shakespearean Biofiction on the Contemporary Stage and Screen* in all of its abundantly engaging dimensions. I begin with general reflections, work to extend the discussion into world cinema and touch on the future research directions of the fresh and exciting field which has been opened up by this innovative collection.

An immediately enabling aspect of *Shakespearean Biofiction on the Contemporary Stage and Screen* is that it alerts us to the latest, multilayered manifestation of the Shakespearean/biographical phenomenon but also to the tradition's deep roots. Representations that combine Shakespeare and a parodic emphasis might be traced as far back as the nineteenth century, as does Lawrence Levine in his book, *Highbrow / Lowbrow*, which, considering the American stage, reads vaudeville, opera and burlesque as forms through which constructions of Shakespeare himself were mediated (1988: 11–82). Just as keenly attuned to the evolution of Shakespearean biofiction is Judith Buchanan's chapter in this collection; as she intriguingly demonstrates, silent screen presences of Shakespeare date from 1907 onwards. Her intricate reassembling of the now-lost film, *Shakespeare Writing Julius Caesar* (dir. Georges Méliès 1907), unearths an early registration of the biofictional Shakespeare iconically wielding his pen.

Firing us to think about time, this collection simultaneously invites us to cogitate context and identify trigger moments. *Shakespeare in Love* (dir. John Madden 1998) is significantly referenced as stimulating a series of later adaptations of Shakespeare the man. A sitcom such as *Upstart Crow* (2016-2020), richly parsed here in chapters by Helen Monks (in conversation) and Ronan Hatfull, also figures as a transformative moment in the popular envisioning of Shakespeare. I wonder, though, if prompts for reimagining are not so much to do with discrete cultural examples as they are with wider cultural currents. Some chapters describe broader flows of understanding and interpretation, and, if we pause over how Shakespeare has recently been rendered, several historicizing factors come into play. Perhaps shaped by the stresses of lockdown, or forged as if in anticipation of it, the Shakespeare that emerges from this collection's discussions is a singularly dispiriting type, troubled with various woes. He is, in Katherine Scheil's eloquent phrase, 'caring but flawed [and] grieving' (90). Or one might cite a comparable expression of Shakespeare in Reed Martin and Austin Tichenor's scintillating RSC *Shakespeare's Long Lost First Play* (2018) in which the man from Stratford is ground down by his knowledge of political realities. As Tichenor speculates, 'the danger of questioning the Tudor myth [and] . . . the risks of casting' (34), all depressively shape the Shakespearean personality.

Elsewhere in this collection, Clara Calvo acutely notes that across a spectrum of Shakespearean biofictions, 'resentment' and 'regret' resonate as leitmotifs, and this is related in no small part to the fact that Shakespeare is increasingly aligned with his family (and his domestic milieu) in the cultural imaginary. Helen Monks, grumpy teenager Sue in *Upstart Crow*, offers a first-hand perspective on the development in her (in conversation) chapter, remarking that 'David Mitchell [who plays Shakespeare] has traditionally played . . . weird . . . awkward men who are trying to fit in . . . social outsiders' (83), linking the actor's past roles intertextually with the series' fraught familial emphases. To situate this recent cultural trend more capaciously, and the concentration on Shakespeare and personal difficulty, we might look beyond biofiction to figurations of other men in difficulty in popular culture – the troubled superheroes with even more troubled backstories of *Justice League* (dir. Zak Snyder 2021), for example, or the cynically drawn Batman in *The Lego Batman Movie* (dir. Chris McKay 2017), part of a franchise insightfully investigated by Ben Broadribb in his contribution to this volume. Interestingly, related superhero tropes have biofictional parallels, as Michael Friedman's chapter on the realization of Burbage in *Will* (2017) (145), and Stephen Purcell's chapter on *Bill* (dir. Richard Bracewell 2015) as an 'origin story' (128), attest. But if the post-millennial era of sadness and angst is refracted in the construction of a more psychologically afflicted Shakespeare, then it is also echoed in readings of the plays themselves. The circuit of influences, inflected towards darkly lensed contemporary Shakespeares, skids across stage and screen, cinema and television, alike, and it is revealing to recognize how cultural trends are mirrored in Shakespeare commemorations. *The Hollow Crown* (2012, 2016) is an apt instance, characterized, as it is, by brooding and unhappy men in fractured relations with family and/or suffering in post-traumatic conditions. Such manifestations of the persons and the plays point up the place of 'Shakespeare' in an elaborate cultural matrix comprised of multiple nodal points and connections.

Indeed, it is worth pondering the extent to which readings of the Shakespearean biofictions introduced in this collection might be complemented by considering other representational forms. Or, to put the point in another way, are stage and screen – and to a lesser extent novels – the *only* forms in which biofiction is pursued? Clara Calvo's chapter is instructive in this respect in that via a discussion of *All Is True* (dir. Kenneth Branagh 2018), it asks us to think laterally across celebrations of heritage, heritage re-enactment, the documentary tradition and the articulation of 'truth, history and national identity' (20) in particular. Without explicitly probing the matter, her chapter also encourages sensitivity to questions around modes of dissemination, programming platform and broadcaster. Here, Aaron Proudfoot's chapter on *Will* is salutary in spotlighting the vital role of the American TNT network (as opposed to the BBC which might more readily have been associated with biofiction of this type). Certainly, the biofictional Shakespeare is not necessarily confined to one national sphere of reception or influence. Stephen Purcell in his chapter penetratingly unravels the premises of the *Doctor Who* episode, 'The Shakespeare Code' (2007), and it is helpful to recall that *Doctor Who* has been broadcast since 2013 in more than fifty countries worldwide (and in Asia either in English or in dubbed or subtitled versions). The fact of these other, transnational domains for the representation of Shakespeare sparks a further question: to what extent is Shakespearean biofiction a American/British/Anglophone phenomenon that debates questions of English/British/American identity and heritage only? Or might other interpretive possibilities present themselves if the sample of examples is amplified?

As Edel Semple remarks in her Introduction, Shakespeare has appeared as a character in *European* literature since the late eighteenth century (2). One might also add twentieth-century cinematic instances, such as the Spanish feature, *Un Drama Nuevo* (dir. Juan de Orduña 1946), in which Shakespeare enters the action to calm the dispute between Yorick and Edmundo, his actors. The Spanish stage has been just as busy in terms of representing Shakespeare; as critics such as Jesús Tronch Pérez have demonstrated, between '1996 and 1998, Spanish theatre spectators were offered four different dramatizations of William Shakespeare, the man and the writer' (2011: 33). Moving forward in time, and into other geographies, the student stage in India is a lively forum for debating Shakespeare's cultural authority. In 2012, at St Stephen's College, Delhi, the 'Shakespeare Society' staged a series of scenes designed to upturn older conventions: in one, the 'writing Shakespeare, played by a male student, [is] interrupted, and encircled, by . . . women directors [who] . . . put an end to his actions with a collective shout' (Ashley 2022: 236). The purposeful and gender-conscious dethroning of the man and his position has a counterpart in several of the productions examined in this collection, including, but not limited to, Morgan Lloyd Malcolm's 2018 play *Emilia*, and David West Read's 2019 West End show *& Juliet*, whose significances Gemma Kate Allred potently underscores.

Opening up Shakespearean biofiction in terms of plural cultural and linguistic categories is, I think, worthwhile. Paul Franssen in his longer study of Shakespeare's literary lives argues that Shakespearean biofiction has historically been accommodated within 'German and Spanish . . . national discourse' (2016: 7), but it remains to be seen if equivalent manoeuvres are the hallmark of the adaptive strategy across a larger sample. In addition, exploring Shakespearean biofiction comparatively might stimulate new arguments about origins (the extent to which biofiction is transnational rather than national in genesis) and methodology (approaches ignited by a global Shakespeare studies). Addressing two pairings of films, one European and one Indian, might help to identify the ideological work of Shakespearean biofiction in non-Anglophone registers.

Post-dating *Shakespeare in Love*, *To be or not to be* (dir. Peter Woditsch 1999), a Belgian-produced short film in Flemish dialogue by a German filmmaker, and *Miguel y William* (dir. Inés Paris 2007), a female-helmed Spanish romantic comedy feature, realize Shakespeare as man and writer across complementary timespans – the twelve minutes leading up to the composition of the 'To be or not to be' soliloquy and a longer period in 1590, one of the so-called 'lost years'. Both, then, are 'early modern' in the sense that they purposefully accommodate Shakespeare in his own time as protagonist, alternately investing, as part of their respective *mise-en-scènes*, in dreamy visuals (*To be or not to be* privileges shots of dripping water, rumpled sheets and dimly lit domestic interiors to suggest a waking into consciousness) and sumptuous widescreen cinematography (the camera in *Miguel y William* pans leisurely over arid landscapes and imposing medieval castles in imitation of heritage-style drama). Crucially, despite art-house/multiplex dissimilarities, the two films revolve around the mystery of how the lines and plays came to be. In this sense, they sit alongside the biofictions introduced in this collection which are likewise preoccupied with Shakespeare's creative process. Shakespeare himself in this pairing of films appears stereotypically, in a nightshirt with quill pen in the short, and in a green tunic with red touches and slouched hat in the feature; these costume decisions indicate an urge to legitimate the representation via authenticating detail.

Standing as 'origin stories', *To be or not to be* and *Miguel y William* limn Shakespeare not so much as individual genius as collaborative artist. For *To be or not to be*, the premise is the dream/nightmare about the dead Hamnet who obtrudes into his father's fitful sleep: in a misty, nocturnal forest, the young boy is decapitated by a knight on horseback and, as only a head, delivers from the ground the immortal soliloquy's opening line. The soundtrack of plaintive ravens and the swish of a sword, and the surrealist editing, locate and underscore writing as a response to trauma. At the same time, however, the short represents the protagonist in the world of the living, ingesting, magpie-like, shards of domestic discourse. Awake, Shakespeare is imagined as unable to remember the line precisely, and here the cheery housekeeper serves as the conduit through which words, semi-recalled and not yet property minted, emerge. 'You're not on stage now!', she reprimands, adding, 'You know the saying, "As one makes one's bed . . . one sleeps."' In the upper rooms, reminiscent of a Vermeer painting, the good-natured squabble sparks invention, Shakespeare recrafting proverbial wisdom, plebeian counsel, and a theatre/life binary to begin to piece 'To be or not to be' together and grow it: his feverish writing develops in concert with the comic servant's unwitting interruptions. For *Miguel y William*, the premise is that Shakespeare, transplanted to Spain to pursue the love of his life, the aristocratic and free-spirited Leonor de Vibero, joins with his sometime rival, Miguel de Cervantes, sixteen years his senior, to write a play his lover has commissioned. Once again, a collaborative theme is aired, although here the emphasis is not on the recollection of a line but the spontaneous flowering of poetry in the context of intrigue. (Shakespeare, in this biofiction, must keep his identity secret from the forbidding Duke of Obando to whom Leonor is affianced against her will.) 'We are making much ado about nothing!' exclaims Shakespeare when the writing of a frivolous comedy is suggested, the title of the play occurring to him unexpectedly, while later, in anticipation of the collaborative work, he erupts into a version of Puck's epilogue to the audience in *A Midsummer Night's Dream*. Each act of writing is a response to situational circumstances or pressures, as when, needing to escape, he commandeers a horse with the Ricardian command, 'My kingdom for a horse!'. With this biofictional Shakespeare, then, resourcefulness – in crisis and in love – is the key characteristic.

*To be or not to be* and *Miguel y William* consort with each other in envisioning Shakespeare in relation to his characters. In *Miguel y William*, these imaginary creations are eventually fleshed out as 'real-life' individuals. 'Leonor, you shall be my Hermia, my Titania, my Juliet, my Ophelia', Shakespeare rhapsodizes when in an amorous embrace, the point being that his lover is the inspirational source for fictive women not yet realized on stage. What the feature portrays, in fact, is the way in which Leonor becomes a Shakespearean character in her own right (if not patron/instigator). In the film's prioritizing of her body and agency, she operates to mediate Juliet (glimpsed at a window/balcony) and Titania (imbued with poetic magic), but works more forcefully as the Dark Lady (singing her version of Sonnet 147) and Desdemona (or Desideria/Desire, as she is labelled). At the close of the film, in a performance of a prototype *Othello* (these are of course Shakespeare's 'lost years'), Leonor steps forward with her own experiential defence: 'when women are unfaithful, the fault lies with the husband . . . take heed, gentlemen! . . . Have we not also affections [and] desires?', she questions. The in-story context for the speech is the Duke of Obando's jealousy; within the logic of the film, however, the implication is that combining into herself the interrogative energy of Emilia, Shylock and Viola, Leonor, through Shakespeare, makes the transition from fictional construct to affective subject. The obverse is true for *To be or not to be*.

In this short film, 'real' individuals – Hamnet, the housekeeper and the actors playing Romeo and Juliet (they visit Shakespeare to suggest the play's ending be rewritten) – give way to imaginative projections, including three witches laughing in the rafters, Puck, playing eerily on a swing, and Ophelia, who, accompanied by a watery soundscape, occasions traumatic memory. But it is the imaginative entrance of Falstaff, rollicking, admonishing and intervening, who makes the definitive impression. Climbing laboriously up the stairs, he appears to write over the fledgling soliloquy, repunctuating the verse and suggesting the crucial/missing second line. Characters create as much as they are created in this biofiction, resolving and ordering what is in Shakespeare confused or inchoate.

In the process of constructing Shakespeare thus, *To be or not to be* and *Miguel y William* mythologize and demythologize Shakespeare in complementary ways. To be sure, in *To be or not to be*, there is low-key domestic incident and drudgery (unwelcome 'beer soup' for breakfast), but this is subordinated to acts of Shakespeare adding and correcting until Hamnet appears again in an inset and the familiar version of 'To be or not to be' is finalized. At this point, Shakespeare breaks the fourth wall, and looks to camera, and we become his collaborators. Dream and 'real life' square, the writerly hand is animated, and Hamnet, captured in verse, does not die but lives on via Shakespeare mythologized. A rather different Shakespeare obtains in *Miguel y William*. Bathetic episodes involving Shakespeare creeping into windows, or spitting out food, reduce the character's cultural kudos, and this is nowhere more apparent than at the demythologizing close. Even if Hamlet's love letter to Ophelia overlays the screen, attention focuses on Leonor/Desdemona, who dances with the assembled, youthful throng, having inherited the dukedom, and revels in her amatory freedom to choose which lover she will.

Concluding in this way, *Miguel y William* offers us a distinctive Shakespeare. The feature seems aimed at promoting Spanish culture at the expense of English/British culture, and not least because Cervantes is represented as the poet of seriousness and maturity in contrast to Shakespeare, the novice brimming with ideas. None of this should be surprising in a film that as Paul Franssen explains, was intended as a companion-piece to 'the quatercentenary of *Don Quixote* and [was] subsidised by the regional government of Castilla-La Mancha' (Franssen 2016: 223). A similar point can be made in relation to *To be or not to be*.

Cross currents of adaptation, then, do not necessarily work uniformly: they can be unpredictable. But, crucially, films such as *To be or not to be* and *Miguel y William* make other Shakespeares available by retooling Anglo-American works that have established Shakespearean biofiction as a genre. This pairing not only suggests transnational circuits of travel but also clarifies the formative power of biofictions such as *Shakespeare in Love* and, to a lesser extent, adaptations such as *Much Ado About Nothing* (dir. Kenneth Branagh 1993), revisiting perennial questions in the process. For instance, both short and feature touch on issues of parentage (the 'how' of poetic production), forming a bridge to Laurence Rickard's chapter (in conversation) about *Bill* by filling in the 'lost years' and contemplating biographical recuperation and loss. In this collection, testifying to a further dimension of the life that remains shadowy, both Katherine Scheil and Paul Franssen explore biofictions about Hamnet, alerting us in their skilled analyses to the interpretive – generic – importance of Maggie O'Farrell's 2016 novel of the same name. Bringing *To be or not to be* to mind, they fruitfully reflect on the ways in which, on stage and screen, the drive to understand Shakespeare through personal tragedy plays itself out. That interpretive move, as *Miguel y William* also demonstrates, is gender aware. Indeed, allying themselves with many of the biofictions introduced in this collection, both short and feature tie Shakespeare to family, nuclear or extended, and conceive of the housekeeper and Leonor as enablers. To finesse the point, Shakespearean biofiction, as this collection showcases, necessitates an undoing of the 'male-centric nature of creation' (58), to adopt Gemma Allred's phrase, and a privileging of female-centric practice. Throughout *Shakespearean Biofiction on the Contemporary Stage and Screen*, indeed, the gendered complexions of realizing Shakespeare are brought to the fore. Germane in this connection is Edel Semple's compelling chapter on one-woman plays centred on Anne Hathaway, Shakespeare's wife/widow, and Emma Whipday's chapter (in conversation) about *Shakespeare's Sister*, her 2016 dramatic disquisition on Shakespeare's mythical play-writing sister. Extending the Shakespearean network of gendered influence is Naomi J. Miller's absorbing chapter on biofictional representations of Mary Sidney Herbert, Aemilia Lanyer and Mary Wroth, on page and stage – a discussion that installs where they cannot be ignored Shakespeare's contemporaries, multiplying the early modern population of rivals, artists and muses. With Viola de Lesseps as impetus, if not Leonor, these biofictions are intricately and excitingly inter-related and inter-sectional.

In contradistinction to *To be or not to be* (1999) and *Miguel y William* (2007), *Angoor* (dir. Gulzar 1982) and *Local Kung Fu 2* (dir. Kenny Basumatary 2017), respectively Hindi and Assamese language adaptations of *The Comedy of Errors*, are 'postmodern' in the sense that unfolding in the present, they represent Shakespeare as an iconic figure, a spectral presence hovering over comic mayhem. At the start of *Angoor*, the camera alights on a framed daguerreotype in a black and gilt frame of a balding, bearded patriarch on the wall, the voiceover intoning, 'This is William Shakespeare . . . a famous playwright of the sixteenth century . . . still considered to be the greatest.' Obligingly, the patriarch stirs (his face flickers) as if in emotional synchronization with the comedy that is about to come to life. Interestingly, however, the face we see bears little resemblance to the famous Droeshout engraving (no earring, no ruff). Instead, this 'Shakespeare' is more akin to portraits of the Indian polymathic philosopher and poet, Rabindranath Tagore, and here the adaptation stages a double bluff, mixing and matching the two in appearance and description: the acronym, 'greatest ... playwright', echoes Tagore's own 1916 paean to Shakespeare, *viśva-kavi* or 'world poet' (Ganguly 2021: 213–15; Gollancz 1916: 320). So does *Angoor*, playing with ideas of twinship and biofictionality, jokily encode Shakespeare as an Indian artist even as it celebrates his worldwide reputation and status. As the final scene closes, we revert back to the daguerreotype: now Shakespeare waves, smiles, winks and points his finger heavenwards. The effect is not 'to assert his authority' (Schwanebeck 2020: 95), as some critics claim, but ironically to pose the question: with whom does Shakespeare belong? Throughout *Angoor*, characters are shot against domestic portraits of Hindu deities (Krishna and Shiva); at this point, then, resolving the issue of his dwelling-place, Shakespeare indicates that he is at one with if not one of the gods (with ourselves as his knowing audience). Part of the pantheon, Shakespeare, in this inset, is treated to an act of indigenization, anti-colonial in spirit but nation-bridging and transcending in effect.

At multiple levels, *Local Kung Fu 2* (2017) is a remake of *Angoor*, copying its blocking, detective novel references and dialogue (although adding digs at Hindi soap operas, kung fu set-pieces, visual gags and distinctively north Indian idioms). What the adaptation also develops is the biofictional Shakespeare: a quarter of the way through the film, when the threads of the story have become particularly entangled, 'Shakespeare' (complete with green jerkin and rolled-up cuffs) steps in *solus* to explicate. Delivering his summary of fractured families in a bookshop (the plastic-backed titles and DVDs hint at classical literary tradition as well as cultures of adaptation), he speaks in measured tones congruent with his *sutradhar* (host/narrator) role. The joke, embellished from *Angoor*, is that in this biofictional interlude there is no illusion of 'Englishness'; rather, the Assamese actor playing Shakespeare, Anupam Baishya, ostentatiously secures his false beard in a mirror, and shows off his watch, all of which marks him out as an impersonation rooted in the here-and-now. The thematic centrality of this brief appearance is underlined in the trailer.[1] Once more in the bookshop, Shakespeare begins to explain the 'truckload of confusion' but is joined by two comic would-be gangsters who are summoned up by his quill. Underscored is a Shakespearean ability magically to body forth character creations but also to learn from another's technological savvy. Referencing 'theatres', Shakespeare is corrected by the gangsters whose namechecking of 'YouTube' and 'downloads' signals the move to digital. In this way, Shakespeare retains a flavour of his older association while moving into the contemporary. Similarly, while Shakespeare is biofictionally repatriated (addressed through the elder brother term of endearment as 'William da'), the elevated ancestry of the film ('Based on William Shakespeare's *Comedy of Errors*') is retained.

Uniquely, this pairing of films does not promote one national constituency over and above another; rather, the emphasis lies with partnerships, hybridity and exchange. So, Shakespeare and Tagore sit comfortably alongside each other, and Shakespeare and martial arts find each other compatible bedfellows. What is illuminated is the easy co-habitation of different cultural registers and signifiers, each hospitable to the other. To reflect on this pairing of films with their finger-pointing Shakespeares is to be pointed back to *Shakespearean Biofiction on the Contemporary Stage and Screen*. In thinking through the transnational implications of *Angoor* and *Local Kung Fu 2*, we are reminded of many of this collection's exemplary discussions. For example, Clara Calvo, in her chapter, identifies the bracketing of two artists – Shakespeare and Austen – in such a way as to suggest that multiple forms inhere in the cultivation of the biofictional Shakespeare, forms with historical, generic and transnational equivalents. Shakespeare the man and writer is mediated across short, feature, adaptation and remake. Whose stories rise to the surface? What subject positions are either queried or validated? To what extent is the biofictional Shakespeare, in transnational guise, put back into a familiar history? These – and many other – questions circulate around Shakespeare in non-Anglophone languages and idioms and across history. Most significantly, perhaps, opening out the biofictional Shakespeare transnationally resonates with Ben Broadribb's reflections on Shakespeare as a global brand and chimes with Edel Semple's observation, in her Introduction, that in the wake of the 2012 Cultural Olympiad and the 2016 quatercentenary of Shakespeare's death the playwright assumed ever more variegated global complexions. Elaborating, Semple argues for more nuanced and concentrated comment on diversity and inclusivity in the field. As the vitality and importance of this collection are absorbed, and as content and understandings accelerate, we will undoubtedly light upon fresh forms and constructions that confirm the biofictional Shakespeare's legacies and futures.

# Note

1 The trailer for *Local Kung Fu 2* can be viewed at: https://www.imdb.com/title/tt6899304/?ref_=ext_shr_lnk (accessed 15 January 2023).

# References

*& Juliet* (2019), Book by D. West Read, Music and Lyrics by M. Martin. Directed by Luke Shepherd [Shaftesbury Theatre, London. November 2019].
*All Is True* (2018), [Film] Dir. Kenneth Branagh, UK: Columbia.
*Angoor* (1982), [Film] Dir. Gulzar, India: A. R. Movies.
Ashley, N. P. (2022). 'Women Punctuating Shakespeare: Campus Theatrical Experiment, the Shakespeare Society and the Insider/Outsider Dialectic', in T. Buckley, M. T. Burnett, S. Datta, and R. García-Periago (eds), *Women and*

*Indian Shakespeares*, 225–242, London and New York: Bloomsbury Arden Shakespeare.
*Bill* (2015), [Film] Dir. Richard Bracewell, UK: Vertigo Films.
*Doctor Who* (2007), [TV series] 'The Shakespeare Code', BBC One, 7 April.
Franssen, P. (2016), *Shakespeare's Literary Lives: The Author as Character in Fiction and Film*, Cambridge: Cambridge University Press.
Ganguly, S. (2021), 'Beyond Bardolatry: Rabindranath Tagore's Critique of Shakespeare', in P. Trivedi, P. Chakravarti, and T. Motohashi (eds), *Asian Interventions in Global Shakespeare: 'All the World's His Stage'*, 213–227, New York and London: Routledge.
Gollancz, I., ed. (1916), *A Book of Homage to Shakespeare*, Oxford: Oxford University Press.
*The Hollow Crown* (2012, 2016), [TV series] BBC, 30 June 2012–21 May 2016.
*Justice League* (2021), [Film] Dir. Zak Snyder, USA: Warner Bros. Pictures.
*The Lego Batman Movie* (2017), [Film] Dir. Chris McKay, USA: Warner Animation Group / DC Entertainment.
Levine, L. (1988), *Highbrow / Lowbrow: The Emergence of Cultural Hierarchy in America*, Cambridge, MA: Harvard University Press.
Lloyd Malcolm, M. (2019), *Emilia*, London: Oberon Books Ltd.
*Local Kung Fu 2* (2017), [Film] Dir. Kenny Basumatary, India: Kuhipaat Films.
Martin, R. and A. Tichenor (2018), *William Shakespeare's Long Lost First Play (abridged)*, New York: Broadway Play Publishing.
*Miguel y William* (2007), [Film] Dir. Inés Paris, Spain: Zebra Producciones.
*Much Ado About Nothing* (1993), [Film] Dir. Kenneth Branagh, UK: BBC Films / Renaissance Films.
O'Farrell, M. (2020), *Hamnet*, London: Tinder Press.
Pérez, J. T. (2011), 'Breaking Shakespeare's Image in Late Spanish Drama and Film', in M. T. Burnett and A. Streete (eds), *Filming and Performing Renaissance History*, 33–49, Houndmills: Palgrave Macmillan.
Schwanebeck, W. (2020), 'The Twin Who Came from Abroad: *The Comedy of Errors* and Transcultural Adaptation', *Shakespeare*, 16 (1): 90–99.
*Shakespeare in Love* (1998), [Film] Dir. John Madden, USA: Miramax.
*Shakespeare Writing Julius Caesar* (1907), [Film] Dir. Georges Méliès, France: Star-Film.
*To be or not to be* (1999), [Film] Dir. Peter Woditsch, Belgium: Flanders Image.
*Un Drama Nuevo* (1946), [Film] Dir. Juan de Orduña, Spain: Juan de Orduña P. C.
*Upstart Crow* (2016–2020), [TV series], BBC.
Whipday, E. (2016), *Shakespeare's Sister*, London: Samuel French.
*Will* (2017), [TV series] TNT, 10 July–4 September.

# INDEX

& *Juliet* (2019 musical)   4, 7, 12, 28, 58–62, 65, 179
#MeToo   11, 59
2012 Cultural Olympiad   4, 185

afterlives   5, 8, 14, 70, 76, 90, 106–7, 157, 169, 173
*Aisha* (2010 film)   22
*All Is True* (2018 film)   1–4, 6–7, 9–10, 13, 19–26, 27 n.3, 72, 89, 91–2, 95–7, 107, 179
anachronism   39, 131, 133, 137, 161, 162, 173
*Angoor* (1982 film)   9, 183–5
animation   8, 21, 39, 167–75, 182
*Anonymous* (2011 film)   4, 9–10, 39, 56, 74, 107, 126–7, 129–33, 163
audiences   1–3, 6–9, 11–13, 19, 24, 26, 29, 32–4, 39, 41, 49–54, 57–8, 61, 63, 66, 69, 71–2, 75–6, 79, 83–4, 90, 100, 106, 108–10, 112–13, 117, 120, 122–4, 126–33, 134 n.2, 134 n.3, 136, 138–9, 141–3, 146–8, 151, 153, 158, 160–1, 167, 171–2, 181, 184
Austen, Jane   22–5, 185

Bardolatry   2, 12, 40
*Becoming Jane* (2007 film)   22, 25
*Bed, The* (2016 play)   4, 10, 12, 69, 73–5
*Bill* (2015 film)   4–5, 7, 10–11, 48–57, 126–8, 133, 160, 163, 178, 183
*Blackadder Back & Forth* (1999 film)   4
*Blackadder Goes Forth* (1983–9 television series)   56, 80, 82, 158

*Blade Runner* (1982 film)   170
*Book of Will, The* (2017 play)   4
*Born With Teeth* (2022 play)   4
Branagh, Kenneth   1–3, 9–10, 19, 21, 27 n.14, 91–2, 96, 179, 182
*Bride and Prejudice* (2004 film)   22
Burbage, James   139, 152, 160–1, 178
Burbage, Richard   8, 11, 138–42, 145–53

Carey, Henry, 1st Baron Hunsdon   63–4
*Celebrity Deathmatch* (1999 claymation series)   4
Chandos portrait   72
*Chariots of Fire* (1981 film)   22
cinema   6, 8, 13, 24, 39, 41–2, 143, 153, 161, 177–80
class   7, 24, 26, 86, 107–8, 118, 126, 130, 132, 155–60, 163
comic book   95–6, 145, 149, 170
*commedia dell'arte*   30
*Complete Deaths, The* (2016 play)   4
*Complete Works of William Shakespeare (abridged), The* (1987 play)   29–30, 32
Condell, Henry   40
Crouch, Tim   4
*Crown, The* (2016–present, television series)   24
Cyclone Rep   4

Dark Lady, The   12, 74, 95–6, 117, 120–3, 181
*A Discovery of Witches* (2021 television series)   5, 118–19

# INDEX

*Doctor Who* (1963–present, television series) 4, 11–12, 34, 39, 126, 129–34, 179
documentary as tradition 7, 20–2, 26, 179
*Dogg's Hamlet* 29
Droeshout portrait 4, 8, 40–1, 157, 168–9, 171–2, 174, 183
Dryden, John 14 n.2

Elizabeth I, Queen of England 48–50, 106, 118, 127–8, 146, 149
Elton, Ben 3–4, 10, 13, 19, 25–6, 78–81, 84, 89–92, 158–60, 162
*Emilia* (2018 play) 4, 7, 11–12, 58–9, 62–6, 121–4
*Emma* (2020 film) 22
Emmerich, Roland 4, 10
Englishness 3, 7, 23–4, 168, 184

family 5, 7, 10–11, 19, 22, 24, 26, 51–2, 54, 60, 69–73, 75, 82, 86–7, 89, 91–2, 95–6, 98–9, 102, 107, 128, 150, 157–8, 178, 183
fandom 9–10, 48, 157, 160
fanfiction 28–9, 31, 35–6, 162
fathers 1, 7, 23, 35, 71–3, 79, 86–93, 96–100, 102, 149, 151–3, 158, 180
feminism 11, 58–9, 72, 74, 96–8, 100, 104–5, 110, 112–13, 122
First Folio (publication) 1, 4, 7, 21, 39–40, 42–6, 55, 118, 168
FitzGibbon, Ger 4, 69–70, 74–6, 77 n.2
Folger Shakespeare Library 30

Gaiman, Neil 95
*Game of Thrones* (2011–19 television series) 143, 161
*Gandhi* (1982 film) 22
gender roles 7, 96, 101–2, 132
*Gnomeo and Juliet* (2011 film) 4, 39
*Good Omens* (2019 television series) 4
Gosling, Mya 168

Greene, Robert 19, 158, 160
guilt 88, 96–7

Hall, Susanna 6–7, 13, 19, 21, 23, 75, 78–85, 89, 91, 96, 100–1
*Hamnet* (2017 play) 4, 7, 10, 86, 89–91
*Hamnet* (2020 novel) 6–7, 71–2, 92–3, 95–6, 98–102
*Hamnet* (2023 play) 4, 6
Hathaway, Anne 4–7, 13, 19, 22–3, 26, 53–6, 60–3, 65, 69–77, 81, 84, 87, 89–93, 96–102, 107, 129, 132, 159, 171, 183
Heminges, John 40
Henry VIII, King of England 34
Herbert, Mary Sidney 8, 118–24, 125 n.4, 183
heritage drama 7, 20, 23–6
*Hollow Crown, The* (2012–16 television series) 24, 178
*Horrible Histories* (2009–13 television series) 4, 12, 48, 52, 133

*I am Shakespeare* (2007 play) 4, 11, 118, 123–4
iconography 7, 168–9
*Imperfect Alchemist* (novel) 118–20, 122
inspired genius 40–3
intertextuality 101, 108, 126, 178

*James Bond* (1962–present, film series) 49, 160
Jarmusch, Jim 5, 156–8, 162
Jonson, Ben 11, 12, 21, 24, 40, 51, 120–1, 130

Kapur, Shekhar 161
*Key and Peele* (2012–15 television series) 4

Lanyer, Aemilia (Emilia Bassano Lanier) 7–8, 58, 62, 64, 118, 120–2, 124 n.1, 139, 183
*Lego Movie, The* (2014 film) 4, 6, 8, 11, 167, 169–75
*Local Kung Fu 2* (2017 film) 9, 183–5, 185 n.1

Lord, Phil  4, 169–71
Lucy, Sir Thomas  19, 24, 26
Luhrmann, Baz  161–2

Madden, John  2–3, 5, 12, 39, 41–2, 44, 46, 127, 129, 162, 177
Malcolm, Morgan Lloyd  4, 58–9, 62–6, 121–4, 179
Marlowe, Christopher  4–5, 8–9, 11–12, 42, 50–7, 130, 133, 138–41, 155–63
marriage  1, 6–7, 19, 22, 24–5, 30, 32, 60–3, 69–77, 75, 81, 86–7, 89, 91–3, 97–8, 122–3, 129, 159, 183
Martin, Max  58
Martin, Reed  28–9, 31–2, 34–5, 178
Méliès, Georges  39, 42–6, 177
Meta-theatricality  28, 31, 159
*Miguel and William* (2007 film)  9, 180–3
Miller, Christopher  4, 169–71
Miller, Naomi  6, 8, 9, 117–25, 183
*Miss Austen Regrets* (2008 film)  22–5
Mitchell, David  80, 82–4, 158–9, 178
Monks, Helen  5, 7, 78–85, 177–8

O'Farrell, Maggie  6, 10, 71, 89, 92–3, 95–6, 98–102, 183
Olivier, Laurence  126, 132, 134 n.2
*Only Lovers Left Alive* (2013 film)  5, 9, 155–7, 162
origin story  8, 11, 39, 50, 52, 128, 136, 138, 145–6, 149, 151–3, 178, 180
Oxford, Earl of, Edward de Vere  9, 10, 39, 127–8, 130–1, 134 n.7

parody  2, 29, 31, 128, 157, 160, 172, 177
patriarchy  60, 65, 69, 71, 95, 97–8, 102
Pearce, Craig  145–53, 161–2
popular culture  3, 5, 9, 11, 13, 32, 33, 59, 124 n.2, 132, 142, 157, 167–70, 172–3, 175, 178

*Pride and Prejudice* (2005 film)  22
*Prospero's Books* (1991 film)  7, 26, 39, 44–5

Quiney, Judith  6, 10–11, 19, 21–3, 25–6, 91–2, 96–9, 101–2, 105, 107–12

Read, David West  58–60, 179
Reduced Shakespeare Company  1, 28–36
repertory studies  8, 136–43
reverse appropriation  8, 136–8, 143
Rickard, Laurence  5, 7, 48–57, 183
*Romeo + Juliet* (1996 film)  161
*A Room of One's Own* (1929 essay)  26, 97, 104, 120
Rough Magic  4
Rowlands, Avril  4, 69–77, 97
Royal Shakespeare Company  6, 29, 169
Rylance, Mark  4, 11, 118, 120, 123–4, 131, 134, 173

*St Trinian's 2: The Legend of Fritton's Gold* (2009 film)  4, 9, 14
*Sandman, The* (2022–present, television series)  4
*Second Best Bed, The* (2012 play)  4, 10, 69–76, 77 n.2, 77 n.4, 97
*Shakespeare 450*  4
Shakespeare, Hamnet  1, 6–7, 10, 21, 23, 25, 36, 72, 80, 86–93, 95–102, 180, 182–3
Shakespeare, William, works
  *Antony and Cleopatra* (play)  75, 118–19
  *As You Like It* (play)  46, 117, 119, 122–3, 140
  *Comedy of Errors, The* (play)  9, 28, 31, 52, 54, 183
  *Cymbeline* (play)  112
  *Hamlet* (play)  3, 29, 34, 53, 62, 74, 87, 89–91, 93, 97, 99–102, 108, 128, 141, 146–8, 157, 182
  *Henry IV* plays  31, 182

*Henry V* (play)   33, 39, 126, 128, 130–1, 172
*Henry VI* plays   52, 142
*Henry VIII* (play)   21, 25, 33
*Julius Caesar* (play)   43, 46
*King John* (play)   90
*King Lear* (play)   54, 81
*Love's Labour's Lost* (play)   63–4, 129
*Macbeth* (play)   28, 31, 61, 74, 128, 132
*Measure for Measure* (play)   26
*Merchant of Venice, The* (play)   160
*A Midsummer Night's Dream* (play)   46, 96, 127, 181
*Much Ado About Nothing* (play)   4, 28, 81–2, 181–2
*Othello* (play)   64–5, 121–2, 181
*Richard II* (play)   131
*Richard III* (play)   31, 52, 131, 141, 146–7, 149–53
*Romeo and Juliet* (play)   39, 46, 60, 63, 107, 127, 133, 182
Sonnets   12, 13, 63, 96, 121–3, 156, 181
*Taming of the Shrew, The* (play)   62, 63, 81
*Tempest, The* (play)   26, 28, 31, 33–4, 44, 72
*Titus Andronicus* (play)   13, 52
*Troilus and Cressida* (play)   14 n.2
*Twelfth Night* (play)   3, 33, 42, 46, 101, 131
*Two Gentlemen of Verona, The* (play)   127
*Winter's Tale, The* (play)   26, 86, 92, 121
Shakespeare Authorship Question   4, 9, 11, 39, 56–7, 73–4, 97, 107, 118, 123–4, 127, 130, 155–6, 173
*Shakespeare in Love* (1998 film)   2–5, 7, 10, 12, 22, 26, 39, 41–4, 51, 53, 59, 69–70, 73, 86, 89–90, 99, 106–9, 111, 126–33, 134 n.6, 145, 149, 160, 162, 177, 180, 182

*Shakespeare in Love* (2014 play)   4
Shakespeare in the Ruins   71–2, 77 n.3
*Shakespeare Live! From the RSC*   12
*Shakespeare Unbound-a Gift to the Future* (play)   4
*Shakespeare Writing Julius Caesar* (1907 film)   7, 39, 42, 177
Shakespeare's family. *See* under individual surnames
Shakespeare's lost years   9, 48, 87, 105, 109, 136–7, 143, 180–1, 183
*Shakespeare's Sister* (2015 play)   4, 6, 10, 104–13, 183
*Shakespeare's Will* (2005 play)   4, 69–70, 87
Sharratt, Mary   120–1, 124 n.1
*Simpsons, The* (1990–present, television series)   4, 33
sitcom   3, 5, 19, 48, 52, 56, 78, 82–3, 85, 89–90, 156, 158–60, 177
slash fiction   162
*Something Rotten!* (2015 musical)   3–4, 12
Southampton, Earl of, Henry Wriothesley   13, 24, 26, 73–4, 109, 128, 134 n.7
Spymonkey   4
*Staged 1592* (2021 comedy sketch)   4
*Star Wars* (1977- present, film series)   53, 142
Stoppard, Tom   2, 29, 109
*Strange Labyrinth*   122–3
superhero   8, 49–50, 52, 138, 145–6, 148–50, 153, 170, 178
supervillain   8, 146, 150–3

Thiessen, Vern   4, 69–77, 87
Tichenor, Austin   6–7, 10, 28–36, 178
*To be or not to be* (1999 film)   9
Topcliffe, Richard   146, 149–53
*Tudors, The* (2007–10 television series)   161

*Upstart Crow* (2016–present, television series)   3–5, 7, 10, 13, 14 n.4, 19, 25, 78–85, 89–91, 93, 107, 145, 155–63, 177–8

*Upstart Crow, The* (2018 play)   4, 5–6, 78, 81, 85

*A Waste of Shame* (2005 film)   4, 10, 13, 96

Whipday, Emma   4, 6–7, 11, 104–13, 183

*Will* (2017 television series)   4, 8, 10–12, 136–43, 145–53, 156–7, 160–3, 178–9

*William Shakespeare's Haunted House* (1998–2019 play)   4

*William Shakespeare's Long Lost First Play* (*abridged*) (2018 play)   1, 4, 7, 11, 28–36, 178

women, early modern   4, 6–8, 10–11, 13, 19–26, 53–6, 58–66, 69–76, 78–85, 87, 89–93, 96–102, 104–13, 117–25, 129, 132, 139–40, 142, 145, 147, 151, 159, 161, 178, 181–3

Woolf, Virginia   26, 97, 104–5, 110–11, 113, 120

Wroth, Mary   118, 120, 122–4, 124 n.4, 124 n.5, 183

www.ingramcontent.com/pod-product-compliance
Lightning Source LLC
Chambersburg PA
CBHW052117300426
44116CB00010B/1703